Suzanne Moore, who now ~~~ Ipswich in 1958. She is a fr~~~ for *The Independent, The Ne*~~~ *Marxism Today. Looking for* ~~~~~ is her first book.

Looking for

Trouble

On shopping, gender and the cinema

SUZANNE MOORE

Author's note

For support and inspiration over the years, thanks to: Helen Birch, Thone Braekke, Martin Deeson, Lon Fleming, Chris Granlund, Janet Lee, my Mum, Kevin McAleer, Siobhan O'Neil, Sally Townsend and Valerie Whitworth.

I especially want to thank Lorraine Gamman for giving such good phone as well as just about everything else. This book is for her and for my daughters, Scarlet and Bliss.

Suzanne Moore

Library of Congress Catalog Card Number: 91-61203

British Library Cataloguing in Publication Data
Moore, Suzanne
    Looking for trouble: on shopping, gender and the cinema
    I. Title
    305.42

    ISBN 1-85242-242-4

First published 1991 by
Serpent's Tail, 4 Blackstock Mews, London N4

Typeset in 10½/13pt Plantin
by Contour Typesetters, Southall, London
Printed in Great Britain by
Cox & Wyman Ltd. of Reading, Berkshire

Contents

Introduction

The themes of this book are really my obsessions. Some are grand — how can we assess the value as well as the price of postmodern culture? Some are not — to shave or not to shave one's underarm hair? But all of them arise out of an attempt to speak both from within and about popular culture and to find a way of speaking that stifles neither its pleasures nor its politics.

As most of the pieces published here were written for general readership from *Elle* to *Marxism Today* to *The Observer*, such considerations have always been practical as well as theoretical. I started writing journalistic pieces as a reaction to the privatisation of knowledge that academia encourages in the hope that if an idea was worth having it was certainly worth sharing and so many of the pieces here are informed by and indebted to debates within cultural studies, feminism and media studies.

Yet these debates like my obsessions do not belong to anyone in particular. Rather they are reverberations that can be picked up and picked out anywhere you care to listen. While lengthy books are written deconstructing masculinity for instance, the question of what it means to be a man is one mulled over endlessly by the tabloids. The preoccupation with the New Man or New Lad or whatever dubious model is being held up for inspection is fuelled by an obvious anxiety. How are men to cope with the changes in expectation that feminism has brought about? Or more basically, what sort of man actually goes out with a feminist?

Likewise, direct and indirect questions about the representation of sexuality permeate every area of our lives — our facts and our fictions. Nowhere is this more apparent than in the great fantasy factory that is

Hollywood and some of the articles were written during my time as film critic for the *New Statesman and Society*. Writing weekly about film means also having to face up to the awkward question of cultural value. Quite clearly, however much one wants to shirk it, reviewing carries with it some sort of evaluative function. It is part of the job to sort out the good from the bad and the ugly.

This has become increasingly difficult as the onslaught of postmodern theory has lead in many cases to a kind of critical evacuation, an apologetic shrug of the shoulders that threatens to swamp us all in a never-ending press release for what's coming soon. If everything is open to interpretation, to radical re-reading then eventually — anything goes. Our energy goes into creatively consuming rather than producing objects of quality. What results is the fetishisation of text at the expense of the context, the subjective over the collective or in a parallel move the personal over the political. At its most extreme point what is lost is any criterion to be actually critical with. For me this suggests not cultural analysis but postmodern paralysis, a cultural politics with the politics surgically removed. More mundanely, people always want to know if a film is worth seeing or not.

On the other hand some of the older, more 'politically correct' ways of seeing seem hopelessly unable to deal with the kind of culture we actually live and love in. With the mantra of class/race/gender in one hand and a checklist of properly ideological contents in the other, we end up with an analysis that fails to grasp all that makes popular culture *popular*.

For these reasons there is much in postmodern theory that attracts me: that is able to describe 'structure of feeling' that we live more accurately than anything else as well as the questioning of the old polarities between high culture and its 'other', low culture. So I have tried to draw on these insights wihout being completely overwhelmed by them. As appealing as it may be to step into the endless sea and abandon all judgements aesthetic, moral and political, I have tried somehow to keep afloat.

What has buoyed me up is another 'other' — feminism. Though at times my relationship to it is as psychotic as it is to postmodernism. During the last four years, when most of the articles were written, I have often longed never to write another word about women again. I wanted to stop going on and on. However because of the experience of sitting through four or five movies a week in which the pinnacle of aspiration offered to us was the prostitute who marries her richest client (*Pretty Woman*), not to mention the real-life difficulties of child-care and work, I'm afraid I haven't been able to shut up women and their place in our culture. Believe me, I would really much rather write about almost anything else. My hope is that one day I will be free to. Until then I guess I'll just carry on Looking for Trouble.

1 Feminism

MEN

Men against men again

It's like a bad horror movie. Just when you thought they had finally left you alone, another one is coming at you. The Living Dead of sexual politics — the anti-sexist male — stalks the land. You might have thought he disappeared a few years back, well and truly overtaken by his more upmarket cousin, the New Man. But you were wrong, he is making a comeback. After all those predictions about the 90s being a more caring decade, what could be more appropriate than a man who cares more about sexism than any woman ever could?

After Paul Gascoigne, Jason Donovan and Cliff Richard have all recently reassured the nation that they are not 'poofs', maybe now is not the time to stick the boot into anti-sexist men. Don't we need some men around who at least give it a go? Whether they regard themselves as male feminists, anti-sexists, pro-feminist, gay-affirmative or just nicer than other men, surely they should be encouraged? Women should resume that delicate feminine position of gratitude and support, as men explain to us just how hard it is to be a man.

Perhaps this is not the fault of individual men. I mean, it's not polite to get too personal about the political, is it? But it *is* the fault of the whole muddle of anti-sexist ideology which is painfully short on theory, politics, or even ideas, and painfully long when it comes to a dire kind of moralism.

Yet that same lethal cocktail of guilt trip and ego trip that characterised and crippled so much of the 'men's movement' is due for a comeback. *Achilles Heel*, 'The Magazine for Changing Men', collapsed in the mid-80s due, they say, to 'a general uncertainty about the role, position and validity of anti-sexist men', but was later relaunched.

A new series of books, 'Men, Masculinities and Social Theory', which touches on the thorny issue of 'men's studies', is explained as 'a separate discipline largely by and for men, paralleling women's studies. The fact that every other academic discipline is unofficially 'men's studies' anyway, seems to have escaped their notice.

The Campaign Against Pornography and Censorship have just held a one-day conference for men where no doubt a bunch of ex-wankers became born-again feminists, more offended by pornography than any woman could ever hope to be. They were addressed by John Stoltenberg, 'America's leading male feminist', and the intellectual guru of self-flagellating men the world over. There was a time when the phrase 'male feminist' was considered to be a contradiction in terms. Not so for John, who, as he explains in his book *Refusing to Be a Man*, realised that he was different from other men. Read this as 'better than other men', though how he mysteriously escaped the oppressive forces of gender construction is beyond me.

That this book comes with endorsements from Alice Walker, Shere Hite and Gloria Steinem is a sign, I think, of how little we have come to expect from men. Even the title is a problem — can you imagine a book called *Refusing to Be a White Person*? All the recent work on masculinity, whether good, bad or indifferent, has stressed the multiplicities of masculinities rather than emphasising the fixed nature of manhood as Stoltenberg does.

This realisation follows feminism's insistence that there are now a variety of feminisms. But Stoltenberg and his colleagues still respond to an imaginary feminism that is united in its demands. It is a frighteningly prescriptive belief-system with religious undertones. Andrea Dworkin is its high priestess and the language is one of conversion. Stoltenberg has seen through 'the sex-class system' even though, as he admits: 'I was born with a penis.' He is now spreading the word.

The word is pro-censorship with a strong line in policing correct sexual behaviour: 'Beware of relying on drugs or alcohol to give you "permission" to have sex, or to trick your body into feeling something that it's not.' This has nothing to do with sexual politics (not my kind anyway) and everything to do with sexual moralism. It has, as the *Achilles Heel* collective acknowledge, also a lot to do with age and class.

Some men may perceive themselves as a vanguard out there fighting for feminism, but if other men perceive them as a bunch of puritanical whingers it's hardly going to have a lot of effect. This stance is partly tied to the history of the men's movement itself, which moved so quickly from the political that it became entrenched in the personal world of therapy, growth and self-expression.

Now all of this is fine. I personally don't care whether men need to go to a men's group to get their consciousness raised or whether they go down the pub to get it lowered. I just don't want to hear about it. But just as early feminist writing was often miserable and confessional, the prospect of a whole spate of autobiographies with men who have grappled with their own masculinity is not something I relish. You know the kind of thing: laughed at in the shower, bad at sports, discovered *Playboy*, series of failed relationships, met feminist, saw the light, became father, life in crisis again . . .

Nor, at a time when women's studies or gender studies are having to fight their ground, do I want a bunch of middle-class men demanding their own men's studies or 'the critique of men' as they call it. If women's studies is not the critique of men, then I don't know what is. What I do want is very simple. Very 70s even, though it still seems impossible for men, sexist or anti-sexist, to comprehend. And that is to give women more space, whether it's pages in a magazine such as this, getting more women into management, or just by looking after the kids.

But this is far too mundane for the tortured world of the male feminist who is too busy searching for his 'emergent moral identity' and it may actually require him to become a little bit less self-obsessed, the poor man. It just goes to show that women are never satisfied. God knows, the next thing they'll be saying is that feminism belongs to them.

Target man

Are you finished with all this feminist crap? Fed up with being made to feel so bloody guilty all the time? Isn't it time you *celebrated* your masculinity instead of making excuses for it?

Just think of all the brilliant things there are about being a man. You can go rock-climbing, wear ties, go 'stagging' on the stock exchange. Best of all you get to shave. You can buy a magazine devoted to just these sort of activities — *Arena*, brought to you by the people who do *The Face*. You could also 'get yourself a *Man*' (the supplement that comes with *Cosmopolitan*) or the ominous sounding *OM* that comes with *Options*. Advertisers have been yearning to plug this particular hole in the market and sell directly to young men — hitherto, the joys of shopping have been traditionally sandwiched between the joys of sex in the porn rags and the zoom lens voyeurism of the camera magazines.

The difficulty of reaching this market lies in 'forcing men to look at themselves self-consciously as men', as Frank Mort suggested in his article 'Images Change: High Street style and the New Man'. Whereas women are used to being addressed as 'Woman' — a sort of bottled essence of half the human race — men define themselves by what they *do*, and buy magazines that reflect their hobbies. In getting men to recognise themselves as part of a community of men, rather than as unrelated individuals, *Arena* has gone for the lowest common denominator of a marketable masculinity and dressed it up as high fashion. While pretending to be esoteric and elitist most of the articles are in fact on shaving, clothes, sports cars and consumer culture. Sex is strangely absent, but we'll come to that later.

More user-friendly than *The Face* in that there is absolutely no difference between the ads and the features — *Arena* is slick to the point of prissiness. Those commentators who saw *The Face* as the ultimate in the fragmented and gloriously superficial postmodern text won't be disappointed. But such an analysis tends to ignore a key factor — gender. As 80 per cent of its readership is already male anyway, it comes as no surprise that the increasingly butch *Face* should finally come out in the form of *Arena* — the *Boys Own* rag it always was at heart.

Like *The Face*, *Arena* pursues the micro-politics of posing. ('Micro' is a very *Arena* word — rock-climbers don't climb rocks, they go 'out on the micro-ledges'.) The rituals and mechanisms of a masculine identity become not a means to an end but an end in themselves — amplifying their artificiality simultaneously deconstructs them and allows them to be reconstructed anew. Thus, as Frank Mort pointed out, men's bodies and clothes become objects of visual pleasure not only for themselves but for other men too. And, I would add, for women. Many of the images he cites are used to sell to women who still buy the majority of men's clothes and cosmetics.

Advertisers seem to have realised that homo-erotic imagery appeals more directly to women than the sanitised versions of male sexuality that are so often served up. The sense of control and objectification it sanctions allows women an active rather than passive gaze. This is exactly the potential that the manager of Wham! picked up on when he first saw them — a homo-erotic tension that made them so popular with the girls. And *Arena* is full of men looking mean, moody and magnificent, reinforced by a manly but narcissistic text. While the female models in so many women's magazines are snarling and defiant, their self-contained state is consistently undermined by references to relationships with men.

Now, I may be confusing homo-eroticism with auto-eroticism (and who doesn't?) but it is exactly this sort of self-containment that worries me. Men becoming self-conscious seems recently to have taken self-containment as its form. Films from *Top Gun* to *The Mission* are about men — women simply don't figure as major interest, because while men can now be objects of the gaze and be emotional, women are simply unnecessary.

I'm not exactly enamoured by the new man version of masculinity where getting in touch with your feelings at the expense of everyone else's seems to be the name of the game, but the fact that so many men are alienated from their emotions remains true. Yet *Arena*, arrogant and asexual, doesn't stoop as low as discussing anything as messy as feelings, relationships or sex (in true modernist fashion, almost everything else — art, power, money is seen as more erotic).

So while *Cosmo* answers 'your most intimate questions' (hapless women still looking for their G-spots) *Arena* and

Cosmo men presumably just 'know'. *Cosmo Man* at least acknowledges the existence of women albeit in peculiar form: as 'victims of Rape', men of course being the other victims: in an interview with Heather from *Brookside* (the perfect *Cosmo* woman and look how she's ended up); and in an article about how divorced women with kids can provide an 'off-the-peg family unit, an attractive option for male baby phobics afraid of the nappy-and-crying syndrome'.

Like *Arena Cosmo Man* features the stubbly Mickey Rourke on the cover ('he's no slave to the shave'). I would have thought the supposedly celibate Morrissey would have been more suitable. *OM* however has no truck with this New Man business and puts the boorish Botham on its cover in order to signify just how phenomenally boring it is. Apart from a few snippets of bizarre advice such as 'you can choose your friend, but you can't choose his tie', *OM* is full of articles about after-dinner speaking, careers and sailing. Is this really what men want?

Frank Mort's article argues that 'a pre-condition for men changing means allowing them some space to debate the issue themselves rather than insisting they conform to a pre-timetabled feminist agenda.' It seems that the space given to them by these new magazines is one in which these issues are not even raised, let alone debated. So although in visual terms masculinity is allowed to be a bit frillier at the fringes, it is still supposed to be as tightly self-controlled as ever. Women's magazines speak endlessly of pleasure — fantasy, desire and dressing up is often a communal activity for girls, more fun than going out itself. But the world conjured up by men's magazines is of lonely boys standing in front of the mirror trying to attach their diamante collar studs. The blurring of gay and straight style which made *The Face* fun has turned into a kind of restrictive coyness.

Consumption becomes redefined as a masculine activity rather than as a passive and feminised one, a by-product is the growing feminisation of images and commodities. This is a contradictory process, and market-led changes in attitudes to shopping cannot necessarily be read as real changes in attitudes to sexuality. And while it may be good to emphasise the positive as well as negative sides to these processes, you only have to listen to conversations in pubs or on buses to know that, for all their pastel pink cardigans and diamante studs, the old double standards towards women and sex still hold good for most young men.

The idea of sexual identity as a disguise or masquerade is a useful one — using femininity as a masquerade, women have been able both to acknowledge and deny the constraints placed upon them. But femininity is about a whole way of *behaving*, not just visual appearance. Similarly, deconstructing the visual languages of masculinity needs to go hand in hand with actual changes in attitudes and behaviour. Otherwise, however it's played around with, the masquerade of masculinity is still the one with real effects and real power.

The brothers grim

In the week when the long-awaited film *The Krays* opened, the brothers grim still had enough pulling power for the *Sun* to put them on the front cover — 'Reg thought a robin was his dead wife'. The *News of the World* reported that a panel of doctors will decide if Ronnie Kray can view the film in Broadmoor while other 'experts' worried over whether having pop stars play gangsters glamorises violence.

Working-class heroes or folk-devils, the Krays may at least

claim to be the only criminals whose activities have formed the basis for a comedy routine — albeit a strangely charmless one. Hale and Pace as the 'The Management' threaten us into buying breath-fresheners by parodying the stupidity and brutality of the original Kray twins until they seem like a pair of gormless thugs. Peculiarly English, peculiarly old-fashioned, lovable almost . . .

Until you remember that they did actually kill people: brutal murders for very little reason other than the lack of what they held most dear. Respect. They wanted to inspire respect. In reality they inspired fear. They confused the two. In our nostalgia so do we. Somehow they have come to stand for a time of innocent crime, a time before muggings and everyday burglaries, before organised drug dealing and anonymous computer frauds. A time when criminals had names and faces and looked after their own. A time when young men like Ronnie and Reggie were only doing what all their class was being encouraged to do — to move on up. It's true that they carved out their own career opportunities. It's also true that they did it quite literally on the faces of their victims. Even now Ron can say, quite casually, 'I have never believed in work, particularly manual work'.

Instead of rejecting all this contemporary mythology, writer Philip Ridley has made the brave decision to further mythologise their story, seeing in this contemporary fable all the elements of Greek tragedy. This may come as a shock to audiences expecting *Sweeney*-style realism or another cocky, Cockney *Buster*-type movie, but it makes for a better film than the hype and the five-year wait.

At times this poetic approach, combined with Peter Medak's static direction, makes for the rather script-heavy feel that is characteristic of many British films. Performance becomes all important. *The Krays* scores highly here, the Kemp brothers work well as the terrible twins.

We first see them growing up in the Dickensian poverty of

the East End. Playing on bombsites, brawling in the playground, sheltering in the Blitz. The film plays upon two particularly powerful strands of the Kray myth: that their extraordinary closeness was in itself disturbing and that their mother's overwhelming love for them was at the root of their problems. Violet Kray believed that her boys could do no wrong and so, ultimately, did they.

Certainly the film surrounds them with stereotypically tough matriarchs and weak men who are regarded as eternal children. Their Aunt Rose bitterly understands that the hardships men went through had nothing on those endured by the women of the time. Yet her outbursts about all the dead babies at the bottom of Victoria Park lake seem out of place in a film which centres on psychology and symbolism. Blaming Violet Kray for her sons' actions seems not only unfair, but untrue.

What is clear both in the film and in interviews is their dividing up of their world into hard men and soft men — their own skewed masculinity — was carried over in their attitudes to women. Ron's gayness —'I'm not a poof, I'm a homosexual' — has been much publicised, but the film suggests it is Reg's treatment of his young wife as an innocent child that led to her suicide. For all their supposed respect for women and the family, chivalry collapses into chauvinism again.

The key relationship for both of them is firmly portrayed as being with each other. They dream the same dreams as though they were in fact one person. Their bond is simultaneously natural and unnatural. The presence of twins is always threatening in a culture that places such emphasis on individuality. Their story even fits into the good twin/bad twin dichotomy that has infiltrated our consciousness through literature and film. Bad twin Ronnie — the psychopath who loves violence and, even worse, is gay. Good twin Reggie with the soft streak, heartbroken by his wife's suicide and led on by wicked Ronnie into stabbing Jack McVitie to death. In his ghosted autobiography Reg Kray denies such an interpretation, taking full responsibility for his actions. Nonetheless the film exploits it to the full.

As does the sharp iconography of those memorable David Bailey photographs. Like so many working-class kids, the Krays couldn't afford to look poor. The fact that they carried sabres under their Savile Row suits does not appear to have detracted from that. Ron still says proudly, 'I'm the smartest man in Broadmoor'.

It was their awareness of image — what Duncan Campbell refers to in his book *That was Business, This is Personal* as 'crime as showbusiness' — that helped both to create and to destroy them.

With their string of clubs, their protection rackets, their charity balls, their celebrity friends, they mastered the art of the photo-opportunity long before it came to be called that. They made themselves glamorous because they believed that gangsters *were* glamorous. Their dealings with the real mafia however proved just how taken in by appearances they were. Ronnie went to a meeting with the mob in the States organised by Alan Cooper and was suitably impressed, not realising that Cooper had merely improvised a gang made up of out-of-work actors and ex-boxers.

Ronnie believed himself at times to be a reincarnation of Al Capone and when everything started to fall to pieces both his and Reg's plots became more and more like James Bond inspired fantasies. They even thought about kidnapping the Pope at one point. Their springing of 'Mad Axeman' Mitchell from Dartmoor was motivated by a desire to flaunt their contempt for the law. And many have said it was this rather than the actual murders that brought about their downfall and their long sentences. By 1969 the romanticisation of the great train robbers was in full sway (and still is thanks to Buster and Biggs, and the late Charlie Wilson). This was the last thing the law and order lobby wanted to happen to the Krays.

After the Profumo affair, which of course has generated its own film *Scandal*, there was a real sense of all the old codes of honour and justice breaking down at both ends of society. If the Krays were a new kind of criminal they merely mirrored a new kind of social arrangement, a shifting of class identities and communities. Even their name, The Firm, was a parody of a new entrepreneurial spirit. Today they look like dinosaurs, and their codes of behaviour and their ethics 'We never hurt any members of the public'—sadly out of date. This, combined with their uncanny ability for tabloid speak ('I was born to be violent') has eased them into the lovable criminal category. Reggie apparently wanted to be portrayed by cuddly Bob Hoskins. They continually hark back to the time when streets were safe to walk on, cleverly positioning themselves as the lesser of two evils.

Yet the only remorse that they express for those they hurt and killed is that they did it themselves, instead of getting their henchmen to do it. McVitie and Cornell were vermin according to Reggie, while Ron describes murdering Cornell as: 'Fucking marvellous. I have never felt so good.'

But simply because the film focuses on the first part of their life, it does inevitably glamorise them. We don't see the trial or their imprisonment. And we don't hear the testimonies of their viciousness that emerged there.

After all these years in prison, they offer a further indictment (if one were needed) of the British system of justice. As barrister Stephen Sedley, quoted in Campbell's book, says, 'We need to remember that hanging is not the only way in which the law can take a life.' The Kemp boys' reptilian charm may remind us that in their heyday the Krays were dangerous to know. Now, however, they seem neither mad or bad. Just sad.

Toy soldiers or wicked willies

Boys will be boys and, given half the chance, so will most men. Growing up is hard to do. Maybe it is easier to switch from infantile selfishness to penile dementia without so much as a glimmer of maturity in between. It is hard enough to live with this fact, let alone see it culturally endorsed by the kind of dreadful films I've seen this week. While *Farewell to the King* is about a white man who becomes king of a tribe in Borneo and *Skin Deep* about a compulsive womaniser in LA, the kinds of macho posturing on display in both movies is not only utterly charmless but completely contemptible. Forget homosexuality — it is the promotion of masculinity *per se* that needs legislating against.

OK, so I've had a hard week. But perhaps I wouldn't loathe these films so much if they were funny or well made. Even on a bad day, I can take a reactionary message if it is wrapped up in shiny enough packaging. If the medium is slick enough, the message matters less. Who can resist a Hollywood blockbuster or, more importantly, who wants to when the *will to resist* is massaged away by the millions of dollars spent on these films? This week's movies, however, are a timely reminder that no amount of money, exotic locations, or grown women impersonating Barbie Dolls, can confer that elusive quality of *irresistibility* on to turkeys such as these.

Farewell to the King is described by director John Milius as the best film he has ever made. He has long been fascinated by a mythical, macho heroism that saw its best moment in the screenplay he wrote for *Apocalypse Now*. But his passion for a raw or 'natural' maleness has led him in search of some pretty dubious heroes. In *Big Wednesday*, Californian surfers were

15

portrayed as lonely existential figures living only for the next wave, while the ridiculous *Red Dawn*, based on the premise of a Soviet invasion of America, led to him being branded a Nazi.

His new film combines his quest for 'real men' with his other abiding theme — that of 'getting back to nature', to a primitive but somehow purer state of being that is freed from the niceties of civilisation. In *Farewell to the King*, Nick Nolte, sounding like Tom Waits and looking like the lion from the *Wizard of Oz*, plays such a figure. One suspects Milius would have preferred Klaus Kinski who, after all, has made a living from roaming round jungles, acting the wild man in various Herzog enterprises. But we have to make do with Nolte as Learoyd, an American deserter who ends up in Borneo at the end of the second world war, and who unbelievably becomes king of a tribe of native people.

Living the life of Riley — complete with blow-pipes and subservient Malaysian women — his blissful existence is rudely interrupted by 'history' in the form of Nigel Havers, a British officer whose mission is to get the tribes to fight the invading Japanese troops. It all results in jungle warfare and a ludicrous bit of male bonding between Havers and Nolte. As Nolte scampers about grunting and communing with nature, Havers tries to convince him that he 'can no longer avoid history'. Havers, whom it is impossible to imagine having a primitive urge in his life, grows to respect and love Learoyd — though both have suitably dumb women to reassure us that it is not *that* sort of male bonding going on. James Fox, as Havers's commanding officer has the best line: 'You've done a hell of a piece of soldiering, but that's not the point'. Exactly.

If *Farewell to the King* expresses, in a botched way, the notion that going back to — or regressing into — an illusory primal existence is laudable, it does so precisely at the expense of 'history' and in doing so validates a particular kind of masculinity as the real thing. Learoyd becomes king of the jungle because colonial and patriarchal impulses don't feel like 'history' or the despised 'civilisation' but like some God-given and perfectly natural right.

Of course the whole point about regression is that you have to grow up to be able to regress in the first place. Which cannot honestly be said for the central character of Blake Edward's sex-comedy *Skin Deep*. The bearded and bland John Ritter is the archetypal Edwards hero, an affluent LA writer with writer's block. He is also a compulsive (and repulsive) womaniser who mouths the old lie — that he can't help it because he loves women so much — rather than the truth, which is that he has a mental age of 13 and more money than is good for him. This is the excuse for a series of encounters with interchangeable Californian girls. To call them bimbos is the equivalent of describing Maria Whittaker as an intellectual.

What this little-boy-lost needs is the love of a good and mature woman, though any sensible female would have more fun blowing her brains out than getting involved with this emotional retard. Still, if you subscribe to the 'wicked willy' view of male sexuality (and sometimes it's difficult not to) and think that men are led around by their dicks, you might like this garbage. Certainly the middle-aged hack sitting next to me in the cinema could identify with this mid-life crisis. He seemed to think the very idea of a condom was hysterically funny.

The clothes, designed by Nolan Miller of *Dynasty*, are incredibly tacky. As Dolly Parton (a woman with more wit in her little finger than this film in its entirety) said of her own wardrobe: 'It costs a lot of money to look this cheap.' It also costs a lot of money to make movies this bad.

The saddest thing of all, however, is the complete lack of a model of mature masculinity. The choice men are offered is to continue to play toy soldiers — which Milius indulges to the hilt — or to be naughty boys, 'wicked willies', which Edwards milks for its sheer ridiculousness.

Yet, surely we only regress both culturally and individually when we cannot face the present, when we cannot accept the consequences of being adult? What saves us from this fate is not the love of a good woman, or even Nigel Havers, but the recognition that regression doesn't work because it is based on an imaginary place that exists only outside both personal and political history.

This is what finally makes the difference between self-awareness and self-indulgence. In other words it is what separates the men from the boys.

▃▃▃▃▃

Prince

Prince Nelson Rodgers has made a career out of playing with himself. Twenty-three instruments in fact. His favourite colour is purple and his favourite foods are Dorito Chips and chocolate-dipped strawberries. He signs his autographs Love God P. He writes the best songs in the world about sex, religion and sex as religion. This much we can establish. The rest is a little more difficult. As one of his lyrics goes, 'I'm not a woman, I'm not a man/I am something you'll never understand.'

This perversity, this refusal to be pinned down either musically or personally to a single identity is what makes him so seductive. Anyway, if you're not turned on by the soundtrack he writes to his 'free-floating one-man orgy' how can you resist a man who has been described as 'a schizoid little tart with a Bible in one hand and his cock in the other'?

Ignoring the fact that the most sublime moments of black

music from Al Green to James Brown have often been produced from exactly the place where religious feeling melts into sexual healing, Prince's 'schizophrenia' is one of his most marketable qualities. With his *BatDance* album at the top of the charts, he established himself as well and truly mainstream, his cross-over appeal intrinsically bound up with his ability to transcend traditional categories.

He wears his eclecticism like a purple heart on his sleeve. The obvious heroes are there — Little Richard, Sly Stone, James Brown — but there in between are Joni Mitchell, Santana and the psychedelic haze of Hendrix. Like Hendrix, Prince turns the usual pop process of white artists ripping off black styles on its head. He picks 'n' mixes the poppiest of white pop, and power-chord rock, with hard funk and jazz.

Live he is magic. As he dances his way into several truly peculiar outfits, he characteristically exhibits a sartorial sense that undermines any coherent notion of 'fashion'. Layering the styles of different decades into a collage that is always more than the sum of its parts, he gets down on his high heels, one minute fellating a microphone the next giving himself to God.

In his private life apparently a Howard Hughes-type hermit, once in public the contents of his Dirty Mind spill out — confused, excessive, strange. He wants it all and he wants it now. Sex is always somewhere between stimulation and *simulation*. Everything and Nothing. It is both Reichian salvation and a reminder of loneliness, loss, death. In other words, of the impossibility of desire.

Yet somewhere in all this polysexual transgression there is a real sadness and ambiguity towards women. They might 'rule his world', he might make a point of employing female musicians and yet you can't help wondering whether he is really interested in making love to anyone but himself, with us watching of course. In *Purple Rain* he seduces Appolonia to the sound of what sounds like orgasmic groaning but is actually the tape of a girl crying played backwards.

From archetypal lonely boy childhood to the perpetual adolescence that only this degree of fame allows, his narcissism prevails. Sometimes it's disastrous as in the awful *Under the Cherry Moon* movie, sometimes it's wonderful pushing him into unknown territories, weirdly fluid identities as in *If I Was Your Girlfriend*.

For you see there is nothing but the movies and lyrics with which to catch hold of him as he slithers from one persona to the next because he never gives interviews and reveals himself only in cryptic coded messages. He wants to be alone and he wants us to know that he's alone. It's as shrewd a career move as any. An image of an image of a star that he played out long before he was a star.

Now, without a doubt, for Prince the day has come. So what will he do next? Prolific as ever, he has written hits for Chaka Khan, the Bangles, Mavis Staples, but as a producer he tends to make everyone sound like (surprise, surprise) Prince. He talks increasingly of his faith in God — well wouldn't you if you were paid £75,000 for saying one line in *Batman*?

Yet the ultimate irony around this most precious of postmodern popstars is that as he has continually transgressed boundaries — sexual, racial, personal as well as musical — discarding and demolishing any notion of fixed identity, he is perceived as a genius, a true individual in the oldest sense of the word. While Michael Jackson, with whom Prince hates to be compared, seeks with increasing difficulty to erase or resolve all signs of difference, both sexual and racial, Prince throws them up in the air and pushes any sense of coherent identity to the limit and beyond, making the very idea seem illusory. Difference becomes simply the starting point for the celebration of desire. And this impulse — frenzied, utopian, disruptive — is more purely subversive than singing *We Are the World* could ever be.

Sometimes, at his most perfect, Prince understands this and he takes us to this place too, dissolving and reforming in some new universe where separation doesn't exist, where bodies and minds come together, free at last of the constraints of gender and ego.

Then the music stops and you fall back into yourself, wondering how anyone could take a pop song so seriously.

—————

Torch Song tightrope

In the TV programme *Out on Tuesday* various drag 'artistes' were discussing the differences between the glamorous images of women that were their stock in trade and real women. The obvious question arose — is drag essentially misogynist? Is it actually an insult to women? 'No,' said one man in a memorably outrageous reply. 'Women are an insult to drag.'

Like it or not, there is a certain truth in this. For drag depends on a kind of hyper-femininity that most real women cannot and do not want to compete with. The best drag flounces about in all the superficial signs of womanhood and then throws them back in your face like a brick wrapped in a feather boa. Drag queens can do what real women are still not supposed to do — talk dirty and fabulously flirty. After all, they are only faking it. Better still, they can do what real men must never do — express desire for other men. By reaching the parts that pure masculinity or femininity can't reach by themselves, drag teeters between jaded stereotypes and genuine subversion. *Torch Song Trilogy* walks this tightrope.

Arnold, the central character of the film, makes his living as a 'female impersonator'. It isn't easy being a drag queen but he has no choice — 'Try as I might, I just can't walk in flats'. Arnold is of course Harvey Fierstein, gravelly-voiced star and writer of the play *Torch Song Trilogy* on which this adaptation is based.

As he puts on his face, Arnold talks straight to the camera about his life and his quest for *lurve*, swerving between emotional vulnerability and devastating one-liners. *Torch Song Trilogy* charts his life through the seventies and in its depiction of the pre-AIDS decade is already an historical document in the way that Mapplethorpe's photographs are. Fierstein, has, in fact, been criticised for not raising the issue of AIDS in what is after all a rare event — a mainstream film about a gay man. Yet the gay community is only a backdrop in a melodrama of heroic individualism.

The original play's three-part form is still present on screen. Acts one and two deal with affairs of the heart. First Arnold is picked up in a bar by bisexual Ed, who is also dating the woman he eventually marries. Next he falls for pretty boy Alan, with whom he builds a loving and stable relationship. Their plans to marry and then to foster a teenager are tragically wrecked when Alan is attacked and killed in the street.

Act three turns to The Family. Arnold goes ahead with fostering David, a young gay teenager who will insist on calling him 'Ma'. But when Arnold's own Ma comes to stay, having lost her husband, she is shocked by her son's new role as parent. Nor can she cope with Arnold's grief over Alan, which he compares to her loss. How can a homosexual relationship come close to thirty-five years of marriage, she demands? Through a stagey and at times overwrought climax Arnold and his mother argue out their differences: she not wanting to recognise his gayness and he refusing to edit his life to suit her sensibilities.

The film ends with hints of reconciliation all round (between Arnold and his mother and between Arnold and the now separated Ed). In so many ways, despite its gay subject matter, *Torch Song Trilogy* is a remarkably straight film infused by old-fashioned values about show business and entertainment.

Nevertheless, *Torch Song Trilogy* raises crucial issues. And how many images of gay people who are not inherently tragic — let alone images of gay parenthood — do we ever see on the screen?

Its sentimentality is made bearable by a campness which threads humour and self-awareness into every emotional trauma. And campness is also exposed as a defence — for in the confrontation between Arnold and his mother, it is she who gets camper and he 'straighter' as he demands once and for all that good old respect.

The film is accessible because it deals in universal rather than specifically gay experience — a process made possible only by the absence of AIDS. Fierstein is interested in families, relationships, fulfilment, in finding oneself — in other words, in the American Dream. His gayness becomes simply an extension of his individuality.

What is heartening about this most liberal of humanist movies is its acknowledgement of the fact that people do change. Every character ends by accepting something that he or she had originally found impossible to live with. But while they 'grow', this growth is only achieved on a personal basis. What Arnold demands are not rights but love and respect. Homosexuality still remains acceptable only in the privacy of the home, becoming a 'threat' the moment it moves onto the street, into the arena of the public and the collective — into the political. And Arnold, feisty and funny as he is, still seems desperate to show that 'Underneath they're all lovable'. Something no heterosexual is ever asked to prove.

Here's Looking at You, Kid!

> All I want is a room with a view
> a sight worth seeing
> a vision of you
> All I want is a room with a view
>
> All I want is 20-20 vision
> a total portrait
> with no omissions
> All I want is vision of you
>
> If you can
> Picture this . . .
>
> D. Harry/C. Stein/J. Destri, 'Picture This'
> (for Blondie)

Virginia Woolf may have needed a room of her own, but by the late 70s Debbie Harry was asking for a 'room with a view', 'a sight worth seeing', '20-20 vision'. That particular object of desire was turning the tables — she was singing about watching and wanting, about looking at *her* object of desire.

Shortly afterwards, Richard Gere was taking a very long time to get dressed in *American Gigolo*, the camera lingering over his body in a way normally reserved for female flesh. The ritual of getting dressed, the pampering and preening of the male body became a mechanism by which movies from *Mean Streets* to *Saturday Night Fever* could effectively relocate the cinematic gaze within the strict confines of narrative structure. Standing in front of the mirror, masculinity could legitimately be displayed. Looking hot meant looking cool, looking sharp meant looking hard. Dressing to kill might mean just that — even goody goody Michael Jackson is panting and pouting to show us that underneath he's really *bad*.

By 1986, however, you no longer needed the excuse of getting ready to go out to show half-naked men: you could show them getting *un*dressed. Nick Kamen's determined unbuttoning of his flies in the launderette was enough to make him an instant success — in a neat bit of role reversal, Madonna had soon whisked him away, and written and produced his hit single.

Something had happened. After years of women complaining about the objectification of their bodies, we find ourselves confronted with the male body on display: cut up, close up and oh! so tastefully lit. For some time now such images of men have been quietly slipping into the mainstream via films, videos and — above all — advertising, selling us everything from jeans to make-up and baby clothes. Yes, by 1987 even Terence Conran had 'sussed' it — Mothercare's spring catalogue featured, instead of the usual blonde mother and toddler, a New Man — naked to the waist with, not one, but two bouncing babies. It now seemed to be less a case of taking the toys from the boys than of getting yourself a 'toyboy'.

This new breed of images of masculinity would not have been possible without two decades of gay and feminist politics which advocated the idea that sexuality is socially constructed rather than god-given and immutable. Hence femininity and masculinity are processes in a state of constant negotiation, not static categories from which there is no escape. Out of this flux steps the image of the New Man (many would argue that he exists only as an image): he is tough but tender, masculine but sensitive — he can cry, cuddle babies and best of all buy cosmetics. He is not afraid to be seen caring but mostly he cares about how he looks. So how do you represent such a man? Well, what's so interesting is that many of these images are culled in both form and technique from a long tradition of softcore homo-erotica, and yet are they being aimed at, and consumed by, women as well as men. Moreover I want to suggest that they appeal to women precisely because they offer the possibility of an *active female gaze*.

As theory lopes in its ungainly way behind what is actually happening I could find little explanation for this phenomenon. When I sought material on how women look at men, I discovered, instead, a strange absence. There is plenty on how men look at women; some on how men look at men; and just a little bit on how women look at other women. But to suggest that women actually look at men's bodies is apparently to stumble into a theoretical minefield which holds sacred the idea that in the dominant media the look is always already structured as male.

But in the end the way that we regard a body of theory is much the same as we regard real bodies. We can disavow the things we don't like, fetishise the bits we do, make do with what is familiar while fantasising about something altogether different . . .

Such writing as there is on the male body tends to offer a reiteration of its stereotyped portrayal: the Stallone-type hard man, the glorified man machine, the celebration of emotional inarticulacy. As Antony Easthope writes:

> This brings up the question of how it is not to be looked at with the eye of desire. This is precisely the look that the masculine body positively denies, as though it were saying, 'Whatever else, not that!' The hardness and the tension of the body strives to present it as wholly masculine, to exclude all curves and hollows and be

straight lines and flat planes. It would really like to be a cubist painting. Or whatever. But above all not desirable to other men because it is definitely not soft and feminine; hairy if need be, but not smooth; bone and muscle, not flesh and blood. The masculine body seeks to be Rimbaud not Rambo.

Certainly many representations of men would substantiate this argument, as Anthony Easthope illustrates, but the key point is to do with the suppression of homosexual desire between men. This suppression, which according to Freud forms one of the foundations of our society, is precisely what renders the cultural representation of masculinity so limited. But its consequences work in contradictory ways. Rosalind Coward suggests that because the male body is not seen as desirable, men remain in control of desire and the activity of looking. Yet this is not without its price: such male dominance is dependent on the sublimation of narcissism (the self as desirable), and the accompanying lack of satisfactory representations of masculinity results in men feeling alienated from their own bodies. So, ironically, as Coward goes on to say:

> One of the major consequences of men's refusal to be the desired sex, however, is that even women have difficulty in finding them attractive. There's a sort of failure of will at the heart of heterosexual desire.

Things have changed in the few years since Coward's piece was written. Although Rambo still rules in some quarters, competing images of masculinity are coming to the fore which *do* show men as desirable. Such images do not suppress desire between men and so their narcissistic elements are made explicit. These images offer the possibility of being looked at with the 'eye of desire', whether it is a male or a female eye. Their capacity to disturb lies in their appeal to both men and women.

The following passage is from an article by Martin Raymond in the free London magazine *Girl about Town*:

> For a lot of people last year's Levis 501s campaign came as a revelation — or should that read revolution. Gone were the product shots, naff jingles and predictable copy lines — instead we had fetish, flesh and fulsome torsos. Those jeans, that flesh, that man. Hey wait a minute . . . yes, but it's true, even for us blokes Levis was one hell of a shock.

The Levis 501s advertising campaign was one of the most successful ever, managing to connect Levis to a nostalgic longing for a simpler time — 'What a wonderful world it would be . . .' and putting 50s style over 60s songs (the lyrics are indeed fitting — 'Don't know much about history'!). But when the camera focused on the leather belt sliding off, the assured unbuttoning of the flies, or James Mardle easing himself into the bath, a different kind of longing altogether was evoked.

This wasn't the first time, of course, that the male body was represented as an object of desire — from the silent movie stars to Smash Hits there is a long if uneasy history of male pin-ups. What was different was that, in a mainstream context, here was a male body coded, in Mulvey's apt but awkward phrase, for its 'to-be-looked-at-ness'. The usual mechanisms that signal erotic spectacle had crossed gender boundaries. As Louisa Saunders puts it: 'Nowadays, the half-naked body you see on TV ads making tasteful love to a bottle of scent won't necessarily be a woman's body.'

As it becomes more problematic to show naked women in advertisements, so naked men come to the fore. The Grey Flannel aftershave ads are a typical example. Shot in grainy black and white, they feature a man, again nude. He looks, not at us, but sideways out of the frame. The picture is cut off at crotch level presumably to leave the rest to our imagination. Again this ad is aimed at women as well as men — and with reason, since it is still women who buy the majority of men's clothes and cosmetics.

And it's not just the advertisers: it's also the people who produce calendars, cards and posters. As the art director of the Athena chain said in an interview in *City Limits*:

> The public want pictures of half-naked men — but all done in the best possible taste! We've played down the macho thing, the men are more passive, there's nothing aggressive.

So alongside all the predictable calendars full of pictures of semi-clad females, 1986 saw the introduction of calendars called *Blues Boy* by Neil Mackenzie Matthews; we also had *Select Men* and *Cindy Palamanos Men*. All three in the same tasteful but suggestive style that could be sold to both men and women. In fact the 1988 *Blues Boy* calendar moves further into the field of multi-purpose sexuality: 'On the reverse of every languid, soft-focus Blues Boy pose is a Blues Girl in exactly the same setting. So depending on which way you hang/swing it gives you a choice of two calendars (Brian Kennedy in *City Limits*). Skilful marketing or a real indication of the blurring of gender boundaries?

What *is* clear, however, is that in both the still and the moving image the camera lens is zooming in on male flesh. In *Top Gun*, where the camera moved effortlessly between cockpit and locker room; or in the American soaps, where it cuts from boardroom to bedroom to catch Jeff/Bobby/Dex just getting out of the shower . . .

> I will give you my finest hour
> then one I spent
> watching you shower
> I will give you my finest hour
>
> All I want is a photo in my wallet
> a small remembrance
> of something more solid
> All I want is a picture of you
>
> D. Harry/C. Stein/J. Destri, 'Picture This'
> (for Blondie)

The finest hour of what has become known as *Screen* theory can't really explain the production or the consumption of the kind of images that I have mentioned. They are certainly not coming from a political avant-garde but are emerging within popular culture as a result of the renegotiations over masculinity brought about by radical political discourses. Obviously, such shifts are precarious and contradictory, yet perhaps they offer the female spectator a different position from those which Jackie Stacey neatly summarises as 'masculinisation, masochism or marginality'.

Dwelling as they have on woman as object of the gaze, many of the theories associated with *Screen* have been vital in understanding the relations of power involved in relations of looking. Paradoxically, however, such theory has also contributed to the repression of the female gaze. For repression is about power too, and as Mary Anne Doane comments: 'In theories of repression there is no sense of the productiveness or positivity of power.'

Likewise there is no sense of the productivity of resistance: to say that women *can* and *do* look actively and erotically at images of men and other women disrupts the stifling categories of a theory which assumes that such a look is somehow always bound to be male.

The appropriation and rereading of certain genres and films by gay subculture as 'camp', the wresting of subversive meanings from popular heterosexual discourses such as Hollywood melodramas, is a way of deliciously disturbing the 'true' story. While homosexuality itself may be repressed, *camp* empowers a gay sensibility that can creatively out-manoeuvre the preferred or dominant meanings of a text. 'Camp sees everything in quotation marks,' writes Susan Sontag. For women this kind of creativity seems to be almost a by-product of the whole process of socialisation. Not only are they surrounded by representations of female sexuality through which they must somehow find pleasure; they live both with the 'power of the image' and an acute awareness of its artificiality. Socially, they are expected to be the 'carers', which involves having to be extremely attentive to visual codes and clues. Indeed looking after babies or small children is skill largely based on being intimately aware of how another body behaves or looks.

It is well documented, by Robin Lakoff and others, that women tend to be able to name slight visual discriminations in colour, for instance. Advertisers aim their more obscure 'lifestyle' ads at women, who are able to pick up minute visual details with great ease. Campaigns aimed at women sometimes deliberately play upon the ability of women to decode the visual clues that signal class and status, such as furniture or interior design. These ads work by making the spectator feel part of a world to which she aspires, using her knowledge to affirm her right to it. Other products, aiming for a wide market, may underplay anything which can be identified with a particular socio-economic group so as not to exclude potential consumers. Avon, for example, use mostly outdoor shots of flowery fields in their catalogues, which are

31

presumably not thought to have particular class or status connotations.

In some ways, then, the very cultural context that weaves the relations of looking into the fabric of power makes it easier for us to unpick it. Nancy Henley's research, for instance, shows that women listen more, look more and are more attentive than men in face-to-face interaction. In public situations, by contrast, men stare at women to assert male dominance, while women look away. But when discussing the way that women look at images or representations of men, we cannot locate them easily in either the private or public sphere. Images on advertising hoardings or in magazines can be looked at privately in the sense that they are always 'just an image' and not a real person who requires a response. Yet on the other hand our access to many images is in and through public space — going to see a film, for instance, involves being part of an assumed audience.

Yet film theory which is primarily about the 'gaze' of the cinema cannot be *simply* mapped on to other media. As John Ellis points out, 'TV is more about the look, and the glance and sound' than the overwhelming cinematic gaze. Video, which puts control of the image within the hands of the viewer, may involve altogether different relations of looking. Clearly, flicking through a magazine is different from staring at a huge poster while waiting for a train, which is different again from replaying a favourite old film on video.

Recognising the contradictions between public and private contexts in which these images are viewed, as well as the differences between the images themselves, means that we cannot be satisfied with a theory premissed on a unified spectator sitting alone in a darkened cinema, luxuriously free of the constraints of race or class, history and other texts. This idealisation is attractive because we could so much more easily talk about the 'female gaze' as though it were an attribute of anatomy' — the rational retina, the iris free of ideology . . . All men could then be offered a choice of operations — straightforward castration or the removal of their phallic cataracts!

What I'm talking about, of course, is *essentialism*, that most emotionally satisfying, but politically crippling, of all discourses. Basically the argument suggests that women *see* things differently — whether it is a landscape or a teacup (see for instance the work of Judy Chicago) — and therefore a female eye behind the camera would automatically produce a different perspective! In some respects this argument runs parallel to the 'unified masculine model' (Stacey) proposed by Laura Mulvey, who returned to Freud via Lacan because here was a theory which stressed the importance of the visual for the formation of the ego.

Briefly put, in Mulvey's terms there are two types of visual pleasure on offer in Hollywood films. One revolves around an active, objectifying look that requires a distance between the viewer and the object on screen. This is the voyeuristic or fetishistic look. The other involves identification with the screen image and so depends precisely on the dissolution of the distance between screen and spectator. Both these processes, Mulvey argues, are structured through the narrative in such a way that the spectator identifies with the male hero and with his objectification of the female. Femininity as spectacle is encoded into the operations of mainstream cinema so that only a radical and deconstructive film practice could disrupt these pleasures. This argument has been tremendously influential and important in getting beyond a simple 'images of women' type of film criticism. Yet because her argument produces only a masculine spectator position, she is forced in a later article on *Duel in the Sun* to assert that pleasure for the female spectator must involve a type of psychic transvestism. A temporary masculinisation is the only way that Mulvey can offer active pleasure for the woman viewer. But the pleasure offered to women by theorists such as Mulvey is linked only with 'enjoying the freedom of action and control over the diegetic world that identification with a hero provides.'

The possibility of the male as erotic object doesn't really exist, because according to D.N. Rodowick:

> Mulvey conceives the look to be essentially active in its aims, identification with the male protagonist is only considered from a point of view which associates it with a sense of omnipotence, of assuming control of the narrative. She makes no differentiation between identification and object choice in which sexual aims may be directed towards the male figure . . .

This arises because, although Mulvey speaks of female sexuality as an oscillation between an active but regressive masculinity and a passive femininity, the terms active and passive remain static. Freud himself noted but never really overcame the confusion that occurs when active/passive becomes automatically mapped on to masculine/feminine:

> 'Masculine' and 'feminine' are used sometimes in the sense of activity and passivity, sometimes in a biological, and sometimes, again, in a sociological sense. The first of these three meanings is the essential one and the most serviceable in psychoanalysis. When, for instance, libido was described . . . as being 'masculine', the word was being used in this sense, for an instinct is always active even when it has a passive aim in view.

Though Freud ends up by saying that there is no such thing as pure masculinity or femininity and that we are all bisexual, it seems that the force of history overwhelmed him into naturalising the descriptions of gender which psychonalysis in fact undermined. Why do active and passive need to be translated into the terms of masculine and feminine? This is a socially constructed convention that, as Stephen Heath points out, has no place in a theory of the subject that is radical precisely in its insistence on the cultural determinations of so-called gendered behaviour.

While Freud discusses the need for the ego to fantasise itself in an active manner, Mulvey maps this on to a cultural masculinity, thus dramatically limiting the options of the female spectator. In contrast, recent work on fantasy and identification by writers such as Elizabeth Cowie points to a far more complex process in which identification may occur with the activity itself, not simply with the subject/object of the representation. According to John Ellis, there are shifting identifications between the images on screen and the varying positions, both active and passive, offered within the narrative. 'Identification is therefore multiple and fractured, a sense of seeing the constituent parts of the spectator's own psyche paraded before her or him.'

So, given the complex and contradictory nature of identification, and the difference between sexual aim and object choice described by Rodowick, we cannot simply assume that gender is coterminous with a predetermined subject position within the text. Preferred readings may not always be preferred . . .

Woman as erotic spectacle brings both pleasure and pain. The anxiety induced by seeing the image of woman supposedly reminds the male spectator of the threat of castration and is therefore displaced by the fetishisation of the image. Through this process, Mulvey argues, the image of woman is once more made perfect or visually complete. In traditional Hollywood genres, such as the historical epic, or the Western, there are also moments when the male body is on display, where male spectacle takes over from narrative. This also causes anxiety, which, according to Stephen Neale, is dispelled through sadism — the body is wounded or punished in aggressive fight scenes and ritualised gun battles. Alternatively, as in films such as *American Gigolo* or *Saturday Night Fever*, punishment may be meted out through the narrative itself. Both these films show the problems inherent in the male body becoming an object of desire.

Yet the overt sexualisation of the black male body in the media unsettles such a line of thought — for it seems that if a body is coded racially as 'other', then in some cases it may be legitimately fetishised. The sublime mixture of fear and desire that such images produce may in fact be at the very heart of fetishisation. Unfortunately the reduction of people to bodies, of complex histories to animal physicalities, is also at the core of racism.

So how do the more contemporary images that I mentioned at the beginning of this essay fit into this scheme of things? The answer is that they don't. What seems to be happening is that now we are seeing the male body coded precisely as erotic spectacle but *without* the accompanying narrative violence. Does this offer women a voyeuristic, even fetishistic look? I'm afraid not, girls. Mark Finch writes in an otherwise interesting article on *Dynasty*:

> Women are not trained to objectify bodies as men are, which implies that *Dynasty*'s codification of men along a *Playgirl/Cosmopolitan* discourse enables a gay erotic gaze through the relay of the women's look.

Now I'm not suggesting that the gay male gaze is not being facilitated by programmes like *Dynasty*, but because so many of the images in question are appropriated or influenced by homo-erotic genres anyway, I want to argue the opposite:

*that the codification of men via male gay discourse enables a
female erotic gaze.*

Explicitly sexual representations of men have always
troubled dominant ideas of masculinity, because male power
is so tied to looking rather than to being looked at. In a
discussion of male pin-ups, Richard Dyer describes the
disturbance caused by presenting men as passive, and the
frantic need to disavow any notion of passivity. Identifying
the hysterically phallic symbolism surrounding publicity
shots of stars such as Bogart, he writes of the totally excessive
quality of much male imagery:

> The clenched fists, the bulging muscles, the hardened
> jaws, the proliferation of phallic symbols — they are all
> striving after what can hardly ever be achieved, the
> embodiment of phallic mystique.

You have only to see a Stallone film or a video of any Heavy
Metal band to recognise the truth of this. Indeed, Sylvester
Stallone crams every available signifier of masculinity into
each frame of his films — which turn into a kind of grotesque
masquerade of manhood, but one that is none the less highly
popular.

Some macho men, however, flirt with this very ambiguity
— Schwarzenegger (body builder turned film-maker), for
example, ostensibly from the same school as Stallone,
consistently loads his films with self-conscious references to
his manliness, which results in a camp sub-text that sends up
the whole ridiculous enterprise. Clint Eastwood, in a seemingly paranoid mood in 1971, made two very interesting films
about what it was to be the object of female desire. In *Play
Misty for Me* he is pursued by a woman who is murderously
obsessed with him, while in *The Beguiled* he plays a soldier
wounded in the American Civil War who takes refuge in a
girls' school — it ends up with the women sawing his leg off to

keep him there. What the loss of a limb signifies depends upon how seriously you take your Freud (or Clint's fear of women).

The striking thing about contemporary images of men is that at least some of them seem to acknowledge and even embrace a passivity that was once symbolically outlawed. The feel is softer, their gaze un-threatening. Many of the ads use black and white photography or moody lighting which connotes that this is just an image — thus a distance can be created between the image and the viewer so that the image may be fetishised precisely as an image. This distance provides the space for the spectator to insert her/himself into the fantasy scenario evoked by many of these representations as the male is marked out as an erotic object.

In the first Levis 501s ad we are offered the secret vantage point of observing a man in the midst of his beauty routine — he doesn't know that we are watching his narcissistic pampering. When he glances at the picture of the girl, his narcissism is momentarily contained — the pleasure in his body is for someone else and yet as the camera focuses on the water covering his crotch and he gets into the bath, the auto-erotic aspects of the image win out. Water, though often associated with female sexuality, has long been used in homo-erotic imagery to signify male orgasm. Just think of all those gushing sounds in Frankie Goes to Hollywood's *Relax* and think of the reason why the record was banned!

'Splash it all over' seems to be a recurring theme — from the post-coital blues boy to George Michael of Wham!. The male body displayed for enjoyment allows women to look actively and powerfully at these private rituals. For a change they are responsible for their own voyeurism and their own desire. In the Nick Kamen ad the relay of looks between the people sitting in the launderette sets him up as object of the gaze — so we too can look. If, in the past, erotic images of men's bodies carried with them the threat of male homosexuality and therefore had to be rendered powerless in some way by being feminised or wounded (the agony is the ecstasy), it now seems possible to represent the male body as a pleasurable object on condition that this pleasure can be contained within 'a narcissistic/auto-erotic discourse.

The slippage into and from homo-erotica is of course inevitable. Unsurprisingly, many of the kinds of images I have mentioned have been discussed from a gay male perspective (see for instance the work of Mark Finch mentioned earlier and of Frank Mort), which tends to underestimate the pleasure that women may derive from such images. Thus Mark Finch can write about *Dynasty*:

> It seems to me that the pleasure for female spectators is in seeing men treated like women, rather than the pleasure of seeing nudity itself: a textual equality to match representations of strong women.

On the contrary homo-erotic representation, far from excluding the female gaze *may actively invite it*. What's more, as many shrewd businessmen have realised, it sells to young girls. When Simon Napier-Bell first saw Wham! on *Top of the Pops* he immediately picked up on the homo-erotic tension between the two boys and saw it as a marketable phenomenon. Many people puzzled over what Andrew Ridgely's role was — he didn't write, play instruments or sing — but the combination of him and George Michael provided visual points of entry into many permutations of fantasy. Many of Wham!'s publicity shots play with classic homo-erotic traditions (George Michael looking ecstatic in the shower, etc.), for it is in this space that men can be presented as desirable. The use of Ridgely is a kind of third term that breaks down the binarism of either identification with the image or the controlling look of voyeurism. What we have here is a far more complicated scenario, one which allows fluid relations of activity and passivity across multiple identifications.

This more mobile concept of desire, which emphasises its productivity, is to be found in Jacqueline Rose's comments on Freud's 1919 essay 'A child is being beaten':

> For what the fantasy of the female patients reveals is the difficulty and structuration of feminine sexuality across contradictions in subject/object positions and areas of the body — the desire of the woman is indeed not a 'clear message' . . . The essay demonstrates that male and female cannot be assimilated to active and passive and that there is always a potential split between the sexual object and the sexual aim, between subject and object of desire. What it could be said to reveal is the splitting of subjectivity in the process of being held to a sexual representation (male or female), a representation without which it has no place (behind each fantasy lies another which simply commutes a restricted number of terms).

So although fantasy may only operate with a restricted number of terms, it can endlessly and creatively rework them. What many of these new images of men do is to leave a gap for the female spectator to occupy, a position sometimes within the frame of the picture, sometimes outside it; sometimes active, sometimes passive. Whereas images of women are fetishised as a disavowal of phallic absence, what seems to be going on here is the disavowal of phallic presence — these men are not presented as all-powerful but as objects of pleasure and desire. They undermine the symbolism of the phallus. As Luce Irigary writes:

> When the penis itself becomes a means of pleasure, and

indeed a means of pleasure among men, the phallus loses its power. Pleasure, so it is said, should be left to women, those creatures so unfit for the seriousness of symbolic rules.

Yet Irigary would be unlikely to endorse my view that women can take pleasure in the kinds of images that I have been describing, for she suggests that female eroticism is linked to *touch* rather than *sight*. She regards the realm of the visual in our culture as intrinsically problematic for women, in that the process of looking always requires a split between subject and object. The transformation of the object of the gaze into the object of desire which is premissed on a difference — a splitting — is therefore regarded as an essentially masculine activity. Women whose auto-erotic pleasure is in closeness, sameness — in what Doane calls 'over-identification' — are unable to distance themselves from images in the way that men are. According to the theory, in terms of visual discourse it becomes impossible for women to become subjects of their own desire.

To escape the ultimate sin of objectification (why is it in itself so terrible?) Irigary retreats into the world of transcendent orgasmic bliss where subject melts into object and where difference dissolves, arguing that touch is the 'true' feminine sense. In a culture where the power of visual images assumes ever greater importance in our lives, this seems to me to be taking the position of the child who shuts her eyes believing that no one can see *her* any more. Touch may be a peculiarly female sense but then so might smell for that matter — and where would that leave us?

While it is crucial to treat women's pleasure as distinct from men's, we must avoid discussing both as though they were fixed outside social conditions. For surely as social conditions change, so do our pleasures. A simple explanation for the proliferation of these new images of men may be found in more liberal attitudes to homosexuality. As homosexual discourse has become public, what was once hidden has become more explicit.

Accompanying these changes there have also been shifts in attitudes to female sexuality. In the 1970s magazines such as *Playgirl* were launched, on the assumption that women could move from being sexually passive to being sexually active by behaving like imitation men and devouring pictures of naked models in ludicrous poses with ridiculous captions. As Margaret Walters writes, 'Such magazines are trying to reduce a woman's feelings to a formula before she knows what they are or might be.' The laughter occasioned by projects such as *Viva* and *Playgirl* compensated for their failure to provide us with anything remotely erotic. If a distance between the viewer and the image is a prerequisite of pleasurable looking, it seems that in this case the gulf was so wide that it could not be filled by any amount of cheap talk about the 'liberated woman'. Ironically, part of these magazines' commercial failure was the fact that advertisers did not want to place their ads on the same page as pictures of naked men!

> One eye in the mirror as you watched yourself
> go by . . .
> Carly Simon

As representations of male homosexual desire become incorporated into the mainstream, they disturb the suffocating dualism of the theory which provides little pleasure for women. Yet is all this to our benefit? Well, like many of the shifts thrown up via the marketplace, I think it works in contradictory ways. So far I have sketched out what I see as potentially positive for women, i.e. an erotic and pleasurable look. Yet not surprisingly what these representations allow, which has so long been repressed, is the 'coming out' of male narcissism. A few years ago, at a press conference in London, Schwarzenegger suggested the boom in male body building was connected to feminism: 'For years men looked at women. Now women are looking back at men.' However, it's not that simple, for, as Walters suggests, 'the male body builder is less concerned with women than with his mirror.'

This would appear to be reinforced by men-focused ads and new men's magazines, such as *Arena*, which promote a kind of 'Look, don't touch' sensibility whereby sexuality becomes a self-conscious status symbol. The idea of smooth sexual autonomy, rather than the messy world of relationships, is the one that sells all those 'personal adornment' products. We're talking strictly *market* penetration here. Listen to Tony Hodges, managing director of the agency that handled the Grey Flannel campaign, speaking about the 'New Man':

> The individual at the heart of this brand is in his early twenties, is discovering himself — discovering what women discovered years ago — that the mirror is perhaps more important than the other person.

Frank Mort suggests that there is positive potential in men becoming self-conscious in so far as it leads to the realisation that they *can* change, rather than thinking of masculinity as an unalterable norm. Yet such superficial changes, so skilfully utilised by the advertisers, will remain precisely at the level of *image* unless they are tied to parallel social changes in male attitudes — unless men are convinced that they need, and want, to change. Caring has to mean more than caring about how one looks. Two decades of feminist demands that men should be more sensitive must surely result in something more than men with sensitive skin?

So are we to welcome this upsurge of male narcissism as a

'good thing'? Or is it just another way of excluding women? Now that men can look good and be emotional, are women expendable? Or are we just trying to pull a homosexual discourse into a heterosexual space?

Such questions arise out of contradictory cultural processes; on one hand culture promotes gay imagery and style in order to get young men as consumers, and on the other, the political climate is increasingly repressive and anti-gay. So although in some contexts the male body is being legitimated as an object of desire, explicit portrayals of the male genitals are still forbidden. An erect penis is still what makes hard porn 'hard'. The right is ever more frantic to preserve its phallic mystique — the erect penis is still supposed to be an object of mystery rather than a bit of a disappointment — so we get uproar at the hint of a Derek Jarman film and a BBC spokesman announcing that there will never be 'an erection at the BBC' (to which someone wittily replied that there would still be lots of cock-ups — and the rest of us thought just a bunch of pricks . . .).

The fear experienced by men of women's Medusa-like stare, which petrifies everything in sight, is in reality a fear that the female gaze will soften everything in its path. Yet this softening has *already* been achieved in many of these new representations of men and such a mythology may actually obscure what is different or disturbing about the female gaze. If a female gaze exists it does not simply replicate a monolithic and masculinised stare, but instead involves a whole variety of looks and glances — an interplay of possibilities.

> We read a text (of pleasure) the way a fly buzzes around a room: with sudden, deceptively decisive turns, fervent and futile . . .

Not for us the singular and silent view of the fly on the wall, instead we must insist, like Barthes' fly buzzing around the room, that our ways of seeing are myriad, our pleasures plural.

Here's looking at you, kid . . .

WOMEN

Material Girl

Of the holy trinity of Material Girls that dominated the 80s, only one is successfully negotiating the 90s. Margaret Thatcher has been reduced to grumbling on the back benches — the House of Commons is where you go when you've got nothing better to do — and Joan Collins to 'acting' for the BBC. *Dynasty* has finally been laid to rest and Alexis Colby has gone to the great bubblebath in the sky. Yet Madonna just goes from strength to strength.

She was the main attraction at Cannes, where her documentary *In Bed with Madonna* was premiered. She has been on the cover of *Vanity Fair*, *The Face*, and *Q*. For some time she has been taught on women's studies courses and, as if anyone apart from himself cares any more, Michael 'Get Into The Groove' Ignatieff pronounced from the great height of his *Observer* column that she was not a proper 'artist'. Instead, he prefers dead Marilyn. After all, there's nothing like dying to bring out divinity in a woman.

Ms Ciccone, on the other hand, is very much alive. More than a 'Lucky Star' has made her one of the most famous women in the world. So why do so many on the Left feel decidedly dodgy about getting into bed with her, despite her eloquent espousal of all the right causes — women's and gay issues, outspoken support for AIDS research, and her continuing insistence on freedom of speech? Shouldn't we be glad to have her on our side?

This unease about her use of sexuality as a power base surfaced again recently in a piece by Ros Coward. Understanding the power of sex or the sexiness of power simply may not be good enough — ultimately it doesn't give women real freedom or real power. But if 80 million dollars doesn't give you real power I don't know what does.

Is she just too hot to handle? On her last tour, the press fell over themselves to tell us that, even kitted out in Gaultier corsets, she was not sexy enough, as though Madonna's aim in life was to titillate a bunch of hyperventilating menopausal males. It it only the little girls who understand, who don't have a problem with simulated masturbation? Or indeed, the real thing? You can't feign an interest in popular culture and then hold back when something gets this popular. Inevitably, any analysis never comes near articulating the sheer physical joy that her performance exudes.

But many also miss her cleverness. She is continually described as *smart*. Not clever, not intellectual, not thoughtful, but smart. As in sussed, sassy, streetwise — a pragmatic kind of intelligence that is continually devalued by those who prefer their feminism to remain rather abstract. Her acute self-consciousness about image, our collective use of star images, and indeed her own constant changes of appearance, gives her career a remarkable consistency.

Sometimes this can be plain embarrassing. The bits in the film where we are supposed to be seeing 'the real Madonna' — bleaching her hair and bitching on the phone — are, like many of her onstage routines, just *too* obvious, too over the top. Too much honesty flips over easily into its reverse. Can we trust anything she shows us? We see Madonna crying at her mother's grave, fellating a bottle, bawling out her tour manager.

We come away knowing nothing. The myth is left intact.

Onstage it is the real Madonna, off it a pale imitation of a star — charming, infantile, obsessive. Madonna knows her place, and it is at the end of a long line of female icons from Garbo to Monroe who, unlike her, were not in control of their own images, let alone their own lives. This skill amply demonstrates her shrewd manipulation of the history of the cinema.

Such techniques of irony and media literacy, though prized in the hands of men, become distinctly troubling in the hands of women — and when turned on to the question of femininity itself, transgressive. The tabloids may have shrieked that she looked like a man in drag, because she so clearly revels in the shiny surfaces of femininity, that what is reflected back is their very artifice. This process, known psychoanalytically as the masquerade, is one of which she is a mistress. It can be used by powerful women as a way of disguising their threat. But the threat remains — to put on femininity with a vengeance suggests the power of taking it off.

Which is what makes the promise of the movie — 'Madonna like you've never seen her before' — even more of a come-on. It feeds directly into the very cultural pre-occupations which she has so successfully exploited — the dichotomy between image and reality. We want our stars both to be out of the ordinary and yet somehow representative of the ordinary. What makes Madonna ordinary is her upfront aspiration to be somebody, to be important. What makes her extraordinary is that she has done it. Her naked ambition makes us even more uncomfortable than her naked body. Women may know what they want, but they are still not supposed to show what they want.

Somewhere along the line, we still like to think that stars are born, not made. Yet many of our biggest stars, like Schwarzenegger, have completely reconstructed themselves. There is nothing natural about this, and Schwarzenegger's assimilation into the American Dream is as bizarre as his accent.

There are no more secrets. Politics too is now openly discussed in terms of appearances and sound bites. Long gone are the times when exposing such conscious tampering with image would have blown apart credibility. Today it is an index of success. Nobody understands this better than Madonna. Whether she is slobbing about in her dressing gown or discussing her art, she reveals very little of herself, but a hell of a lot about the mechanisms of stardom, and that peculiar state of permanent adolescence which our culture calls 'fame'.

Hi, I'm Anneka-Fly Me

These days we're all into tele-travel, whether it's David Attenborough bumbling around Borneo or watching reports about holidays that we will never go on. But some people it seems get around more than others — take Anneka Rice for instance who makes her living dangling out of helicopters and shrieking.

In the programme *Treasure Hunt*, she dashes around Britain by helicopter, pursued by camera men and instructed politely by the middle-class studio contestants to look for 'clues'. Invariably she finds them just in time and the competitors get a cheque. So what clues are there to *her* function in such a patently ridiculous programme? At the beginning we are told that she acts as the 'eyes and ears' of the studio contestants. But then one wonders why can't they simply get into the helicopter themselves? No, it has to be action woman Anneka who gets airborne because more than the 'eyes and ears' of the programme she is of course the body. Voted last year's 'rear of the year' by the people who decide such things, *Treasure Hunt* pivots on Anneka's appeal.

She plays over-excited daughter to Kenneth Kendal's slightly bemused father-figure. (No wonder Kenneth looks so out of it — reduced from reading the news to this!) He is supposedly in control of the proceedings but with his air of ironic detachment manages always to mishear Anneka and be consistently unhelpful to the guests.

But that doesn't bother our Anneka who flirts with him anyway — she might as well, seeing as she flirts with everyone else — the helicopter pilot, the camera men, the contestants... She certainly is amazing, keeping her brand of breathless enthusiasm going for the whole show. Hers is the TV vocabulary of excess — everything is 'absolutely staggering', 'incredible' and 'totally exhilarating' and her ecstasy reaches fever-pitch as the seconds on the clock tick away.

She inhabits a hyper-emotional world where you can't help feeling she could orgasm over a cup of tea. This total lack of unselfconsciousness, though, is the key to her success. Gauche and giggly she seems to have stepped straight out of a *Bunty* comic where she was the slightly naughty head girl. Her 'sexiness' is totally adolescent — the girl can't help it because she doesn't even realise she's doing it. She is allowed to be physical because she is presented as not yet grown up — Daddy's favourite daughter is uninhibited because she simply doesn't know any better.

The image of a physically capable and daring woman — which she undoubtedly is — is undermined by the fact that she isn't ever in control of where she is going but has to be instructed by other people. Thus she is kept in a state of permanent ignorance. Yet for Anneka ignorance seems to be bliss, as she careers around screaming 'Hi, there' at embarrassed looking bystanders. Relentlessly she keeps up her inane but ecstatic banter. 'Hello Donkey', she shouts at a disdainful looking donkey, 'Oh look — Ye Olde Folke Dancing,' she screams as the helicopter hovers over yet another quaint village.

For you can rest assured that the clues she has to find won't be situated on Broadwater Farm or the Falls Road, but in the rural England of a tourist brochure, a place untroubled by conflicts of race or class. This construction of 'Englishness' has little to do with the reality of living in Britain in the eighties. As with the more exotic travel programmes nasty things such as politics are not supposed to interfere with our enjoyment. Armchair tourism allows only a very limited view of other people and other places. *Wish You Were Here* — the holiday review programme which also features Anneka Rice testing our Action Holidays — offers a very bland and sanitised perspective of the rest of the world. Holiday resorts appear to occupy little pockets of time and space somehow outside of their geographical location. So remarks like 'Beautiful beaches without the usual problem of beggars' can go unquestioned.

After all these programmes are literally about escapism — endangered species has to refer to exotic animals not parts of our own species. England has to be the rustic paradise of 'One Man and his Dog', folk-dancing and thatched cottages — not the urban, multi-ethnic, class-ridden society it actually is. Past struggles and contemporary politics have to be repressed for the myth of merry England to maintain its power.

But then Anneka is just a good old-fashioned funloving girl so these things don't seem or aren't allowed to enter her consciousness. Instead we are offered Anneka as the ultimate avenging angel. Aryan and aerobic — what more could you want in a woman?

Green light spells danger

The other day I had an unexpected visit. I opened the door to a smartly dressed middle-aged couple. 'Are you concerned about the environment?' the man asked. 'Kind of,' was my sheepish answer until I realised that he was rapidly producing all those weird and wonderful pamphlets that are the trademark of the door-to-door God squad. I don't know why I should be surprised that Jehovah's Witnesses are marketing themselves as environmentally friendly. After all everyone else is. I'd just never realised before that the Apocalypse was really the ultimate in eco-disaster or that Jesus Saves should now read Jesus Saves so that He may Recycle. But there you go.

Saving the Planet is a laudable enough aim either for a politician or a religious fanatic. It must be uncontroversial because even Hope in thirty-something wants to do it. Young Sammy Rodgers in *Brookside* is at it too (when she is not swigging gin in her bedroom), badgering her mum to buy ecologically sound products. 'I'm not made of money,' is the pragmatic reply.

Being for Saving the Planet is like being for democracy or for freedom. It's a pretty hard thing to be against. While pompous press editorials argue over whether the Greens should be a 'proper' political party or a pressure group, and despite the feeling that the rush for supermarkets to go green may be little more than a cynical manipulation of a middle-class fad, the fact is that our overall awareness of green issues is increasing.

When you get past the unnecessary packaging and hype, however (Green Book Fortnight, Green Shopping Day, Earth Day, etc), it seems that many greens have taken the feminist slogan 'The personal is political' to such an extreme that the political has disappeared altogether. Much green literature has replaced political analysis with wishful thinking, so it's no surprise that environmental issues can find a home in both the National Front paper *Bulldog* and the *Guardian*. It's a thin line between eco-fatalism and eco-fascism.

This lack of a coherent philosophy is at its most apparent when it comes to women's issues. There is a keen recognition that because women make most of the smaller purchase decisions, they are at the forefront of green consumerism. Yet no one is talking about how much more work a green lifestyle actually involves or how much more it actually costs. To read through the endless consumer guides, with their lists of do's and don'ts, you would think everyone had a nice house with a garden, a husband and enough free time to make-do and mend, as well as grow their own herbs. The reality of most women's lives — the double shift of work and kids — is never discussed except as something vaguely undesirable.

On the other hand, just because women have babies, they are supposed to be fundamentally closer to nature and more concerned with the fate of the planet than men. Socially it may well be the case that women are forced to think about the consequences of their behaviour in a way that men are not, but does this mean we have to swallow whole the myth of the 'natural woman', surely one of the oldest stereotypes in the book? Women can only represent nature while men continue to control culture. And one of the key ways men control culture is precisely by defining what nature is.

Be it Mother Nature or Mother Earth, nature is routinely defined as female. So before you know it real-life females start getting defined as little bits of nature — awkward, unpre- dictable animals that we are. This tendency is not new but what is happening is that much New Age and green writing invites us to celebrate this in a completely uncritical way. From Mother Earth to earth mother in one fell swoop.

Instead of denying the tenuous link between women and nature, some women have chosen to reinforce it, calling themselves eco-feminists. They view ecological concerns as intrinsic to feminisim. This utopian desire for 'a global ecological sisterhood' may obscure differences of class and race as it brings together a bizarre mishmash of mysticism, morality and the more mundane business of everyday activism. At its most banal it simply echoes radical feminism's division of the world into 'all that is good is female, all that is bad is male', then bungs in a few half-baked ideas about grieving for trees. I can think of plenty of good reasons for wanting to save the rainforest, but to claim that it is because the trees are your brothers and sisters has to be the most unconvincing. The earth has been repeatedly raped and battered by man and his horrid technology. It is only by celebrating all these good old feminine virtues (forget the vices) that we will get back on the straight and narrow.

Many British greens would perhaps not go as far as this, though it's interesting that they too stress the importance of feminine rather than feminist values. Janet Alty, spokesperson for the Green Party, admits that she hates the earth mother stereotype, yet says, 'I'm not happy with feminism in its adversarial, confrontational mode; I think you have to give people the benefit of the doubt. And I don't think individual men want to be aggressive. Inside they are deeply unhappy. The problem with feminism is that it tries to seek power over men and that's not getting us anywhere.'

Talking cosily about consensual power-sharing is one thing, but sharing means that those who are now in power have to give some of it up. And whether it's men or multinationals, there is little will for them to do so. Harping on about harmony, balance and responsibility isn't exactly going to bring down the walls of capitalism. Or is it? Bernadette Vallely of the Women's Environmental Network suggests that perhaps women look at power differently. 'It's not about who gets most money. Power to a man might mean being the head of a nuclear industry but it might be something different to a woman in a feminine world. Equality is not about women being nuclear physicists. It's about empowering women to say, "No, I don't want to be a nuclear physicist", by giving equal status to motherhood. The earth mother is not what hippies said she was in the sixties. We're in the nineties now and we have to re-evaluate these stereotypes.'

The under-valuing of motherhood is an old current in feminist thought and remains a key issue. But a politics based on maternity will be severely limiting for women in the long run. In the abstract motherhood may be sacred but sadly history has shown that mothers as well as fathers have been party to some of humanity's worst crimes. Having children may make some women understand the interconnectedness of all living things, but then so can certain drugs.

It is in practice that the cult of motherhood and a green lifestyle interconnects with everything. Except the modern world. Being a green parent can be a mammoth task involving preventing your child interconnecting with anything as pernicious as TV or junk food. Green consumer guides turn kids into vigilantes ready to spring their down-trodden parents at any moment, while their poor mothers scour the shops for organic vegetables, wash nappies (disposables are out) and look for the nearest bottle bank.

Women who never in a million years would buy a book on household tips are being bombarded with prescriptive ideas, many of which are themselves recycled from the war and before. Women used to use baking soda and vinegar to clean because there were no specialised products to do it. Though Bernadette Vallely insists it's not a case of going backwards, she recognises that she has given up things many women wouldn't want to. For instance, she uses re-usable sanitary towels instead of tampons.

However, there *is* an undercurrent of looking back in much green thinking. Indigenous cultures are romanticised as ecologically friendly natural people who live often in abject poverty because they innately care about the planet. Indeed

Jean Liedloff's influential book on childcare, *The Continuum Concept*, was written after the author had spent two and half years with Stone Age Indians in the jungles of South America. She recommends that we sleep with our babies as they do and carry them around all the time for at least the first eight months. 'The difference between our way of life and that of the Yequana is irrelevant to the principles of human nature we are considering,' she says, demolishing both cultural diversity and cultural aspirations. Do Yequana women carry their babies because they want to or they have to?

The big names of the Green Movement, the ubiquitous, Jonathan Porrit and David Icke, also pay lip service to this idea of feminine values at the expense of explaining properly how green policies and politics will affect women's lives. Yet the really big environmental issues, such as overpopulation, are implicitly feminist questions. Time and time again it has been shown that birthrates go down voluntarily only when women's conditions improve. It is these everyday conditions that get forgotten in the rush to the green hypermarket.

Women's participation as shoppers may put them at the vanguard of green consumerism but, as Shelagh Young, deputy editor of *Green* magazine, says: 'Where it is possible to make choices over consumption, it's really only the small things that are green. These are the products that make up the hard work of shopping which is mostly done by women. When it comes to the bigger items — decisions mostly made by men — things haven't changed that much. You can't really get a green stereo, car or TV.

Where green politics and feminism do coincide is in their woolliness about the mechanisms of change. There are huge systems that work to preserve the status quo and hoping men will be nicer doesn't actually make them nicer, any more than asking multinationals to clean up after themselves makes them do it. Embracing feminine values at the expense of feminism means that green politics are not a new way of doing things but the same old story recycled and repackaged. Isn't it about time women who live in green houses started throwing stones?

━━━━━━━

The odds of getting even

'Sweet is revenge — especially to women.' So said Lord Byron a long, long time ago. One can't help feeling that Byron's idea of the perfect act of revenge, a great drama of pain and passion, might have been something grander than spooning Pedigree Chum into the pockets of your spouse's best suit or cutting up his knickers.

In the modern world, such incidents are routinely reported in the tabloids. Headlines such as 'Scissors Sizzler chops up Y-fronts' or 'My Fatal Attraction to a Pizza Revenge' — about a jilted woman who pestered her lover by having scores of pizzas and skip-loads of scaffolding delivered to his business — are commonplace.

With their magical combination of juicily adulterous sex and righteous female resentment, these stories are always good for a laugh. Or a cry, if you really think about it. For, in between the nudge and wink at male duplicity and the sneaking admiration for a woman who gives as good as she gets, is a tangible sense of women's powerlessness — a sense that, despite a symbolic display of female anger, nothing changes.

The *Sun* loves examples of 'Great ways you got your own back on your cheating fella', as though washing his silk shirts in Domestos and pricking holes in his condoms — or your cap — makes everything all right.

In reality, women's revenge is often a peculiarly domestic form of violence that uses women's inside knowledge about their men's habits. Itching powder in his pyjamas; laxatives in his lunch. Some women do go and smash up his car, his boardroom or his mistress in order to publicly humiliate him, but they rarely touch the man himself. They do get mad, but rarely even.

In fantasy, however, female revenge knows no bounds. All those over-achieving soap queens and heroines of the 'humping and hoarding' novels are driven to more and more improbable activities to get back at some creep who once raped, ruined or rejected them.

Fantasy revenge is a kind of wild justice and a source of great pleasure for female readers, who implicitly recognise that while striving to destroy one particular man may not be right, it's not wrong either. The popularity of Fay Weldon's novel *The Life and Loves of a She-Devil* bears this out.

Self-styled 'domestic goddess' Roseanne Barr plays the wronged wife Ruth Patchett in *She-Devil*, Susan Seidelman's new film of the book, which opens on Friday. Barr has said: 'This is not a movie about revenge, this is about justice.'

Though the story has been considerably — and disastrously — toned down for the film version, it is still good to see Ruth turn She-Devil to slowly extract her revenge against her pathetic husband and his new love, the impossibly frilly Mary Fisher. The fact that Mary is played by the impossibly perfect Meryl Streep no doubt adds to our enjoyment of her downfall.

In the black comedy *The War of the Roses*, Kathleen Turner plays another woman who gives as good as she gets. She destroys her husband's car and makes pâté out of the pet while he saws the heels off her shoes and pisses in the meal she has prepared for her friends.

An American couple who carried on like this in real life have just had their story made into a movie called, appropriately enough, *I Love You to Death*, starring Kevin Kline and Tracey Ullman.

Fran Toto made five unsuccessful attempts to murder her philandering husband Tony. He ended up alive, but in hospital, and she went to prison for four years. They are now happily reconciled. Fran says of the man she tried to kill: 'He's quite safe now.'

This case, though, is unusual. When women get violent, it is often directed at the other woman. Just occasionally there are stories of a wife and a mistress who join forces to get their own back, but these are seldom reported. The initial grudging admiration that female avengers attract, collapses into outright fear and hostility when men are actually physically assaulted. The chilling story of the dentist who extracted five teeth without anaesthetic from a man who crashed into her car was reported without the usual sniggering tone.

Revenge may be sweet, but it is not about being sweet. The She-Devil proclaims: 'I want revenge; I want power; I want money; I want to be loved and not love in return.' Revenge literally destroys her as she turns herself into a replica of Mary Fisher.

The motive for revenge comes from the dark recesses of infantile helplessness. Little boys may learn to turn their anger into aggression or assertiveness, but little girls are more likely to grow into women feeling guilt, envy or depression. To want revenge is to acknowledge both that you are a victim and that the social mechanisms for justice in our culture does not take account of the power imbalance between men and women.

Revenge only comes easily to those glamorous women in the K-Shoes ads. It's not like that in real life, although Anna Ford (who doused TV-am's chief executive with a glass of wine after she was sacked by the station) or French National Front leader Jean-Marie Le Pen's former wife, Pierette Le Pen, (who posed as a scantily-clad maid in *Playboy* after her husband said she could do housework for a living) have made spectacular public gestures.

Most of us, however, would not go to the lengths that Ruth Patchett goes to as the She-Devil, though we may well wish thrush upon the object of our man's desire. In the end, revenge is motivated by helplessness — Ruth remains obsessed with her hopeless husband.

So, when we celebrate these avenging angels or devils, are we not simply reinforcing our position? Because real power is not about getting back at someone when you have been wronged, it is about striking the first blow. This is something that men understand only too well. There is an awful lot of false security in being a victim and these token outbursts of anger are too easily mopped up.

Simone de Beauvoir wrote: 'Women are comrades in captivity. They help one another to endure their prison, even help one another prepare for escape.' By all means get mad and get even, but above all get out.

A call to underarms

Beatrice Dalle had masses of it in Betty Blue, Madonna used to have it but hasn't got it any more. Kylie Minogue looks like she never had any in the first place. I'm talking, of course, about underarm hair — a subject little discussed outside the pages of women's magazines where it is routinely referred to as 'a problem'.

'Even nature makes mistakes' reads the copy in one of the numerous adverts for depilatory creams promoting the myth that nature intended women to be smooth and hairless. Such ads manage to invert the truth until the natural, ie hairy, armpit has come to be seen as unnatural. Yet what could be more unnatural than bunging a load of foul-smelling chemical cream under your arms? Immac may now come in Red Rose fragrance but in this case a rose by any other name smells just as vile.

Perhaps that's why so many women are slaves to the shave, ruthlessly eradicating any stray hair that dares to poke its head out. Recently, however, more and more women sport underarm hair and obviously don't give a damn about who sees it. This is not the hairier-than-thou puritanism of seventies feminism because these same women shave their legs, wear make-up and have no qualms about looking 'feminine'. So what's going on?

Like our attitude to everything else, the way we feel about body hair is conditioned by culture and class. So, generally speaking, British and American women are encouraged to be hairless, while in Latin countries body hair is considered erotic. Likewise my mother's generation see underarm hair as a sign that you have not only 'let yourself go' but are probably dirty as well.

Such strong reactions are unsurprising because underarm hair is undoubtedly sexual. Whether or not it is sexy is a matter of opinion. Visually it forms a rhyme with pubic hair with the added attraction of being mostly hidden then suddenly visible. Its purpose is to trap and intensify the sexual stimuli of the underarm secretions. If all this sounds a bit primeval, then it helps explain the embarrassment it causes for it not only reminds us of the fur of our animal ancestry but, even more disturbingly, of our animal urges. If cleanliness is next to godliness, then hairiness is sin itself. As Germaine Greer wrote in *The Female Eunuch*, hairiness is 'an index of bestiality and as such an indication of aggressive sexuality'.

In our society any kind of active, let alone aggressive, sexuality is the prerogative of men only. So, as many feminists have argued, it is no coincidence that the ideal of adult womanhood — the obligatory smooth, slim figure — is actually reminiscent of the powerless, adolescent girl. To remove body hair is also to remove the evidence of puberty. In our culture hairiness is equated with strength and virility, so to see a woman with body hair is like finding a stray piece of masculinity on a female body.

However, such codes are not inflexible. Many male body builders shave off all their hair to exhibit their oiled muscles. Maybe this is why the hairy armpits Madonna displayed so brazenly in *Desperately Seeking Susan* are now as sleek as the rest of her new toned-up body. As a badge of defiantly deviant femininity, they fitted her bad girl reputation. For my money, though, the true heroine of the underarm hair world has to be Patti Smith whose androgynous image was way ahead of its time.

Today's icons are far more predictable. Is anyone surprised that Michelle Shocked has hairy armpits and Sam Fox doesn't? But how come we never see models of any kind with underarm growth? Do modelling agencies go in for compulsory hair removal? Models One agency told me that they have no policy on this: 'It's just an unspoken rule; it's more practical.'

Likewise Isabel Koprowski, editor of *Forum* and *Penthouse*, revealed that she has never seen photographs of models with underarm hair, though 'men's tastes do vary. We have had letters in *Forum*, for instance, from men who fantasise about women with pubic hair up to their navels.' This is highly unfortunate as the advent of the euphemistic 'bikini line' means many women are furiously reducing their pubic hair to a one-inch strip.

Despite this, however, the idea that women are spending enormous amounts of time and money in order to conform to some male ordained stereotype doesn't seem altogether true. Many men I spoke to were indifferent on the subject, while some women were totally horrified by the very thought of body hair. Writer and columnist Julie Burchill said, 'It's disgusting! Who wants a big beard growing under their arms? I always refer to them as ideological armpits and my motto is, 'If it moves, shave it!''

Martin Amis, on the other hand, has a far more *laissez-faire* attitude. 'As I put in one of my books that armpits were surprisingly good value erotically, I've got no objection to underarm hair. Both shaved and unshaved armpits are fine, though I think it's a bit much to ask women to do it. Stubble is horrible, though; it just looks too masculine.'

There is no such thing as designer underarm stubble, it would seem. Nearly everyone I spoke to was unanimous in their distaste for the plucked turkey effect. Dylan Jones, editor of the men's magazine *Arena*, professed to not liking stubble but denied that *Arena* had any policy on the subject. He thought there should be no social stigma attached to hairiness: 'At *Arena* we take our women as they come.'

Jones did say, however, that most men find hairy legs unappealing — a view that was echoed by author Hanif Kureishi. 'Women with hairy legs should be arrested by the police and made to shave them, then forced to read an Anita Brookner novel three times. I don't mind underarm hair as I'm quite a hairy person myself, but stubble is a killer.'

Mel Steel, a twenty-five-year-old publicity worker, would be one of those arrested under the Kureishi regime. She gave up shaving at seventeen with the onset of a feminist conscious-ness and egged on by some German boys who thought the whole idea of shaving was ridiculous. Nowadays, however, she says, 'I simply can't be fagged to do it.' And she added that while sunbathing the other day, a man approached her with the unusual chat-up line, 'I'd love to lick the salt off the hairs on your legs.'

The range of male reaction to female body hair is indeed huge. Richard Matthews, a 24-year-old barrister, finds underarm hair 'comforting', while 21-year-old car trader Jason Penn thinks 'It's horrible! Women will be having hairy chests next. I wouldn't go out with a girl with hairy armpits — I'd probably shave it off for them. The women in Spain make me feel ill.'

Mark Perryman of *Marxism Today* is also not keen. 'I don't like to see underarm hair blowing in the wind. I don't like hairy men, so why should I like hairy women?'

'Deodorant dandruff' is another common dislike. But on the whole this is not an issue on which opinions divide up into neat sociological categories. The image of the militantly hairy lesbian, for instance, is shattered by Mandy Merck, series editor of Channel 4's lesbian and gay series *Out on Tuesday*. 'I hate my underarm hair and shave it off every day. But I don't mind it on other people; it can be quite erotic.'

The charm of the underarm, then, is open to debate. Is it mere pretension to suggest that the new trend of shaving legs and leaving armpits as natural reflects the state of contemporary feminism? Certainly there seems to be no one political line any more. Women are pleasing themselves rather than conforming to the explicit ideology of pure feminism or the implicit ideology of pure femininity. It may seem both illogical and contradictory to shave one part of your body and not another. But, when you think about it, isn't this exactly what men have been doing for years?

Fatal fantasies

Democracy works in mysterious ways. So mysterious in fact that in the week that we are supposed to elect our EuroMPs, most of us don't have a clue about which of this faceless bunch of bureaucrats is supposed to represent us. But if my EuroMP looked like Charlotte Rampling I think I'd remember her.

In David Hare's new film *Paris by Night* she plays such a creature. As Clara Paige, up and coming darling of the right, she is an ambitious Euro MP who appears to have it all. Her political philosophy is as immaculate as her clothes. Her image is of a successful Tory career woman, a woman who instinctively knows about hard work, ambition and the need for order.

Typically the price of her brilliant career — even in the work of a right-on dramatist such as Hare — is a messy private life. Apart from a hopeless alcoholic husband, Gerald (the wonderful Michael Gambon), Clara is plagued by anonymous telephone calls. In the middle of the night, a male voice breathes down the line, 'I know who you are. I know what you're doing.' Could this be Michael Swanton, a one-time business partner ruined by Gerald, who is trying to blackmail her? Or someone else?

Clara escapes through her work to Paris, to a conference where her brisk, but charming, manner wins over not only her colleagues but a young industrial designer, Wallace (Iain Glenn). She has dinner with him at his brother-in-law's house: this is where we see Hare's impossibly romanticised view of an extended family: good food, agreeable argument, witty conversation and sweet French kids. The richness of this scene provides an over-stated and over-simplified contrast to Clara's own impoverished family life, yet seems characteristic of a film which, while appearing to be a sophisticated indictment of Thatcherism, relies almost entirely on sloppy 60s ideas.

This is nowhere more apparent than in the treatment of Rampling's character. Clara Paige is duplicitous, not simply because that's the nature of politics, but because that's the nature of women. Thus, like our leaderine herself, Clara can be the best man for the job. The right-wing woman provides an excuse for the insidious misogyny so well practised by members of that protected species — the lefty playwright.

Hare also uses a form — that of the noirish thriller — in which it is almost compulsory for the strong female character to be obliterated. But Rampling must be used to being destroyed in just about every film she appears in. Paris provides a backdrop for her downfall, as visually stunning as Rampling's face, shot for much of the time in dramatic close-up. But even this cannot compensate for some appalling dialogue which may well sound meaningful on stage but, as a film script, is awkwardly pretentious.

'I shall walk around Paris all night,' says Clara significantly after her date with Wallace. On her stroll she meets Swanton and pushes him in the Seine. Women just can't help acting on impulse even it it means murder. The plot, as you may have gathered, gets as bloated as the body that is fished out of the river. Clara loses her cool as she tries to rationalise what she has done. Only Wallace knows the truth, but after a couple of love scenes, he is not going to tell.

And we are back to that old chestnut — the difference between private lives and public morality, which has never struck me as solely a problem for Tory politicians. What I object to, however, in this film is the way that this everyday conflict is played out through one-dimensional notions of sexual difference.

This successful working woman is successful because she represses traditionally feminine qualities. She says at one point that she hates shapelessness, promiscuity, softness. Her hardness, her relentless endorsement of the need for strong leadership and self-help is seen somehow as a denial of herself rather than as a consciously chosen worldview. It is only with Wallace that she reveals her other side.

For Hare this contradiction is what destroys her. And yet, as long as left-wing men such as Hare continue to articulate the machinations of conservative ideology and femininity in such a crass way, right-wing women will remain little more than fantasy figures. Conservatism is not some mutation from 'natural' femininity or some kind of hormone imbalance that upsets the ability of women to vote Labour!

It goes without saying that right-wing women are much more than fantasies. They may well also, however, have a better understanding of the political nature of the fantasies constructed around power and gender than their critics. Fantasy has no problem at all with contradiction. Countless commentators have pointed out the inconsistencies in Thatcher's public persona — but this has not diminished her position. She and her imitators seduce by denying sexual difference and promising an imaginary resolution of it by, as Bea Campbell says, uniting 'patriarchal and feminine discourses'.

In the limited and linear thought of certain parts of the left, this unity is a contradiction in terms and therefore not theoretically viable (as though contradiction is somehow an untenable and unliveable phenomenon). Practically, it sustains some of our most powerful politicians and popular fictions.

Maybe that's why David Hare's 'heroine' ends up riddled with bullet holes, while both Mrs Thatcher and Alexis Colby/Dexter can wear a string of paradoxes around their necks as if they were pearls.

Happiness is a warm gun

Kathryn Bigelow is a woman who knows what she's doing. This seems to make some people very uncomfortable. In an interview in the magazine *Elle*, director Bigelow is described as a 'steel magnolia' with 'no chinks in her denim'. Few male directors would be examined thus to discover if 'underneath they are all lovable'; but then Bigelow is a woman in a man's world — a woman who will persist in making films that deal with decidedly unfeminine subjects like violence.

Add to this the facts that she has a background in conceptual art; that she has made two very stylish cult movies; and is good-looking enough to model T-shirts in the current campaign for The Gap shop: and you can see why people are so desperate to find some hint of vulnerability.

They certainly won't find any in *Blue Steel*, the move into the big time that has made her 'the hottest female director in Hollywood'. *Blue Steel* is an extraordinary film in many ways. Bigelow likes to take an established genre and bend it into something altogether different. Having tackled the biker movie in *The Loveless* and the vampire genre in *Near Dark*, in *Blue Steel* she takes on the violent action thriller and stands it completely on its head, mainly by having a woman as the central protagonist.

Jamie Lee Curtis is Megan Turner; we meet her as she is dressing for her graduation ceremony from the New York Police Academy. As she buttons up her blue shirt, laces up her regulation shoes and scrapes her hair back under her cap, the opening sequence also lingers on her pride and joy, her shiny new gun. She has always wanted to be a policewoman because, as she wryly quips, 'I've always wanted to kill people.'

Within twenty-four hours on the beat, she has shot an armed robber who is holding up a supermarket. But, when the gunman's weapon cannot be found and no witnesses come forward, she is suspended from the force for killing an unarmed suspect. The gun is actually in the hands of Eugene Hunt, a charming commodities broker who, unknown to Megan, was at the shooting.

Eugene is fascinated by Megan and engineers a chance encounter that leads to an affair. She is overwhelmed by his attentiveness, not realising, as of course the audience has done by now, that he is an out-and-out psycho who is responsible for a number of motiveless killings in the city. This theme of the tough cookie — the professional woman — who gets involved with the obviously dangerous man is nothing new. In many ways it is a flaw in the script. Glenn Close did it in the particularly nasty *Jagged Edge*, Cher did it in *Suspect*, Theresa Russell did it in *Physical Evidence*.

It is as if women, even ruthless career women, cannot be trusted ever to separate the public and private sides of their lives. For Megan, the two collide dangerously when it turns out that the killer is using bullets with her name on them. This makes her a vital key in the murder investigation. So, despite being suspended, she is suddenly promoted to detective. From here the plot takes a number of even more improbable twists and turns, as Megan realises that Eugene is the killer.

We catch tantalising glimpses of Megan's family background. As a reaction to her mother's downtrodden passivity, Megan smashes her father up against the wall, handcuffs him and takes him in for arrest. Though she eventually lets him go, her whole character is based around a refusal to be a victim. If there is to be violence, she will be in control of it.

It is this knife edge between being in and out of control that Bigelow exploits to the maximum. When Megan shoots the armed robber, she is both completely terrified and totally cold. This is an amazing scene, and in terms of the narrative, the primal one: it is when Eugene first sees her. To Eugene, Megan has unlimited power. She has a gun and uses it. If the gun is a phallus, she is in complete possession of it. This woman, who 'has it all', so to speak, is both enormously attractive and enormously threatening. Just as Megan knows how to use a gun, Bigelow understands the power of the fetish. Her other films, after, all have been about leather, bikes and vampires.

This makes American critic David Denby's accusation that she is somehow turning 'uniforms, violence and guns into fetish objects' all the more ridiculous. Bigelow is simply exploiting what our culture *already* fetishises. But she unsettles their power by literally putting them in the hands of women. Megan gets to shoot and kill and be wounded just like the hero of a thousand cop films. This is a significant contrast to what usually happens when a woman picks up a gun. How many scenes have you sat through where the woman is in possession of the weapon — until it gets kicked out her hand at the last moment?

Bigelow is helped enormously by a stunning performance from Jamie Lee Curtis. She of the 'perfect' body and the less-than-perfect face manages to be feline, physical and androgynous, all at the same time. When she is on screen, you just don't want to look at anyone else. Bigelow has said that she wanted Curtis to play a kind of 'Everyman', her thesis being that our identification in action movies is not gender-specific. A woman watching a Mel Gibson film, she says, is 'riding Mel Gibson's ride'.

Yet this runs contrary to much of the psychoanalytically inspired film theory that leaves so little room for the female spectator. The process whereby a woman viewer identifies with a male hero has been described by film critic Laura Mulvey as a kind of 'psychic transvestism'. It is perceived as somehow inauthentic. Indeed, Megan actually steals the police uniform that covers up her femininity, in order to get back to the centre of the action. Megan's power, according to this line of argument, is illusory, lying as it does in the phallus/gun. She has merely appropriated it — it will never belong to her fully.

But the moment when she drags herself up to blow away Eugene also blows away such pessimistic theorising. Not only is this incredibly powerful; it is highly unusual for a mainstream movie. You leave the cinema believing not only that, against all the odds, Megan has made it in a man's world by taking on male violence, but also that she has done it by *knowing* what she is doing. You might wonder what the phrase 'Happiness is a warm gun' might mean for a woman; but you won't wonder why interviewers are so busy looking for the chinks in Bigelow's armour.

Close-up as the cookie crumbles

When Mickey Rourke says to Kim Basinger in 9½ *Weeks*, 'Close your eyes and just lay on the floor,' we know that she is in for something more than a midnight snack.

Here is the man who has everything, including a well stocked fridge full of rude food — cherries, strawberries, olives, jelly, pasta and syrup. She gets to taste it, he gets to watch and we get something resembling an extended Cadbury's Flake advert.

Food as foreplay is an image that has been repeatedly used in the movies, from the famous banquet scene in *Tom Jones* where the couple wiggle asparagus suggestively at each other, to the heroine's aggressive swallowing of her pasta in *Nikita*. The couple in *Tampopo* do strange things with raw eggs, the woman in *Ai No Corrida* does even stranger things with boiled ones.

Brando is evidently not a Flora man, as everyone found out in the notorious scene in *Last Tango in Paris*. And the sight of women tasting, licking, dribbling and gulping, idly fellating everything from frankfurters to chocolate bars is a common one. It may be a highly eroticised image, but like many male

71

fantasies, it is a relatively uncomplicated one. It's oral and obvious.

But for women, food is not just a symbol. A piece of chocolate gateau may represent heaven on earth or a thousand calories, but rarely is it thought of as just dessert. The relationship between women and food is both social and sexual and, more often than not, secret.

Women eat, binge, fast and vomit in private. They feel uncomfortable and anxious around food in public because they know they cannot trust themselves. This is not a natural reaction — if it was, we could simply eat when we are hungry — but a cultural one.

Fat is a feminist issue because food itself is a feminist issue. Women are responsible for providing nourishment for others yet at the same time are bombarded with images of perfect bodies and exhortations to diet.

Yet rarely do we see this anxiety represented in films. Which is why Henry Jaglom's film *Eating*, currently showing in New York and to be released here in the autumn, has got many people talking about their consuming passions. What Jaglom has captured, through interviews with young women, is the obsessional nature of this most intimate of relationships.

His female interviewees use food both to reward and to punish themselves. Food is not only about sex but, more fundamentally, about love. It is, after all, the first way we receive love, unconditional, boundless, wordless love. And our appetite for it is insatiable. Desire and hunger meet at the breast and many of us spend the rest of our lives confusing the two.

Without a doubt, eating is more reliable than sex and often more pleasurable. You never have to fake satisfaction. But like sex, it is also presented as forbidden and dangerous because of the ever-present threat of losing control, of getting fat, of being no longer desirable.

As one woman in *Eating* says, 'I think I'm still looking for a man who could excite me as much as a baked potato.' Why have an orgy when you can get what you really want in Spud-U-Like? When Sally fakes an orgasm in the diner in *When Harry Met Sally*, the woman at the next table tells the waitress, 'I'm having whatever she's having.'

Yet few films actually show women in the slog of preparing food — Glenn Close's attempt at rabbit stew in *Fatal Attraction* can hardly be counted. Perhaps because the reality of shopping, cooking and cleaning day in and day out is as tedious as it is uncinematic. Chantal Ackerman's *Jeanne Dielman, 23 Quai du Commerce, 1080 Bruxelles*, is regarded as a feminist classic precisely because it shows domestic labour such as peeling potatoes in real time instead of the usual edited highlights.

Film food is usually of the 'And this is one that I prepared earlier' variety. Families sit round to sumptuous meals that have just miraculously appeared on the table, maintaining the invisibility of women's work on screen as well as in real life.

An exception to this is the wonderful *Babette's Feast*. It centres entirely on the preparation of one glorious meal which Babette cooks lovingly for the pious inhabitants of a remote Jutland village. The culinary magic she weaves is a direct challenge to the doctrine of austerity by which the villagers live. It is a last supper celebrating life, not death, and the taste that lingers is one of sensuality rather than self-sacrifice.

In the movies, however, women are more likely to use food as compensation than celebration. While men go and get drunk or kick ass, women raid the fridge or, like *The Witches of Eastwick*, gather round the TV with bowls of popcorn to discuss the lack of men in their lives.

Eating is not just a substitute for sex but the first thing that women turn to in a crisis. Just occasionally, we catch a glimpse of what happens when this relationship gets out of hand. For if food is sex, eating disorders are commonly perceived as a flight from problematic sexual identity.

Freud's classic hysterics have been updated into a legion of bulimics and anorexics, some as young as nine years old.

The flip side to the model sucking on a Flake while the phone rings — an image, after all designed to appeal primarily to women — is the anorexic twin in Mike Leigh's *Life is Sweet*. The idea of eating as an erotic and private pastime is taken to its logical conclusion. After refusing to eat with the family, we see the young girl taking out a padlocked case of Mars Bars, cramming them into her mouth and then silently vomiting into a carrier bag.

This is not naughty or nice, just plain disturbing. Yet the current advert which tries to persuade us that herbal teas are also as forbidden as cream cakes operates on precisely such a premise. We only want what we believe we shouldn't have.

And once we start, who knows when we will stop? We live in fear of ourselves because we are brought up to believe that female appetite, once stimulated, is uncontrollable. Our relationship to food is often used as a cheap metaphor on which to hang a critique of all kinds of consumerism by supposedly radical directors, from David Byrne's *True Stories*, in which the laziest woman in the world is fed by a machine, to Percy Adlon's *Rosalie Goes Shopping*.

Yet it is in the smaller and personal worlds of the soaps, rather than in the cinema, that eating occupies a more central place. Miss Ellie presides over many a family meal in *Dallas* but never actually eats anything, while Alexis Colby would, at strategic points, bite the head off a stick of celery in a manner that can only be described as frightening. While most of *Neighbours* opens up in open-plan kitchens, both *Roseanne* and *The Golden Girls* are very knowing and very funny about what food means to women.

If men's relationship to food is far more innocent and straightforward, nothing could be more revealing than Agent Cooper's sheer delight in cherry pie. Compare this with Norma's frantic efforts to get everything just right for an illustrious food critic's review of her diner. The critic turns out to be none other than her mother and Norma's mashed potatoes fail the test.

That women are trapped in these ambivalent feelings around food is not surprising when you consider that, on one hand, they are referred to as edible items (crumpet, cherry, cheesecake) and, on the other, are bombarded with tales of women who are destroyed by what they eat, from Eve to Snow White to Weightwatchers. If this is love it is tainted love because, while men are encouraged to express themselves and their anger, we are told to swallow it. And we do, literally.

The politics of eating is so shot through with contradictions for women that we end up in vicious circles of excess and denial. We are Desperately Seeking Something but, unlike Madonna, dare not stuff ourselves full of junk food.

Cinematic images hardly ever catch the pain and the pleasure of these activities, perhaps because most of them are made by men. Or perhaps it is a secret that we want to keep secret. Yet the connection between many women's feeling of powerlessness around food and their powerlessness in the real world is undeniable. Such lack of control is more than a metaphor. It is enough to make you eat your heart out.

Women who read too much

Are you a Woman Who Loves Too Much? A Smart Woman Who Makes Foolish Choices? Is the man in your life suffering from The Peter Pan Syndrome (men who have never grown up) or maybe he has just got the good old Casanova Complex? (Ditto.) Would you say your problem is The Wendy Dilemma — When Women Stop Mothering

Their Men; or The Cinderella Complex — are you still waiting for your Prince Charming? Perhaps you should really learn How to Love a Difficult Man or better still How To Forgive Your Ex-Husband.

Answered yes to any of the above questions? Believe me, I can help you. Your problem is a simple one. You are A Woman Who Reads Too Many Self-Help Books. A fully paid-up member of the burgeoning Victim Culture, your idea of a good time is to curl up on the couch, put on a Billie Holiday record and read about other people's problems. Or, even better, your own. It's exquisitely painful to find out that you came from a dysfunctional family, that you are a 'man-junkie' who is routinely attracted to misogynists, alcoholics and all-round low lifes; that you repeat these patterns endlessly in circles of self-destructive behaviour because . . . well, it hurts so good.

The literature of Victim Culture relies on the fact that somewhere, sometime most of us, women and men, have been victims. But it thrives on turning a problem into a life-long profession, a crisis into a drama, in which you, dear reader, can be assured of the starring role. Maybe you don't see yourself this way. Don't worry, you will. As the blurb on the back of *The Cinderella Complex* says, it is 'A book in which — *whether she likes it or not* — every woman will recognise herself.' Victim Culture leads you to believe that everything is basically your problem, if not your fault; that if only you could change, everything would be wonderful. It feeds on women's general dissatisfaction and yet advises us to turn inwards at a time when we should be turning outwards. It turns social problems into individual anxieties and provides personal solutions to fundamentally political problems. For whatever they say on the cover, the solution most of these books aspire to is a cosy, stable relationship with a cosy, stable man.

Forget ambition, work, travel, friends, children or any of

the finer things of life. Helping yourself translates into either getting (or keeping) a man. Men may want to learn *How to Win Friends and Influence People* or *How to Increase Sales and Put Yourself Across by Telephone*, but it is assumed that they are successful individuals who have some kind of life outside the chaotic world of relationships. Women, on the other hand, are often addressed as little more than a bundle of neuroses: 'I'm Okay, You're Not Okay' is the subtext.

'You are addicted to men and emotional pain,' Robin Norwood cheerfully advises us in *Women Who Love Too Much* as she provides case history after case history in which supposedly intelligent women lacerate themselves in masochistic relationships. Read how Arleen, Trudi and Mary Jane had 'good sex in bad relationships' and generally let themselves be walked over by shitty men who have about as much idea of an adult relationship as a gerbil.

Yet it is not these male emotional illiterates who are in therapy, moaning to their friends about how she never calls, or lying in bed with a box of Kleenex reading *Men Who Love Too Little*. Just as women are bombarded with advice on every aspect of their appearance, so too are they the consumers of these endless emotional exercise regimes. They must change, adapt and remould themselves in that elusive quest for 'happiness'. Men may need a little surface grooming, but women physically and psychologically go for the burn. Even if it is acknowledged that the man is at fault, it is still the woman who has to do the dirty work of trying to change him. Take this extract from *The Peter Pan Syndrome*: 'Once you understand the final picture of The Peter Pan Syndrome, I'm certain you'll be moved to help in any way possible. For with all their rage, denial and procrastination, the lives of the PPS victims are filled with sadness.' In other words, the man may be a pig but somehow it is the woman's duty to try to rehabilitate him.

If she fails at this she can always go back to the dating game with the aid of *How to Find Your Ideal Man*. If you thought love was about excitement, spontaneity, even perhaps sex, forget it. This book makes bonking as boring as banking. The language of love is replaced by that of business. Thus we learn about Romance Management techniques and the Lease-Option approach to love (living together). The deal we are trying to close is, of course, marriage, but then how can you resist a book whose dedication reads '. . . to my husband Neal. Had we never met, I'd probably be in real estate instead of romance.'

The author goes on to address the problem of finding a decent man and the lack of suitable partners for women. She includes an Availability Chart (married men are okay as long as they don't have kids), a Plan of Action in which you must ask yourself, 'How many hours a week am I committed to finding a relationship?' (believe me, it's a full-time job) and a vocabulary list to help you word your Lonely Hearts ad. (What kind of person describes themselves as magnificent, inspiring or scintillating?) When you finally get to go out with a man you must continue to police your behaviour in ever more bizarre ways. Having researched him 'in much the same way you would research a company you would consider purchasing', you mustn't slouch in your chair or have any 'unstructured time' together in case 'he presses for sex'. You must, however, 'talk slowly, in a low voice', 'hide any prescription drugs' and get rid of any 'excess sexual energy with a good work-out'.

When such ridiculous standards of behaviour are set it's no wonder that many women are doomed to failure, which only serves to reinforce their victim status. And that is the ingenious paradox of these books — while promising power, they promote powerlessness; while appearing to offer solutions, they are actually part of the problem.

Of course, self-help books appear far more sophisticated than this. Often American in origin, they are written in fluent psycho-babble by people who always claim to be doctors or therapists. Some are well-qualified I'm sure, but some, one can't help suspecting, bought their doctorates off the back of a lorry in deepest California. Because there is no denying that a successful self-help book can make its author an awful lot of money. Victim Culture is a lucrative business.

They offer a kind of DIY therapy that is one part philosophy to two parts platitude. But these books promise a lot more than any therapist ever could — a cure for a disease you didn't realise you had. And they do so in a style that is immensely pleasurable to read — the confessional. If you remain unconvinced by countless case histories, they get to you by sheer force of repetition. The central message is repeated time and time again as if you were a five-year-old. After this drilling, if you didn't admit at the beginning that you were a 'relationship addict' you sure as hell will by the end of it.

And yet, somehow, this stuff still speaks to us. I have two friends, both intelligent women, who swear by *Women Who Love Too Much*. They have totally different lives and backgrounds, yet both have said that they felt this book described their lives with stunning accuracy. How can this be? Like horoscopes, perhaps, we see what we want to see. Indeed, scientists researching the accuracy of astrology often use something called the Barnum effect. Barnum statements are generalised personality descriptions such as 'Though you are a friendly person, at times you are shy'. The Barnum effect says that people tend to find these statements accurate even though they could apply to anyone. For example, if your man 'forgets important dates like birthdays', or 'yearns to be close to his father', then, according to Dr Dan Kiley, he is a candidate for *The Peter Pan Syndrome*. These statements could apply to most of the male — and female — population.

Like astrology, self-help literature operates with simplistic typologies. Fun maybe, but as serious observations, seriously lacking. *Smart Women Foolish Choices* offers us four types of unsuitable men (why stop at four, I wonder) — the Clam, the Pseudo-Liberated Male, the Perpetual Adolescent and the Walking Wounded, plus tests to find out if you are a 'Love Addict'. This obsession with addiction is fundamental to the self-help genre. It is also very worrying. Complex behaviour is explained away by questionable theories of addiction. Women, we are told, are addicted to love, to men, to relationships, even to violence. In other words, the girl can't help it. Believing you are an addict puts the ball firmly back in your court. It is not men who are at fault, it's you. Why bother trying to improve the world when you can improve yourself? But blaming and anger are not an option. 'Angry women frighten men,' we are warned. Though as Shere Hite points out: 'Anger unexpressed can become a fear which pervades everything, leading to a perpetual low-level anxiety. Indeed, women's frustration and/or anger is responsible for much of the psychological counselling, tranquillisers and so on that women use.'

The whole goal of books such as *How to Forgive Your Ex-Husband* rests on not expressing any anger at all. So when Al phones Janet to say he is not going to come up with the alimony payment this month, which she is relying on to pay the rent, she is told to thump a pillow in private and to start her own business so that she doesn't depend on him for money. She is given the example of a woman who bought a can of spray paint and a stencil: 'Going from door to door, she offered to paint address numbers on kerbs. Within one month her earnings were in excess of two hundred dollars a day.' Even more unbelievably, Janet is expected to be grateful that he gave her advance warning that he wasn't going to come up with the goods.

Flagellating oneself at the same time as shouldering all the responsibility for a failed relationship hardly seems the way to bolster a woman's self-esteem, which is ironically what these books promise to do.

When such thinking is applied to actual physical illnesses, it becomes downright dangerous. It's one thing taking responsibility for oneself but another to believe that the cause of cancer is the harbouring of deep secrets or that diabetes results from sorrow and sickle-cell anaemia from a feeling that 'one is not good enough'. What such books abdicate is any sense of social responsibility, everything is reduced to an individual and relentlessly internal level. Just as we know certain diseases are connected with poverty, why can't we admit that female dissatisfaction has as much to do with social conditions as it does with individual psychology — or would that be too dangerous?

The power of positive thinking is a wonderful thing, but will it really make a difference? The lists of affirmations and rules of Victim Culture make the slogans on T-shirts seem profound. Are sensible adults really supposed to go around repeating such rubbish as 'Fewer Expectations Lead to Greater Aliveness', or 'Growing up Means Giving up Daddy'.

The last thing that women need is to be encouraged to expect less from life, to shut themselves inside the claustrophobic world of pure emotion. Then again, it's far less threatening to have hordes of women going around mouthing these inanities to themselves in their isolated searches for the Ideal Man, than women getting together, saying out loud what is really wrong with their lives and demanding real change. And *really* Helping Themselves . . . to what they want.

The great awakening

Where do babies come from? You wouldn't know if you spent your time watching the direly cute rash of baby movies. From *Baby Boom* to *Three Men and a Baby*, the facts of life became fiction and babies miraculously appeared from nowhere. But then babies can be the ultimate yuppie accessory, especially if they come pre-packed, immaculately conceived and dumped on a doorstep.

To actually think about where babies really come from is in some ways the ultimate yuppie nightmare. Efficiency — either in the boardroom or the bedroom — doesn't prepare one for the messy business of parenthood or more specifically motherhood.

So I was looking forward to *The Good Mother* directed by Leonard Nimoy (of *Star Trek* fame) because the title alone seemed to confront some of the issues that last year's movies had been avoiding. Unfortunately the movie manages to evade as many questions as it poses.

Anna (Diane Keaton), a divorcee, *is* a good mother involved in a relationship with her six-year-old daughter that looks like something out of a nappy advert. But then she meets Leo. Their relationship immediately throws new light on her character. After picking each other up in the launderette, they embark on a passionate affair. Leo (Liam Neeson) is that cliché of the liberal imagination — an *artist* who is able through a bit of oral sex and a night in a blues club to sexually awaken Anna.

Sex for women, at least in these types of films, seems to work rather better than Heineken: it not only refreshes parts of them previously unreached, it seems actually to turn them into completely different people. Having had her parts refreshed. Anna is no longer repressed or uptight and she, Leo and Molly live in unwedded bliss. That is until Mr Uptight himself — Anna's ex-husband — decides to apply for custody of Molly, having found out that Molly has touched Leo's penis.

The whole ethos of Anna's newly found openness is shattered. What follows is, as the director says, a clash between the permissive attitudes of the 60s and the 80s reactive morality.

What *The Good Mother* highlights is that neither the confused 60s ideas about sexual openness — it's OK for children to see their parents naked — nor the 80s moral backlash actually deal with the uncomfortable areas between children's sexuality and sexual abuse. The wishy-washy and and lax ideology of 'letting it all hang out' can't fully acknowledge the power that adults have over kids, just as it couldn't acknowledge the power men have over women. Yet current attitudes, as illustrated in Cleveland, are about protecting children rather than granting them autonomous rights — they are certainly not about redressing this power imbalance. *Virgin*, a movie by Catherine Breillat, is impressive because it grants its fourteen-year-old heroine, Lili, a sexual autonomy far beyond anything that the adult Diane Keaton seems to get.

Lili, bored out of her mind on a caravan holiday with her family, is desperate to lose her virginity. Sulky and pretentious, Lili is that wonderful adolescent mix of existential angst and Madonna posters on the wall. Having escaped for a night out with her older brother, she meets Maurice (Etienne Chicot) an ageing would-be playboy. They are both fascinated and repelled by each other, but this is no easy seduction. Lili wants Maurice but is scared, and Maurice wants her though he is disgusted at what he is doing.

The sex scenes are not an easy ride either. Shot in real time rather than the slow-mo or the edited highlights of most sex scenes, they are frank and fumbling, disturbing and unusual in their depiction of unfulfilled desire. Yet as a real relationship develops between Maurice and Lili, it is she and not he who is more in control of the affair.

Delphine Zentout manages to be both a child and a woman without ever succumbing to that male fantasy of the virginal child-woman. She is stroppy, difficult and defiant. Eventually she fucks a boy she doesn't even like. As soon as the act is done she gets up, finally relieved of the burden of virginity. Bertrand assumes that she must love him as it was her first time. 'Arsehole,' she replies and flashes a smile to the camera that shows that, for all her confusion, she is far more in control of sexuality than the countless Hollywood heroines who, twice her age and despite their wonderful careers, always seem to end up flat on their backs waiting to be 'awakened'.

Modern Romance

Why not start with a climax? 'He lifted her, sweeping her up in his arms and carrying her out through the door, up the wide staircase to his room. She had never been here before. He threw her down on the bed and she felt herself pinned beneath the weight of his heavy body . . . She was lost, submerged, floating in a world where time ceased to count.'

This world where time and a few other things besides cease to count is, of course, the world of romance fiction. It is a floating world peopled by men who are as hard as steel and women who are soft and yielding and radiantly beautiful. This is the place of reckless moments and overwhelming desire — the place of true romance or true rubbish, depending on your point of view.

Yet even those who dismiss romance fiction as escapist

rubbish have to accept its staggering popularity all over the world. It dominates the market place completely from Europe to Japan, from the USA to Australia. In 1982 alone, 250 million women bought a Mills and Boon book. This trend appears to have peaked in the mid-80s but by 1987 a quarter of all books read in the UK by women came under the category of romance fiction. Despite this, these books are never shortlisted for literary prizes or celebrated alongside the burgeoning fiction that is being produced by the feminist publishing houses.

Instead, romance fiction is routinely dismissed by critics as formulaic fantasy that is badly written and mindlessly consumed. Feminists in particular view these books as sugar-coated versions of an oppressive ideology. The sole aim in life of the essentially passive heroines is to get their men. You start off sinking into his arms and you end up with your arms in the sink. From adolescence to old age, they say, romance for women is presented almost as a series of freeze-frames: the first kiss, the wedding, the honeymoon and so on. The long hard stretches of reality in between are barely mentioned. The timelessness of such fantasies suspends itself over and above the banality of everyday life, unable to represent social change or harsh realities.

In my experience, however, women who read romance (at least 50 per cent of women read them at some time in their lives) are not confused idiots with an inability to recognise the difference between these mass-produced fantasies and their own existence. Their dissatisfaction is often easily articulated and only eased by returning again and again to these repetitive narratives — hence the metaphor of addiction that they often use to describe their reading habits. This dissatisfaction is also mirrored by the heroine of the novel. She too is desperate for her life to change. As Tania Modelski, author of *Loving with a Vengeance*, says, 'If the popular culture heroine and the feminist choose utterly different ways of overcoming their dissatisfaction, they at least have in common the dissatisfaction.'

These, after all, are books written by women for women. So why are they treated with such disdain? Well, that's part of the answer. The things women enjoy, from soap opera to melodrama to romance fiction, tend to be castigated by male critics as superficial and over-emotional trash, while football and detective fiction are elevated to semi-mystical heights. The fact that romantic novels are enormously popular serves to discredit them further. How can anything which sells in such quantities be 'great literature'? A prerequisite of joining the literary canon is, after all, a degree of inaccessibility.

On this, left and right-wing moralists unite. These novels are intrinsically stupid and masochistic. Just like the women who read them, in fact. Yet the refusal to take seriously women's pleasure in popular culture is not a viable position for anyone who is actually interested in changing the reality of many women's lives. It may be the fact that the pleasures of romance are currently harnessed to a patriarchal system and used to endorse all kinds of questionable activities — monogamous marriage as the only expression of female sexuality, for example. But it does us no good simply to deny those pleasures. The idea that a few consciousness-raising sessions and the odd evening class can make us give up these regressive pleasures is a serious underestimation of the power of fantasy. Instead, as feminist writers such as Ros Coward, Alison Light and Tania Modelski have argued, these pleasures may have to be our starting point.

Nor can all romance fiction be lumped together as it so often is by its critics. Not all romances are written by Barbara Cartland. Nor do they all involve a virginal nurse and virile young doctor. They range from twee historical romances to sexually explicit bodice-rippers where the heroine is often a sexually active 'vixen' who has to be tamed by the hero. And then there are the increasingly popular blockbusters written by authors such as Shirley Conran and Jackie Collins. Commonly known as Shopping and Fucking, or Humping and Hoarding novels, these often chart the meteoric rise of a young woman whose desire for sex is only exceeded by her desire for designer labels. In blockbusters, the heroines want it all and they usually get it.

What we get are the details of how they get it. Sometimes this involves the usual romantic description of endlessly vague orgasmic sex, but more often than not the sex scenes are characterised by a shocking degree of honesty. In Shirley Conran's *Lace*, for instance, sex between Pagan and her husband Robert is described as him dutifully stabbing at her with 'the marital chipolata'. Meanwhile, she has discovered her clitoris and 'can masturbate to a climax in five minutes'. She knows how long it takes because she has checked it with an egg-timer! This sort of thing is enough to make Barbara Cartland turn in her mascara.

The emphasis on female sexual pleasure, along with the restructuring of impossible power relations between men and women into an essay resolution, offers the reader, as Alison Light argues, 'an imaginary control'. It makes heterosexuality seem both easy and desirable. She goes on to say: 'The reader is left in a permanent state of foreplay, but I would guess that for many women this is the best heterosexual sex they ever get.'

Other women have taken this line further, arguing that romance fiction operates as a kind of pornography for women. The American writer Ann Bar Snitow has convincingly examined the similarities between these fantasies that are produced for women and pornography, which is after all the key way that sexual fantasy circulates between men. Misogyny may be one content of pornography, but another, she says, '. . . is the universal infant desire for complete and immediate gratification, to rule the world out of the core of passive helplessness.'

Certainly, romance shares some of the central characteristics of pornography. Everything is set in a kind of eternal
present, sex is a transcendent force which breaks down all
boundaries and every contact is highly sexualised. The
routine tasks that women carry out every day become
somehow charged with sexual potential — she might see him,
he may be watching her. As the heroine is struggling to take
control of her life she is suddenly swept away on a tide of
sexual feeling. While porn fetishises parts of the body,
romance instead fetishises emotions — the constant antici-
pation, waiting, hoping that our heroine has to go through,
the battle of wills that invariably occurs before blissful sexual
union can take place.

If romance fiction, however flawed, is one of the few
cultural expressions of female sexuality, we still have to take
on the question of passivity and the fact that so often in these
novels the woman ends up happily subordinated to the man
of her dreams. Understanding the unconscious processes at
work may not refute these charges, but it does help to explain
their continuing attraction. In some ways, the fantasies that
these books activate are regressive and infantile, but the
desire for helplessness, abandon, 'response without responsibility' are not simply fantasies about masochistic passivity
but about the *human* rather than purely female desire to
merge completely with another person. Unfortunately, this
pleasurable desire to give up all responsibility becomes for
women mapped onto the social expectation that they are
sexual objects, rather than sexual subjects: they simply have
to attract men's desire rather than fulfil their own.

But this is where the blockbusters, however individualistic
their ethos, offer some hope of change. These are *conscious*,
not unconscious, fantasies. The female characters in these
books are strong and independent women. They like sex, but
accept that sometimes it can be wonderful, and sometimes
not. They may want marriage, but ultimately they want the

power that only financial independence will give them. They want to be in control of their own destinies.

Jackie Collins, who writes such books, sees herself as such a woman. As her new book is made into yet another mini-series, she wants things done her way. 'I think the women that I write about would completely approve of that because what they have is control over their lives . . . total control.' Maybe it is a fantasy, too, but it has nothing to do with the traditional female masochism of romance. And as millions of women will testify, it is one that they can live with. 'This,' she says, 'is my kind of feminism, anyway. Isn't it yours?'

The merry life of Windsor

A few years back a businessman in Devon had the figurehead of his ship made into a likeness of Barbara Windsor. 'Barbara was my first and only choice. She's got the most famous and best loved chest in Britain,' he said at the time. Well if France has the face of Catherine Deneuve carved into its public monuments to represent the spirit of the country, who better than Barbara to represent Britain? She is after all a national treasure. For Barbara's boobs have a definite character. These are not the anonymous breasts of a page three girl — the Windsor bosom represents an attitude and an era that is peculiarly British.

In the flesh she is far prettier than she appears on television. Rather than the bubbly and brassy figure beloved by the tabloids, she is a well dressed and delicate woman, who treats everyone around her with warmth and respect. It is only that wonderful dirty laugh that reminds you that this is the girl whose bra popped off in *Carry On Camping*, who played the Earl of Bristol's daughter (who else?) opposite Sid James' King Henry, that this is the woman for whom the word 'saucy' was invented.

Although she only appeared in eight of the twenty-nine Carry Ons it is this image that has stuck. 'I'll never shake it off now. I thought that when I got to my forties I'd be offered character parts like Diana Dors was, but it hasn't worked out like that.' Too few people realise that she is a versatile performer who has played everything from pantomime to Brecht, Lionel Bart to Brendan Behan. 'At the time I just thought of it as another part of my career. I mean at one point I was doing a Carry On in the day and *The Threepenny Opera* at night. It wasn't till all those compilations were shown and Ronnie's case came up that I became fodder for the popular press. I don't call it the gutter press because I still like to read it'.

Ronnie is Ronnie Knight, the man she has married to for twenty-two years and who was at various times charged with murder, arson and robbery. Though this relationship is central in her autobiography, *Barbara: The Laughter and Tears of a Cockney Sparrow*, Barbara has also been remarkably candid about her affairs with other men including Sid James. 'I did the book to get in there first as I'd heard there was going to be an unauthorised version of my life. But at first I did it all wrong, I got these two people to ghost it who made me sound so boring, so theatrical — you know me, me, me, I just wanted something honest.'

The book details her affairs, her abortions, the bad times as well as the good with the lack of pretension that makes Barbara so endearing. It is dedicated to her mother with whom she always had a difficult relationship. 'She wanted me to be dark, leggy and posh and I was short, fat and loud. But when she died I found this letter she had written to me — better than any letter that a man had written to me — saying what a wonderful daughter I was. But she could never say it to me when she was alive. I think that's what is good about today — I hate the bloody AIDS thing — but at least people are more open. I mean we never spoke about sex and when I got pregnant, she carted me off to Streatham for an abortion and I came straight back and did it again. She never sat me down and said 'This is where it's at'. When I went into showbusiness I was fourteen going on ten not fourteen going on twenty-four like they are now.'

Within a year Barbara suddenly found 'I had these enormous bosoms — 38D — I just couldn't understand it all.' It is this curious mixture of naivety and knowingness that characterises her image and the appeal of the Carry Ons themselves. 'All I ever showed was half a boob and that was only because bloomin' Hattie (Jacques) pulled my arm. I think one time I showed my bottom and in another film there is half a buttock but it was all so quick, all so nothing. I mean there was Vanessa Redgrave next door doing *The Devils* and letting it all hang out.'

It is the seaside humour of the Carry Ons that still fascinates today's comics. And Barbara herself manages a quite anarchic sexuality that disrupts everything in sight. What she excels at is not so much being sexy but playing with the signs of sexiness — big boobs and big hair in the same way that Dolly Parton has done. 'Once upon a time you had to be a caricature, you don't now'.

The actors in a Carry On don't play doctors and nurses, they play *at* being doctors and nurses in much the same way children do.

Apart from the affair with Sid James ('I got into it reluctantly but don't get me wrong he made me feel wonderful. He thought I was Monroe, Streisand, Bassey and Glenda Jackson rolled into one'), Barbara also remained close to Kenneth Williams.

'I can't believe he's gone, I miss him so much. How could

he die of an ulcer? I've had an ulcer but you shouldn't die of things like that these days.' He even went on honeymoon with her. 'He said: "Honeymoon? How can it be a honeymoon — you've been having it off with the bloke for two and a half years. It's a holiday and I'm coming with you." He did and he brought his Mum and sister. It was disastrous. He and Ronnie used to go off to nightclubs together and I'd be left!'

The first time she met him however she was very nervous. 'It was the first Carry On I'd done and I'd heard Kenny could be difficult. I'd also heard he hated Fenella Fielding. Anyway in the first scene I did with him he was dressed up as a spy and I blew it. He went "Oh ducky, *Do* get it right" and I just came out with "Oi, don't you have a go at me with Fenella Fielding's minge hair all round your moosh." It was the start of a wonderful friendship.'

But then Barbara has always been a very unthreatening kind of sex symbol. 'I'm not a threat — how could I be — I'm four foot ten and a half? I've always been silly sexy not threatening sexy and I've always made other women feel important. I like women. Anyway you go into any pub and you'll find a barmaid who looks like me.' She laughs when I tell her that a friend of mine said that when he was eight, he didn't know what sex was exactly but he knew she was it.

And she seems genuinely surprised by the reaction of people like Jonathan Ross and Harry Enfield. 'Jonathan just hounded me into going on his programme. He came up to me in Stringfellow's one night and said, "Look, Barbara, I love you, if you come on my show I won't take the piss out of you." He has pictures of me and Sid all over the place. It was the same with Harry Enfield.' She made an hysterical appearance as a Greenham Common woman with CND badges pinned to her nipples on Enfield's spoof Norbett Smith — A Life. 'I said I'm fifty-two, I can't play that twenty-two-year-old *Carry on Camping* girl. But he begged me.

'I was really scared when I first met Dawn French. I'd read

that she hated all those stereotyped blonde ladies. But she came up to me at a first night and was lovely to me. I asked her to forgive me for playing all those roles and she said "Darling, that was a stepping stone for people like us." So I suppose one day Dawn and Jennifer will feel old fashioned and think "How did we do those things?" But honestly they treated me like a goddess.'

And so they should.

CHILDREN

Hiding in the wardrobe

Peter York once described the period from 1968–80 as 'Babytime' — a kind of anorexia of the soul. He was talking about the regression in style terms at least to childish clothes and decor. Kickers, those shoes with primary colours, big eyelets and big laces, were just scaled up baby bootees that epitomised the jokey Peter Pan look. Along with plastic hair slides, stripey socks, dungarees (adult babygros?), Mickey Mouse watches and enamel badges saying things like 'head prefect' or 'I am seven', this style seemed symptomatic of the 70s embrace of all things childlike. An expression of a very grown-up desire for a second childhood.

All that was a very long time ago. These days if you were to plunder the average kid's wardrobe, you would be hard pressed to find cutesy pastels and Start-Rite sandals. You would more likely come across junior Doc Martens and imitation RayBans. These days everyone wants to be ultra grown-up. Even children.

Children's clothes are big business. The fashion market for kids is booming, rising by half a billion pounds in the last five years alone. The market for babywear in particular is expanding at the rate of 10 per cent a year. Currently there is more profit to be made from kids' clothes than from kids' toys.

There are a number of reasons for this. More women are having their children later and having fewer of them. Consequently, the spending on each individual child increases. People buy new clothes for their kids rather than making do with hand-me-downs. There is also a far bigger choice and range of clothes available. I knew things were really changing when I could buy my two-year-old a black sweatshirt from Mothercare instead of having to put up with yukky shades of pink and green.

Retailing outlets from Mothercare to Next have pushed many of the major stores to revamp and relaunch their own ranges. And it's now easy to order your sprog a hot little number from the BG (Boy Girl) range in the Next catalogue.

And it's certainly not just the top end of the fashion market that is fashion conscious. In any street market it's now possible to buy kids' clothes that are replicas of the latest look. Last year as soon as puffball skirts hit the shops you could buy them for two-year-olds down the market. The best incentive to potty training is the promise of a tiny pair of boxer shorts the minute he is out of nappies.

For girls you could try a silky French knicker and camisole set (age three and up!) from the usually sensible Marks and Sparks. The truly trendy among you will have already bought their kids a miniature pair of blue suede Doc Martens from Red or Dead in Covent Garden that look great with little leather jackets (customised of course).

There have been other times in history when children's clothes were scaled down versions of adult garb — often these were periods of pre-revolutionary decadence and such fashions were confined to the upper classes. Paradoxically, the royals dress their kids now in a style much reminiscent of the fifties when childhood was a well-demarcated state. It's working-class parents who spend a fortune on high-fashion for their little ones.

But how far can all this go? When 'junior' make-up was

introduced a couple of years ago there was a muffled outcry. Although the various types of eyeshadow and lipsticks were billed as educational toys, designed to improve 'hand and eye coordination', many people felt that the idea of encouraging three-year-old girls to slap on make-up was morally reprehensible.

It's interesting that this particular product should be regarded as outrageous when the rest are not. Perhaps it's because it hit on one of the most vulnerable taboos of our society, that of children's sexuality. We may want our kids to look like smaller versions of ourselves or to wear the clothes that we secretly yearn to wear, yet we are shocked at the thought of make-up and 'sexy' underwear because we still want our children to be treated *as* children.

Mini-pops, that paedophiles' paradise of a TV programme where little girls gyrated in Lurex pants and sequinned boob tubes, was taken off the air after many complaints. In the light of Cleveland it seems astonishing that such a programme ever got made in the first place.

However, the one topic that has been ignored both in official reports and in many of the excellent feminist analyses of Cleveland is precisely this question of children's sexuality as both *active* and *normal*. This no way means that sexual abuse is anything other than an horrific abuse of power, but to deny this most radical of Freud's findings plays into the hands of the moral right.

To insist that children are sexual beings means that we must treat them as individuals and listen to their demands rather than simply regarding them as passive property that needs always to be protected. Children's rights must be a fundamental part of the much vaunted concept of citizenship. Episodes such as Cleveland demonstrate our schizophrenic attitude towards children.

There is such tremendous pressure on all of us to be grown-up, sensible, hard-working and mature, it's not surprising that we hand this pressure down to our kids. In the culture of the image the look is the thing. But although they may look like adults, children have hardly any more rights than they ever have had. It's sad that while the new generation may look immaculate in its designer togs, the British attitude towards children still remains that they should be *seen* but not *heard*.

_____

Hung-up on Father Christmas

It always strikes me as rather weird that while most parents spend most of the year advising their kids not to talk to strange men, come Christmas time those same howling infants are bundled onto the lap of a peculiarly clad man and expected to reveal their secrets to him. Yes I'm talking about *Father Christmas* — that cheery bearded patriarch without whom it would appear no Christmas is complete.

I know all about HIM, in fact I've become quite an expert because these days HE is the main subject of all conversation with my four-year-old daughter. I might not have got round to buying the presents yet but it looks as if I've bought the myth lock, stock, and barrel. And once you start the whole damn business, believe me, you get drawn into the web of lies from which there is no escape. Unless, that is, you are prepared to speak the unspeakable and admit that Father Christmas does not . . .

It seems that the need to believe in, or at least for our children to believe in Santa is as strong in adults as it is in children. This perfect stranger who breaks into your house in the middle of the night not to *steal* but to *give*, offers a kind of unconditional love and generosity that most of us can't quite manage. Children get given presents simply because they are children — all they have to do is tell him what they want and promise to be good. And parents get the thrill of taking instamatics of little Jo on Santa's lap. Well, it's all for the children really isn't it?

Now I'm all for fantasy but it seems that this particular one is so pervasive that there are few alternatives — where are the stories about Mother Christmas with her radiation free reindeer? As a feminist, do I really want another hero, another God-like man for my daughter to worship? Worse, why do I want her to think that all the time and energy that will be spent giving her a 'proper Christmas' is in fact the work of a man she meets once a year?

But children aren't stupid, are they? She has already started asking questions about the 'Real Father Christmas' negotiating a difference between those that are just 'dressed up' and the real thing. Four-year-olds are not going to be palmed off with any old simulation and she has sussed that it's only the 'real' ones that give you 'real' i.e. big presents.

And all of us — adults — seem desperate to find this authenticity as well. When I asked at Selfridges who exactly Father Christmas was, how exactly he was selected, I was told that, 'Selfridges has the only real Father Christmas.' Which is funny because, when I asked at Harrods, I was told that their Father Christmas was also 'the only real one'.

However real they are they certainly earn their money. The Selfridges' Santa sees 500,000 children a year and its theme 'Out of the nursery, into the night with Father Christmas' (Eat your heart out Angela Carter!) will guarantee such numbers again. The walk through to Santa's grotto takes half an hour and is full of automated displays involving 'teddy bear's fantasies'.

In Harrods' 'Edwardian Christmas', Father Christmas's caravan is approached through cages of stuffed animals as well as live performers. 'It's a fabulous, magical experience,' says Vicky Kershaw. 'There is silver glitter — magic stardust all over the floor. It sticks to the children's shoes and it's still there when they get home.' Isn't it just lovely to know that this fabulous experience will involve having glitter trailed through your carpets for days afterwards?

Though these West End Santas will ask for sherry and mince pies to be left out, I have heard of far more socially aware Father Christmases who, in poorer areas, just ask the kids to leave out bread and water. And perhaps in the end, having given in to the whole thing, the best we can hope for is that whatever Santa Claus votes it certainly *isn't* Conservative. Ok, he might be a bit macho and tend towards authoritarianism, but he isn't the model of a typical Thatcherite subject. He gives and he cares. This rather anonymous, rather old-fashioned, old man makes it possible for the community to give to itself, and us all to give to each other. He has all the advantages of Jesus without any of the hang-ups.

And, as I've explained to my daughter, the rest of the year he devotes himself to radical causes. It's not for nothing he wears red you know . . .

Politics of choice

Film critics don't cry. I mean can you imagine Barry Norman or Alexander Walker fumbling for a Kleenex during a preview? No, instead they say they find a film 'moving', 'powerful' or 'penetrating' to show that their reaction is based on considered judgement rather than dubious emotion. It is as though emotional involvement is thought somehow to preclude, or be divorced from, critical assessment. Yet for many film-goers, being reduced to tears is the mark of a great movie — though I'm not sure how many men would admit to having a bit of a sniffle.

Weepies are usually associated with silly and sentimental films and yet the least sentimental film I've seen in a long while certainly made me cry. Chris Menges' directorial debut *A World Apart* is set in the South Africa of the early sixties. Like *Cry Freedom* it explores apartheid through the angst of a white family but, unlike *Cry Freedom*, its unblinking stare catches the contradictions as well as the heroism of its characters. This is largely because the story is told through the eyes of thirteen-year-old Molly Roth. Jodhi May gives an extraordinary performance as a girl trying to come to terms with her parents' political activism and its very real effects on her life.

Written by Shawn Slovo, daughter of Ruth First and Joe Slovo — the exiled ANC leader — *A World Apart* is a true story based on her childhood. As Molly Roth's middle-class parents become more involved in the struggle against apartheid, her father is forced into exile and the personal costs of their politics are borne by the whole family. Molly is taunted at school about her 'traitor' father and also experiences a lesser but equally painful form of exile — her friends are not allowed to see her anymore.

When her mother is taken into detention, her family seems to be breaking apart and Molly runs after the car crying, 'don't go Mummy, don't go,' as if her mother were choosing to leave her. In a sense, through her activism, her mother is choosing a certain path that leaves her daughter with no choice whatsoever.

This exclusion from the world of politics, of struggle, of secretive goings-on and from her mother's decisions leave Molly confused and isolated. Barbara Hershey plays her mother, Diana Roth, and appears unusually hard and defiant not only with the authorities but with her own children. Like so many 'radicals' she unreasonably expects everyone to share her total commitment and she is willing to sacrifice not only herself but those close to her for the greater good.

When Molly complains that she never sees her mother, Diana asks her instead to consider the plight of Elsie, their black housekeeper, who is also separated from her family. But this idea of thinking of others worse off than yourself is as good as useless to a child demanding love and attention. Molly is resentfully and rightfully angry and issues that most contradictory of demands, 'don't treat me like a child!' — for what she needs most of all *is* to be treated like a child.

It is the impossibility of reconciling motherhood with political activity that tears apart not only her family but Diana Roth herself. Though she is incredibly brave, the film itself is brave in its portrayal of her, showing her as an admirable, but not necessarily likeable, heroine. The chinks in her emotional armour are filled with defiance and lipstick even in her prison cell. But however much she suffers or is mistreated, the most tortuous question that her interrogators ask her is also the most ordinary: 'What kind of a mother are you?'

In less dramatic ways this is the question that prevents so many women becoming involved in politics. How can you leave your children for hours, days, weeks to go to meetings, demonstrations, conferences? Political activism, while appearing totally selfless, often seems to require a peculiar kind of selfishness.

Yet the film makes clear that for the black people of the townships these questions are still a luxury. There is no choice between the 'personal and the political'. Like Molly, who as a child is disenfranchised politically, who has no say over her own life, and who feels totally powerless, the situation under apartheid breeds desperation.

The strength of *A World Apart* is its relentlessness. One longs for a break, for a lighter scene, for things to be all right just for a little while, not to be reminded continually of just how bad things are. But the regime that created apartheid will smash a skull. This film bears witness to this unremitting violence and to those who fight against it. See it and weep.

━━━━━━

Birth and Death

I am not really in a position to write this column. Or maybe I am in the perfect position to write it, as I have spent the last week slumped on the sofa, watching the war. And waiting. Waiting for something to happen. And waiting to go into labour.

Like most women in the last week of pregnancy I am not blooming. I am big, bored and uncomfortable. The baby has gone past the sell-by date given by the hospital, but there is not a lot I can do except dig in on the frontline. If it wasn't for the Great Video Game in the sky, I'd probably be reduced to watching *The Young Doctors*.

In between Dimbleby and Paxman, I avidly follow Miriam Stoppard's advice: 'Start to neglect parts of your domestic life. Allow the non-essentials to slide and don't worry about them'. Then I worry about that. After all this is the woman whose husband has just run off with Felicity Kendal. I read reports that convoys of 'our boys' are hopelessly blundering about in the desert, completely lost within thirty miles of the Kuwaiti frontier.

They don't even have basic maps. Mass graves are already being dug. There is nothing that destroys morale more than seeing bodies lying around. This is not tasteless. This is war. Lulu's record 'Boom Bang-a-Bang'; now that is tasteless, according to BBC, who have banned it, alongside 'Give Peace a Chance'.

A psychologist is brought into the studio to comment on

'stress'. At least it interrupts the flow of retired vice-marshalls. He informs us that 'even soldiers have nervous systems and respond to life-threatening signals'. Some even resort in the middle of a battle to lying motionless in a foetal position.

Well, this is certainly what the war is doing to me. I scan the papers daily but there is less and less information and more and more detail. My six-year-old daughter has ominously started making paper aeroplanes and dividing them into teams. Yellow, blue, green, pink. Is she playing war? No, she is 'playing airports'. Am I getting paranoid?

A neighbour asks when the baby is due. 'All battle-situations at the ready,' he comments, and then is totally embarrassed at his choice of phrase. I don't mind. Maybe it's my hormones, but there seems something increasingly similar about the language of war and the language of childbirth. All is euphemistic denial of the one fact of both. Pain.

Sheila Kitzinger, childbirth guru, talks about the 'functional' pain of labour as though somehow it reduced its intensity. I wonder how long it takes to be burnt alive in a blazing Tornado? Is that 'functional' pain too? At least in the post-Gazza era in which we now find ourselves, several soldiers have admitted to a level of fear that makes them cry their eyes out. Officers' stiff upper lips have trembled as they resort to psychobabble about teaching their boys to 'confront their feelings'. You can see it's a damn sight more difficult than getting them to confront the Iraqis.

But as the men in suits — the politicians — give way to the men in the studios — the experts — it seems too obvious even to mention the fact that these days there is hardly a woman's face to be seen on television. But then, how many ex-air commanders did I really expect to be female? And there are not even that many men's faces. The same old commentators are wheeled from channel to channel to comment on the same snippets of film. It's a lucrative business. One American general who was fired for revealing that the US would bomb 'downtown Baghdad' is now working for CBS. In two months he will earn what he earned in a year working for the Pentagon.

The other morning, two TV channels were reduced to discussion of whether there had been too much war coverage. Whatever else, the media is scoring a direct hit on itself. CNN may have already won the war, but media dissent or even scepticism has been severely carpet-bombed. Misinformation, disinformation or plain bloody lies have been delivered right on target. Whatever happened to postmodern cynicism? How come we have believed what we have seen and seen what we have believed?

John Pilger may point us back to the lessons of Vietnam or even the Falklands, but we also live day-to-day with distorted coverage of Ireland and it doesn't seem to bother us too much. In fact over the last week I have had more sympathy with the likes of Max Hastings who say quite simply that it is the job of the press to reflect the government position. At least you know where you stand.

A few days ago when I was hooked up to a foetal monitor, a midwife rushed in, not to ask how I was, but to see if I knew the latest on the war. 'No, nothing much has happened, except they've bombed Tel Aviv.' Yet already the urgent need to know what is happening is fading. Because we are realising what television cannot admit; that nothing much happens for long periods of time. How long before we lose interest? Who really understands the politics of the Middle East anyway? Isn't a game of Scuds versus Patriots a lot easier to play?

Tony Benn is right to be dismayed at the talk of 'firework displays bigger than the Fourth of July', but he's wrong to deny that on some level this is what war has become. I can say this because I am lucky enough to live in the other gulf — the gulf between the personal and the political — that such events open up. And because death is still as difficult to imagine as birth; both are hidden away. So we all resort to clichés like, 'Even in war, life goes on.' And so it does.

I flick through *Name Your Baby* with its 'Special Baby Personality Horoscope'. I wonder what sign Saddam is. The baby will be an Aquarius, just like those famous peace-lovers Ronald Reagan and John McEnroe. Thinking of a boy's name is harder than thinking of a girl's. The only one I can come up with is Scud. Scud Moore. I quite like it. Sounds like an American novelist.

——————

Maternal melodramas

Modern motherhood is simply wonderful. It's hip, fun and so very easy. Just look at all those poor, blank babies dragged down catwalks or staring out from magazine covers cradled by their model mums. *She*, one of the few magazines with rising circulation figures at the moment, has cleverly relaunched itself as the magazine for 'women who juggle their lives'. Though I've never met a child who could be successfully juggled, in the new myth of motherhood *anything* is possible. You too can be like Neneh Cherry, eight months pregnant and dancing in a Lycra dress on *Top of the Pops*. You too can be like Fergie, able to jet off for the best skiing without a moment's worry about a babysitter. Or you can even be like pampered Paula Yates, call your children ridiculous names, pay for nannies so you can promote your exclusive underwear collection and then write a book that says women with children really shouldn't work.

This may all be a long way from the image of the downtrodden, self-sacrificing mother, but whether the new myth is any easier to live with than the old myth is debatable. Culturally, the representation of motherhood *per se* still seems impossibly difficult, resting as it does on the lethal combination of denial and idealisation.

This is one reason why many feminist film scholars have turned to the classic melodramas of the 30s and 40s, a genre exemplary in its ambiguous representation not only of motherhood but of femininity in general. Before this recent rehabilitation, melodrama was routinely dismissed as a lower form given to embarrassing stylistic excess. That this was the very quality cherished by its largely female fans is no coincidence. Popular female pleasures have always been castigated by the (mostly) male guardians of official culture.

One of the best-known movies of the sub-genre dubbed 'the maternal melodrama' remains *Stella Dallas*, the 1937 film starring Barbara Stanwyck as the girl from the wrong side of the tracks who marries above her station but never manages to hide her origins. Eventually she gives up her daughter for the higher goal of upward mobility. Thousands of noses must have been blown during the final scene, in which Stanwyck stands outside in the rain watching but excluded from her daughter's society wedding.

This is the scene deeply etched on the memory of Val, a character in Marilyn French's novel *The Women's Room*. 'How they got us to consent to our own eradication! I didn't just feel pity for her; I felt that shock of recognition . . .' she says. Yet *Stella Dallas* has been read very much as a film of its time expressing an underlying anxiety about the disruption of traditional sex-roles during the Depression. Why this anxiety should always focus on the figure of the mother is another story.

And why there is a 1990 remake of this film is still another. That Hollywood is still floundering about trying to make 'women's films' or at least cope with the changing demographics of cinema-goers is one possibility. Enter Bette Midler, hardly known as the self-sacrificing type, in the Stanwyck part. Though maybe this is the reason that the divine Miss M has recently been given to crowing about the joys of motherhood. You'll be pleased to hear that it has made her go 'mushy'.

Indeed mushy might be the best word to describe the whole of this film. Unlike her last film, *Beaches*, which was an effortlessly weepy female buddy movie, *Stella* is so contrived that it is more likely to provoke laughter than tears. Apart from Midler's dire wardrobe and almost vaudeville performance, the basic components of the story don't survive the update from the 30s to the 60s.

Stella mark two is a sassy barmaid who has a fling with a dapper doctor, gets pregnant and has to go it alone. Though the fluorescent ribbed jumpers may tell us it's the 60s, nothing else does. There is no contraception or abortion and no single mothers around. There is only Ed Munn — played by the ubiquitous John Goodman of *Roseanne* fame, who appears to be the US's all-round best friend—for support.

Stella, nevertheless, survives until Jenny becomes a teenager and she realises that she cannot provide the kind of background that any upwardly mobile adolescent requires: 'books, museums, art-stuff.' So Jenny swaps her hunky leather-jacketed boyfriend for a wimpy WASP in a blazer and gets packed off to live with her Dad. Dad by now has acquired a properly sophisticated girlfriend who, instead of telling children to shut up, says elegantly, 'Less is more.'

She is in sharp contrast to Stella, for whom 'More is more', which is why Stella ends up outside the window in bag-lady garb, and the new girlfriend inside at Jenny's wedding. Much of this is ludicrous, the operations of class so crudely drawn as to be totally unbelievable.

Are we to believe, for instance, that all working-class

American youth are druggie delinquents while their upper-class counterparts are drug-free paragons of virtue who want nothing more than to work on literacy programmes for the underprivileged? Are we to believe that inter-class marriage is still the only way for women to change their lives? And are we to believe, as we did in the 30s, that a mother's desires must always be sacrificed for her daughter's needs?

The punishment in the classic maternal melodrama for a woman who steps out of place is this separation from her child — duty and desire being mutually exclusive. Midler, like Stanwyck, is also punished for being too obvious, for trying too hard. Her very appearance is a 'masquerade of femininity' rather than an acceptance that femininity must always appear totally natural.

What Linda Williams describes as 'the device of devaluing and debasing the actual figure of the mother while sanctifying the institution of motherhood itself' is as reactionary now as it was fifty years ago. We are still left with the 'ultimate unrepresentability' of motherhood. Do the contemporary heirs to the classic melodrama — the soap stars — offer any more hope? If you want self-sacrifice 90s style, just tune in to the long-suffering Sheila Grant of *Brookside* or Pauline Fowler of *Eastenders*, for these are the ever-present flipside to the designer-baby brigade.

Eternal childhood

There is something about Australia that is not very grown-up. I say this not out of some jaded English imperialism but because the way that Australia often chooses to represent itself is as a country of eternal childhood, perhaps even

eternal immaturity. This is a genuine immaturity, a gauche-
ness that is both charming and innocent and one that
ultimately wins the day. Both as *Crocodile Dundee* and as
himself, Paul Hogan exploits an ignorance of urban etiquette
that literally disarms would-be muggers as well as under-
mining the snobbishness of British tradition.

Against the 'done too much, much too young' of worn-out,
cynical old America, Australia offers itself up, in its tourist
literature at least, as the real thing — a youthful country,
uncorrupted by the excesses of the American Dream and
unspoilt by the stifling repression of British culture. To some
extent this image has been reinforced by many Australian
films, even those that have been critical of such a view. The
so-called Australian New Wave was often bathed in a glowing
nostalgia. Films such as *Picnic at Hanging Rock* are memorable
precisely for their loving reconstruction of an uncertain past.

More recently, however, a new breed of film-makers, the
New New Wave, most of them products of the Australian
film schools set up in the 70s, have been producing much
darker films, ones which refuse the myth of Australian
innocence. The brilliant *Ghosts of the Civil Dead* by John
Hillcoat and Evan English and Richard Lowenstein's *Dogs in
Space* are both extremely uncomfortable films. Now we
have a remarkable first feature, *Celia*, by one of their
contemporaries.

Though set in the late 1950s, *Celia* is no cute exercise in
nostalgia, despite the fact that on the surface it may sound like
yet another rites of passage movie. It is, in fact, a disturbing
tale about the end of childhood and the end of both personal
and political innocence. Celia, played stunningly by Rebecca
Smart, is nine years old, a wilful little girl who lives in a world
peopled by fantasy beasts called Hobyahs. Her life changes
when her grandmother dies and a new family moves in next
door. They become her friends though her family disapproves
of their communist views. As they are being harassed for their

beliefs, Murgatroyd, Celia's beloved pet rabbit, is also under threat because of the government's nation-wide rabbit cull.

Turner plays wonderfully on the paranoia surrounding communism and the demonisation of the humble bunny as it is turned from pet to pest. Bizarre and horrifying archive footage of rabbits blinded by myxomatosis underlines the fear of being overrun by vermin, or, worse, those of left-wing persuasions. Yet, with great subtlety, Turner also manages to weave in all kinds of other themes. Although Celia's father may find her politics abhorrent, he is attracted to the wife of his new neighbour. She, in turn, is disillusioned by the chauvinism of organised activism though she still manages to encourage Celia's mother to be more independent.

Celia sees all this going on and decides that she will resist. In a shocking climax, which forcefully suggests the shattering of childhood innocence, Turner manages an unsettling moral ambiguity which describes rather than judges the actions of a powerless, but knowing, young girl. This ambiguous tone disrupts any notions of pure guilt and pure innocence, suggesting a far more mature response to Australia's own past than any amount of pretty period drama.

What *Encounter at Raven's Gate* might tell us about present Australia apart from the fact that it is full of UFO's, Verdi-loving policemen and sexually frustrated farm women, is anyone's guess. This sci-fi horror movie directed by Rolf de Heer has been described as the best thing to come out of Australia since *Mad Max* — and it certainly has a lot going for it except a comprehensible plot.

It more than makes up for this with atmosphere, special effects and ludicrous dialogue. Set in a deserted landscape, it centres on an isolated farmhouse run by Richard, with is wife Rachael and helped by his brother, ex-con and ex-punk Eddie. Strange goings on go on all over the place, not least between Eddie and Rachael. She hangs around the farmhouse in a red satin slip and matching lipstick (well, you would, wouldn't you?) until Eddie succumbs in the shower. Meanwhile Eddie's barmaid girlfriend is being murdered by a lunatic opera buff who also happens to be the local policeman, machinery starts and stops all by itself and their nearest neighbours' bodies have been welded together by an unexplained 'presence'.

Richard, who is getting weirder himself, seems not to notice what is going on under his very nose, let alone that the outback is being invaded by aliens. In a fit of pique he demands to know, 'What the hell has happened to the shower curtain?' This may be complete nonsense but it looks great and is explained, in the end, by a sinister 'astro-physicist'. 'The encounter was total.'

Unhappy families

All is not well in the heart of that most sacred bastion of society — the family. If you believe what you read you will know that this most fundamental institution is under attack from a multitude of directions. Promiscuous single parents, campaigning homosexuals, morally-irresponsible television programmes and, of course, feminists who claim that the family is the site of woman's oppression par excellence, are all seen to threaten normal family life. You might wonder how something as supposedly natural and institutionalised can feel itself to be so fragile and flimsy.

A number of films may in part provide the answer. For although they are 'about' families, they all point to the emptiness of traditional family life.

Family Viewing is an extraordinary film from a Canadian

director, the wonderfully-named Atom Egoyan. As far as video technology is concerned it would appear that the family that plays together is erased together. At the centre of this blackest of comedies are father and son, Stan and Van. Stan is a semi-catatonic video salesman who can only be turned on when the camera is switched on or by second-hand telephone sex. Sandra, his hapless mistress, is instead preoccupied with seventeen-year-old Van who is increasingly worried about 'not feeling connected.'

As his father erases home movies of Van's mother who has 'run away' with home-made remote control porn, Van visits his Armenian grandmother who has been put into a seedy nursing home, in an effort to retrieve his past.

Egoyan cleverly mixes different kinds of film — the authentic looking jumpy home-movies providing another texture to the stilted apartment scenes which he shoots on video. Using the inane laughter of sit-coms on the soundtrack, he flattens out these traces of family life so that we are always reminded that they are in Godard's famous words 'just an image'. With ridiculous anti-naturalistic dialogue the film is in turn hilarious and desperately sad.

In the midst of all this alienation Van conspires to construct another kind of family with his grandmother and Aline, the young woman who works for the telephone sex service patronised by his father. Pursued by the obsessive Stan, they become once more the objects of surveillance. Throughout the film we are aware of the presence of video cameras — in shops, lifts, hospitals and hotels — and of the way that this everyday surveillance coerces us all into behaving 'properly' wherever we are.

Family Viewing succeeds in posing all sorts of questions about memory — about a culture that records everything but remembers nothing, in a brilliantly haunting way. But why, oh why, do all these arty directors from Wenders to Godard, and now Egoyan, have to resort to that tired old metaphor of prostitution whenever they want to conjure up a bit of alienation? Why couldn't Aline have worked in a shop instead of selling sex to pay her mother's nursing-home bills? My own suspicion is that while parading as some kind of critique, prostitution is vaguely titillating to male directors and audiences. All those screen whores service the fantasies of thousands of the right-on men who sit there believing that, come the revolution, they could take them away from all this.

What is interesting about *Family Viewing* is that the nuclear family looks so perverse and sinister by comparison with Van's self-created family who actually provide love and care.

Yet we all know where 'pretend family relationships' can lead to, don't we? For it is homosexuality that is perceived to undermine the very basis of familial life. As usual, no amount of theorising can express the stupidity of this idea as eloquently as the words of an 'ordinary person'. In the American documentary about gay rights, *Rights and Reactions*, an elderly gay woman says: 'When people say I'm a threat to the family — I think of my kids, my grandchildren, my son-in-law.' In the background protestors who believe that 'we should do away with gays if possible' hold banners that say it all: 'Tradition, Family, Property.'

Which is why a short New Zealand film, *A Death in the Family*, should be compulsory viewing, Andy, dying of AIDS, goes back to New Zealand to be looked after by his friends. Unlike the British television dramas *Intimate Contact* and *Sweet as You Are*, which presented AIDS as essentially a crisis for the heterosexual family, *A Death in the Family* puts Andy's dying and its effect on his gay friends at the core of the film. When his conservative family, who have never accepted his gayness, come to visit, it is once again the *real* family that appears emotionally impoverished.

The film never glosses over the realities of an appalling loss. Andy says himself, 'This is one bitch of a death.' I, for one, don't subscribe to the idea that learning to die is somehow good for you. When it comes to AIDS, tears are not enough. Many people dying of AIDS will not get a place in a hospice, let alone have a network of friends to care for them. *A Death in the Family* is an elegant and quietly intense film.

It seems that those who portray the family as under siege from pernicious outside influences have got it (deliberately?) wrong. What is tearing the family apart is the eruption of tensions that have always existed *within* the family. What these films suggest, in quite different ways, is not that we should all go off and live in communes, but that it is possible even in the midst of the fallout from the nuclear family, to make new kinds of families, new kinds of communities.

In the light of Cleveland and Clause 28, 'pretended family relationships' have never seemed like such a good idea.

Heroes in a half-shell

There were several *Teenage Mutant Hero Turtles* at a kid's fancy-dress party I went to recently. One inventive mother had made the shell of her little boy's costume out of egg-boxes painted green. I thought this was by far the best effort, and said so to my daughter and her friends. They snorted derisively, all agreeing that the best-dressed turtle was the boy who had the bought costume — the one in the official Turtle merchandise. They thought the home-made 'hero in a half-shell' was 'stupid'.

Like many adults, I obviously have a misplaced nostalgia for a home-made children's culture — one made out of old egg-boxes and imagination rather than one that you can simply buy into. The truth is that kids always have made, and always will make, their fantasy life out of the detritus of consumer culture; though, as concerned parents, we tend to believe that, despite the phenomenal amounts of money we spend, our children's lives are impoverished by this kind of ready-made culture.

And you can't get more ready-made than the Turtles 'phenomenon'. From toothpaste to tracksuits to Retro Mutagen Ooze, it's all been sewn up. *Today* estimated that if you bought all the Turtle spin-offs at Christmas, you could easily spend £1,000. Ninja may have something to do with 'the art of invisibility', but not as far as the marketing men are concerned. And even if you never buy a single item, the Turtles are now so well-established a cultural referent that *Spitting Image* can parody them as Teenage Mutant Hero Turds — 'They come from the sewers.'

The film itself, although the most successful independent production ever, is actually the most insignificant of the products. But don't tell the kids that. Directed by Steve Barron, it is relatively low-budget and low-concept. It doesn't even look special, and the Turtles themselves, produced by Jim Henson's Creature Workshop, are lumpy, rubbery things, able to muster only a few facial expressions.

None of this really matters. All they have to do is to incarnate the mythology that the kids will have learnt from the much faster-paced cartoons. We first meet them when Raphael (all the Turtles are named after Renaissance painters) rescues April O'Neil — a 'beautiful young television reporter' — from muggers. We are constantly reminded that New York City is falling apart because of the silent crime wave; but the four turtles live underneath the urban paranoia with their Ninja master, Splinter, in the sewers.

Splinter is a large rat, an immigrant from Japan who has looked after the Turtles since they were babies. A pretend family relationship? Having found them in a pool of radioactive ooze, he has seen them grow into upstanding Turtles, who can not only talk, but whose first words were 'pizza, pizza'. These mutant Turtles have also picked up a strange lingo that is a cross between black street talk, Valley speak and Surfer jargon. They are hip dudes who incorporate a range of influences from the mutated creatures of Japanese comics to the more traditional American superheroes.

Unlike many superheroes, their appeal to kids rests on the fact that they have a mental age of about eight. This is most apparent in their treatment of April. Although they think she is a real 'babe', there is no question of inter-species sex — they are not *that* mutant. They just gaze on, embarrassed by displays of affection. I say 'they', because, apart from different-coloured headbands, there is no way of distinguishing one Turtle from another. Characterisation is not a strong point.

Nor is there much of a plot. The Turtles are soon battling against the Shredder and his evil gang of disaffected kids, who also live underground. The Shredder's feud with Splinter goes back a long way, as he murdered Splinter's master, Yoshi. In line with current trends in American films, the Japanese are portrayed as the ultimate villains: yet, at the same time, Splinter mutters a lot of cod-oriental philosophy, and the fighting is all martial-arts-based. This is nothing new in kids' films either — even *Star Wars* went in for a bit of pseudo-eastern mysticism. As is to be expected, it is soon absorbed into the American Way.

The Turtles' much-vaunted multiculturalism is shallow. If, as some have suggested, it's a whitening-up of black street culture, it is also literally a sanitised denial of it — just like the sewerage-free sewers that the Turtles live in.

A parallel story running through the film, as the Turtles struggle to rescue Splinter, is that of Danny and his father, who are also struggling towards a reconciliation. Danny's waspish father is April's boss but, like the Turtles, Danny appears to have no mother. In its own way, this is yet another movie about father-and-son relationships that squeezes out women. Indeed, all the Turtles at the kids' party I went to were boys. As with the Bart Simpson craze — another white, 'black', boy — there is not a lot going on here for girls to pick up on.

There are the usual self-reflexive media jokes — 'It's a Kodak moment' — and catchphrases — 'I could go for little deep-dish action right now' — but nothing as sophisticated as you get in any *Gremlins* movie. Turtles may cry like Gazza but, like him, they also seem to have suffered the arrested development that passes as heroic masculinity. When I asked Ben, a four-year-old fan, what was so great about these heroes in a half-shell, he said: 'They fight.' 'What do they do when they are not fighting?' I ventured. 'They run to fights.' And that's about it. But don't tell the grown-ups.

2 FANTASY

FEAR

Killjoy Culture

Hearts of darkness come two a penny these days. 'The horror, the horror' that both Conrad and Coppola strove to suggest has now become 'the hype, the hype'. So you want to delve deeply into the putrid imaginings of murderers, rapists and torturers? You want to rip open the fleshy underbelly of 'the way we live now' and watch the blood and guts slowly ooze out? Well, feel free. After all, as good old Jim Morrison sang way back when, 'This is the end, My friend.'

If it's dismembered bodies you are after, forget the Gulf. Get yourself to the movies. Curl up with a novel. Watch *Twin Peaks*. The new psycho-killers are everywhere and they make Norman Bates look adorable. After the air-brushed whimsies of last year — *Ghost* and *Pretty Woman* — Hollywood has got horrible. But the slasher at a teenage slumber party has grown up. The 90s villains are slick, sexy and sophisticated. What more could a girl want in a serial killer? Anthony Hopkins as Hannibal 'the Cannibal' Lecter in Jonathan Demme's *The Silence Of The Lambs* is 'witty, charismatic, artistic and, in a twisted way, a little gallant'. It's a pity that he also happens to eat people.

Patrick Bateman, hero of Bret Easton Ellis's *American Psycho*, is also described as 'handsome, sophisticated, charming and intelligent'. He just gets his kicks out of sex with severed heads and putting rats in women's vaginas. Patrick Bergin also stars as a serial killer, in *Love Crimes*. And in case you should think that this is a peculiarly male or even American psychosis, you will be glad to know that David Lynch's daughter Jennifer is directing *Boxing Helena*, which stars Kim Basinger as a woman who is cut into pieces and put into boxes by another loony man.

Helen Zahavi's radical feminist/radical revenge novel, *Dirty Weekend*, in which the much put upon Bella spends a couple of days killing men, is to be made into a film by that well known radical feminist director Michael (*Death Wish*) Winner. The novel, endorsed by Andrea Dworkin and Julie Burchill, was described in *The Observer* as 'more offensive than pornography'.

So what are we to make of all this? Is it all some terrible *fin-de-siècle* decadence, a sign of immoral times, proof that we have become so desensitised that anything goes? Probably not, though the 'ban it and burn it' brigade would like to have us think so. Yet I do think that the lack of critical debate, never mind critical terms in which to discuss these things, is severely limited. For a start the attention paid to these films and books reflects an enormous critical snobbery. There are and always have been far worse novels and films around whether you call them exploitation movies, trash novels or genre fiction. It's just that they don't get reviewed in the pages of the Sunday supplements.

We know *American Psycho* is Literature with a big L because Norman Mailer has publicly defended it. *The Silence of the Lambs* is not some teen horror flick, it's an artful film by an arty director. In other words, it is only when these things enter middle-brow culture that we begin to make a fuss about them.

But the fuss we make often boils down to little more than an argument over good and bad art. If *American Psycho* works as a novel, is well written, then maybe its scenes of sadism are excusable. Defenders of Ellis offer us aesthetics over politics — the right of the artist to force us to look at intolerable material in whatever way he or she pleases. Those who would ban the book, such as the American National Organisation for Women, care little for the aesthetics of mutilation. Ellis himself speaks of his generation's 'need to be terrified' after an adolescence spent watching every kind of violence on the news and at the movies.

What bothers Mailer about the novel is the tone. It is a monotone. The details of dying are described in exactly the same way as the details of dinner. Mailer longs for some revelation about Bateman's inner life, his motivation. This is little more than nostalgia for the familiar characteristics of the bourgeois novel. Any point that *American Psycho* might be making is precisely about the meaninglessness of the 'spiritually disgusting' 80s.

What disturbs me, however, is the laziness of the metaphors of murder and rape. Is there really no other way to reflect the breakdown of society, than by breaking up — literally — the bodies of women? However cleverly this is done, it still seems to indicate a poverty of imagination, never mind a problem for the women who watch and read this stuff. The argument that artists and writers are simply reflecting what they see around them still doesn't explain so many male writers' fascination with these themes. Nor does it explain why we continue to conjure up evil in such a purely individualistic way — locating it in the disturbed minds of a few alien creatures who are somehow both inside and outside of society.

It is remarkable isn't it, that the expression of all these 'one-off' psychopathic minds should result in acts of a desperately similar nature? And as unglamorous as it may be to say so, this is culturally determined. Focusing on these skewed individuals, however, is far more interesting than asking about their anonymous victims or looking at the everyday and collective violence that surrounds us. Yet, as Ellis says, we are prone 'toward fantasy, but it's often a mean-spirited horror-show fantasy', and such fantasies have little time for real moral conflict or ambiguity of any kind. How we regard such fantasies, though, does not have to be so simple. The choice is not between aesthetics or politics – any judgement we make, for we are all critics here, has to include both. Because this stuff isn't going to go away – never mind Safe Sex, welcome to Safe Death.

Filming by numbers

Peter Greenaway is a clever, cultured man who makes clever, cultured films. So clever, in fact, he managed to get a special programme on Channel 4 just to explain his *Fear of Drowning* — both a guide to, and an analysis of, *Drowning by Numbers*. In it he sounds like a man with a plan, someone with a trick or two up his sleeve: precious, pretentious and profound — rather like his films.

There is by now an almost standard set of critical responses to his work and he is respected as an arty and inventive filmmaker even by those who regard him as too clever for his own good. The argument goes something like this: his earlier work remains 'interesting but indulgent', the beautifully filmed *Draughtman's Contract* is regarded as a turning point in bringing together his cerebral concerns with charm and elegance and, most importantly, commercial suceess. The follow up, *A Zed and Two Noughts*, was for some critics once again marred by his ruthless formalism which forces out feeling. This school of thought prefers *Belly of an Architect* which is celebrated for the power of Brian Denahy's performance — for once strong enough to flesh out Greenaway's stylistic devices, making the whole thing far more user-friendly.

Basically it seems that we can only stand difficult ideas if they are sugared by a little naturalism or at least some recognisably good acting. Yet in a cinema so barren of experimentation shouldn't we be grateful for Greenaway's intelligence? In *Fear of Drowning* Greenaway has the courage of his convictions and returns to the territory of *A Zed and Two Noughts* and *The Falls*, refining his themes and literally playing his ideas out. My complaint is not that his cleverness gets tiresome (which it does) or that the human element is missing (which is irrelevant), but that if he is going to depend on ideas alone he will have to get some new ones!

Accusations of pretentiousness are fairly redundant, for Greenaway understands that cinema is *always* about pretension — a film is never real but a game that the audience agrees to be part of. In *Drowning by Numbers* games, small and large, are the preoccupation of Madgett (Bernard Hill) and his strange son Smut. They devise a game for every situation, intoning the rules and regulations that turn even the smallest event into a kind of ritual. Madgett is the local coroner and becomes involved with not one, but three, women all named Cissie Colpitts, and all of whom drown their husbands. In love with each, he becomes entangled in their games as he pronounces the drownings 'accidental death' rather than murder in the hope of procuring sexual favours. The plot unfolds with the precise symmetry we would expect: there are three drownings, three funerals and three failed seductions. Intertwined with these stories is the sad tale of Smut and his longing for the mysterious skipping girl.

Set in idyllic, magical English countryside, *Drowning by Numbers* is shot in rich autumnal colours, all gold and amber and overflowing with overripe fruit like some mad harvest festival. Greenaway is wonderful at unearthing an Englishness

125

that is essentially pagan, full of maypoles and mayhem. Children's games reveal themselves as metaphors for fertility, loss, death and decay.

Just about every scene is reminiscent of one painting or another from Breughel to Rackham and if you are an art historian you can pat yourself on the back every time you get it right. Another favourite game for the childish or élitist amongst us.

But if games and riddles are primitive ways of ordering the world, Greenaway is also engrossed with all the ways we try to pattern what would otherwise be chaos. Classificatory systems, from numbers to alphabets to lists, are his obsession. All through the film we can count the numerals from one to a hundred which appear as the narrative unwinds.

This fascination with structure, random taxonomies, with the very form of things, is always at odds with the themes of *Drowning by Numbers*. The content is in fact that old staple of the art movie — sex and death. These messy instincts, that are never fully controlled, are the undertow of all the imperfect systems that try to control and define our experience. As a meditation on the impotency of hyper-rationality in the face of unconscious desire, the film has its moments.

Yet, despite his sophistication, Greenaway plays out this dialogue between the conscious and the unconscious in the most stereotypical of ways. The male characters, all non-swimmers, represent a desperately masculine rationality with their ludicrous games. They all end up done in one way or another by the enigmatic women who naturally have a great affinity to water. It is thus femininity that somehow holds the key to the deeper knowledge of sex and death. Witch-like, the women share not only the same name but an unspoken bond that gives them a special power.

Greenaway, like so many other men, seems to think that he is flattering women by showing them as mystically all powerful. This elevation of women to a transcendant womanhood, however, obscures all the far less mystical power relations between the genders. If women are innately more powerful than men, why should anything need to change? More mundanely, Greenaway's cinematic gaze remains distinctly male so Joely Richardson, the youngest and the most conventionally pretty of the women, spends a great deal of time with her clothes off.

And this is part of the difficulty. Though clearly Greenaway would like to submerge himself in the forces of love and death and the whole damn business, he also wants to contain and control them. Urbane and academic on television, I wondered what made him need to explain so carefully every twist, every plot device, every idea in his film. Surely once a movie is made, the way audiences read it is beyond the filmmaker's control?

If I was your analyst, Peter, I'd tell you to loosen up. I'd also tell you to go and see a film where three women *really* do get away with murder — *A Question of Silence*.

Beating times

Oh, the things we do for love . . . and publicity. When the invitation for a screening of Julia Roberts's film *Sleeping with the Enemy* arrived, out of the envelope dropped a wedding ring. It's a neat idea, if you fancy spending your life wedded to Mr Murdoch's Twentieth Century Fox. I promise to love and cherish it alongside my free *Dick Tracy* stickers and my *Great Balls of Fire* flashing badge.

It's debatable how far such gimmicks account for the success of certain films, but this one has already done very good business in the US, and Julia Roberts is proving that she is more than just a Pretty Woman. Based on the novel by Nancy Price, it takes liberties with what is basically a feminist thriller, turning an everyday tale of wife-beating into a domestic horror movie.

Julia Roberts plays Laura, the perfect wife to Martin Burney (Patrick Bergin). She makes sure his supper is always on the table, that the towels in the bathroom are always straight, that the tins in the kitchen cupboard are correctly arranged and that she is at all times sexually available. Here is a woman who not only fakes the odd orgasm; she fakes her entire life, for Martin controls her every move. One part anal-retentive businessman to two parts sick psycho, he punishes her physically and mentally, until she lives every moment in a constant state of terror.

Their superficially perfect marriage is rotten to the core. He started beating her as soon as the honeymoon was over. Roberts uses her aura of fragility to portray a woman who flinches every time someone makes a sudden movement. Until one day she decides that she isn't going to take it anymore . . . Having faked her life, she now fakes her death and runs away to an impossibly golden American town full of marching bands, checked tablecloths and home-made apple pie.

Within about a day, she has found herself a New Man (literally). Ben just happens to live next door, have a beard, teach drama and be endlessly patient and understanding. He guesses her secret — none too difficult, seeing as the woman is a nervous wreck. So she, or course, begins to feel safe. Which is a big mistake, because Martin has found the wedding ring she has flushed down the toilet and is out to get her back. Then the film changes gear, sliding into a full-scale horror mode. With a score by Jerry Goldsmith, who also wrote the music for *The Omen* and *Poltergeist*, the tension builds, with the camera tracking Laura as the classic woman-in-peril.

Martin may be a monster, but what *Sleeping with the Enemy* does is to treat him, filmically, exactly as if he *were* a monster. As director Joseph Ruben says: 'I'm not interested in making a movie about the occult or the devil. I think there are enough scary things going on in the house next door.' Yet overlaying a tale of sexual violence with the conventions of the horror genre works both for and against the movie. It has been described as 'just Julia Roberts and a psycho in an old dark house', but if this is formula film-making, the formula still has a purpose.

Only when Laura trades in her clapped-out 80s man for a nicer, newer 90s model do things start to work out for her. And here the limitations of the chosen genre become apparent. For while the film effectively heightens the drama of her situation, it veers further and further away from a more uncomfortable reality: that the reason most women carry on being battered is often rooted in their economic dependency on the men they live with.

What this does is to situate Laura's story entirely within an emotional, rather than social, arena. But that's Hollywood for you. Both in her old life and her new, she lives in a social vacuum. Where are her female friends, for instance? Nevertheless, the film does what it does with economy and style, superbly conjuring up an atmosphere of terror without showing much actual violence. And it appeals to those of us who would not fork out to see some worthy, naturalistic production about battered wives.

When Martin gets his come-uppance, the audience I was with clapped and cheered. That is at least some advance on the shouts of 'Kill the bitch' that accompanied *Fatal Attraction*. Our sympathy is entirely with Laura. But by making Martin a vicious monster, he also seems exceptional, which is something, unfortunately, I can't say about wife-beating. Like many violent men, he is alternately loving and brutal, but it is no coincidence that he is represented here as an entirely 80s man: all immaculate suits, investment dealings and computer screens. As with Patrick Bateman, Bret Easton Ellis's sexy serial murderer, these American psychos are presented as the ultimate outcome of a decade of greed and brutality.

The yuppie nightmare genre which dealt, often sympathetically, with yuppie fears, has mutated into something altogether different. In *After Hours* and *Something Wild*, for example, our identification is with the confusion of the male protagonist whose world has suddenly turned upside down. But in this film, in *Vampire's Kiss* and in Ellis's novel, what we are now afraid of is of the yuppies themselves.

The times are definitely changing. These yuppie-monsters are invariably male control-freaks who are losing control, not only financially but emotionally. Their morals are also in recession. And while it may not scare them, it sure as hell seems to be terrifying the rest of us.

The death of intimacy

Catholicism is responsible for some pretty scary things but none of them as bad as some of the sub-genre of horror movies it has unwittingly inspired. *The Unholy* is one such atrocity, silly enough to make you yearn for the good old days of *The Exorcist*.

Even more strange is the fact that Catholicism in its more mystical manifestations is both genuinely frightening and genuinely fascinating. Full of the compulsive/repulsive imagery that the best horror is about, it demarcates the sacred and the profane so precisely, spelling out its taboos so exactly that any self-respecting audience just aches for them to be broken. Priests are crying out to be tempted, virgins to be violated and altars to be desecrated.

The Unholy certainly has all this but it lacks the imagination to do anything with it. *The Unholy* 'apparently thrives on pure souls, on priests and virgins', which provokes one of the latter to gasp to Father Michael, 'Make love to me, father,' in order presumably to kill two birds with one stone.

Father Michael (Ben Cross), you see, has miraculously survived a fall from a seventeenth-storey window and has been made pastor of St Agnes. Once he finds out that the last two pastors had their throats ripped out, even this remarkably thick priest starts to get suspicious. What follows is the classic confrontation between good and evil with evil, as always, appearing the less bland option. The demon in this film supposedly tempts by taking the form of whatever it is that its victim most desires and then kills in the act of sinning. This might be an interesting proposition except that all that priests desire, according to this film, is the same air-brushed woman in a net-curtain.

And just as the representation of desire is formulaic, so is the depiction of evil. When we get to see the demon in all her glory, it is a laughable hotch-potch of left-over special effects — a kind of *vagina dentatis* on legs that licks its way into Father Michael's crotch.

But then that is what you would expect from a film that uses two women kissing in the abyss that hellishly opens up underneath the church to suggest the ultimate in horror. Simplifying the battle between good and evil into the old battle of the sexes number, with wicked women tempting chaste men, is not only dubious but makes for a boring and repetitive movie. The more exciting possibility — the exploration of the anomalous area between the sacred and the profane, the evil and the erotic — is sacrificed on the altar of a circular male fantasy that blames women for the desire they incite in men. And it's ironic that no special effect, however good, has been as successful in conjuring up the 'evil' of femininity as the Catholic church itself.

▬▬▬▬▬

To hell and back

976 Evil is a horror film directed by Robert Englund, Freddy of *Nightmare on Elm Street* fame. Basically another wimp's revenge movie, it's a perfect example of how contemporary horror has become what Philip Brophy describes as 'a saturated genre'. The pleasure of a movie like *976 Evil* depends precisely on its ability to embrace the clichés and conventions of other horror films — on this genre's amazing capacity to eat itself alive.

Like so many of these teen horror flicks, it is set in a small American town conjured up as usual by a diner, a church and a school, in some indefinable time that may be the present but could be the 50s. Somehow, this hazy conception of time and place serves to intensify the events in the film — it seems enough to simply suggest 'normality' at the beginning of the movie, as we know that by the end this will be overturned. Since the audience is already complicit in the knowledge that everything is not what it seems, then it doesn't matter if things never seem too real or too accurate in the first place.

In this way the tackiness of the film-making is in itself a source of pleasure that gets reabsorbed by the text. While other genres strive for flawlessness, horror is often able to turn its flaws into virtues by overplaying them — by actively inviting the audience to recognise them.

This is why the most horrific sequences can be the most hilarious while the humorous scenes be so sick that they leave the nastiest after-taste. The wimp in *976 Evil* is Hoax, a fumbling no-hope adolescent who gets picked on by the local high-school gang. He idolises his cousin Spike who is cool enough to have a pony-tail, a motorbike and a girlfriend. They both live in a house dominated by Hoax's weirdo mother 'Aunt Lucy' — a monstrous mother in the long line of maternal madwomen from *Psycho* to *Carrie*. Aunt Lucy is a religious nut with a penchant for ridiculous wigs.

While she witnesses a modern-day miracle — fish pouring out of the sky — Hoax has been getting up to other things. By dialling a telephone answering service he has been talking to the devil who promises him special powers. And sure enough the quietly odd Hoax soon turns into a reptile with extended finger nails and is slashing faces in the boys' toilets. As his body changes into something completely different, he extracts revenge on everyone including, of course, his mother.

This link between adolescent sexuality — the feeling of a body changing, growing, being out of control — and its grotesque exaggeration in horror movies has often been discussed but this element may explain the genre's continuing fascination for young audiences. What is disturbing is that in so many of these films the responsibility for unleashing these horrific powers is laid squarely at the feet of the female characters.

Hoax's inability to break free from his mother's grip (in all these films the father is always absent) as well as his rejection at the hands of Spike's girlfriend is what finally turns him into the devil incarnate.

The only thing that appears to be able to save him is Spike's rendering of the American Dream — 'We'll drive cross country on our bikes, on the open road, get a couple of babes...' But, alas, the devil has got his hooks in and anyway the family home has literally turned into hell with the kitchen covered in ice and a gaping fiery abyss appearing in the living room. It's reassuring to know that Hoax is not impressed: 'Once you've been to hell, everything else pales in comparison.'

What remains the most shocking thing about this kind of movie is that although hell is loosely bound to vaguely religious imagery, it is made abundantly clear that it is actually located in the heart of the family and in the minds of its young men.

─────

Murder most foul

What does it feel like to kill somebody? To turn a person into a corpse? How long does it take to squeeze the life out of someone? How hard do you have to hit to smash a skull?

Never having committed murder I glean my insights into these matters from the movies, and occasionally the news. And from what I can see, death looks pretty easy. Cinematic violence is slick, quick, never bungled and even the most gruesome deaths only take a matter of seconds. The news, when it is allowed to, frequently hints at a different story, one that is much slower. Film of Israeli soldiers repeatedly beating the arms of captured Palestinians with small boulders until the bone breaks — not once but in several places — indicates the dull routine of torture. The sheer bloody effort of breaking a human body requires a determined efficiency. Only then can it appear to be so easily accomplished.

In this way murder, which is illegal, and execution, which some would make legal, are not much different. In the places where the death sentence is law, such as parts of the US, the act of execution is highly medicalised (as are the more sophisticated techniques of torture). That is a sign of our *civilisation*. In places like Iran executions are brutal affairs.

That is a sign of their *barbarism*. It might take longer to die in an electric chair than to die of a broken neck caused by hanging, but let's not get obsessed by tasteless details.

It is exactly the tasteless details of death that are the subject of *A Short Film about Killing*. Made by the Polish director Krzystof Kieslowski, *A Short Film about Killing* is shocking in its single-mindedness, its unflinching stare at murder and execution. Its stark title gives a hint at the enormous power of its directness. It is part of Kieslowski's project to make a film for each of the ten commandments and this one takes up the fifth commandment, thou shalt not kill, as its motif.

Shot through a wash of yellowy filters that emphasise the bleakness of Warsaw, the film is almost plotless giving it the feel of a documentary. Yatzek, a charmless drifter, murders a taxi driver with no apparent motive. He is then given the death sentence despite protests from his earnest young lawyer. That's it. Yet the film grabs you by the throat from the very start, forcing the audience to be witnesses to every awful detail of the two killings. Nothing could be more horrific than the almost interminable strangulation of the taxi driver until you see the laborious preparations for the hanging: the oiling of the machinery, the tray under the trap door to catch the urine and excrement of the swinging corpse.

We cannot be sympathetic to Yatzek after we see what he has done. But somehow his institutionalised murder is even more terrible. He doesn't go to his death in the proud but resigned way we are led to believe occurs, but screaming for his life. Even the argument that the purpose of execution is as deterrent rather than punishment seems irrelevant when faced with the logistics of killing.

This extraordinary film won the international critics' prize at Cannes. It is filmmaking of immense concentration and gut-clenching clarity. The relentless pursuit of its simple theme — thou shalt not kill — which is at its very core, marks it out from so much contemporary cinema where ideas are regarded as decorative additives rather than the driving force of a film. Because Kieslowski is driven to question, so are we. Here he has made a film which is unbearable to watch. That is precisely why we must watch it.

Murder is also at the heart, or rather the soul, of *Heathers*, a blacker than black high-school comedy. This too is a superb film — which twists every convention of 'the high-school movie' until it hurts.

Directed by Michael Lehmann from an ace script by Daniel Waters, it stars Winona Ryder as seventeen-year-old Veronica — a girl who has everything. Rich, popular, pretty and clever, and about to be accepted into the élite of the cliques at school, which is run by the supremely bitchy and colour-coordinated Heathers — three girls all named Heather. Veronica, however, fantasises in the privacy of her own diary about killing the top Heather. When she teams up with JD, a seductively psychotic teenager who has watched far too many Jack Nicholson films for everyone else's good, these fantasies start to get serious.

JD's expertise at turning murders into fake suicides soon becomes too much for Veronica who decides she must stop him. By now the film has mutated into a kitschy and beautifully observed satire on high-school movies, adolescent angst and the death-wish at the heart of American culture. Exaggerated colour and fabulous unreality *à la Blue Velvet* highlights the exaggerated and weird emotions expected of teenagers.

In between brilliant lines like 'fuck me gently with a chainsaw' and 'Bulimia is so 87', *Heathers* exhibits a dark maturity. Veronica begins to understand that 'death gives' — that we assign to the dead qualities that they so obviously were lacking in their life. She writes: 'Dear diary, my teenage angst shit has a body count.'

In another genre, the horror film, teenage angst inevitably

leads to all kinds of horrible goings-on. The onset of puberty in sleepy American towns seems indelibly connected to poltergeists, dream-monsters and a great deal of disembowling.

In the mannered hysteria of *Heathers*, this angst is revealed not as a supernatural event but as perfectly *natural*. If adolescent depression is caused, as some analysts have argued, by the first realisation of mortality, then *Heathers* pushes home the cultural repression that is part of all those teen mythologies.

It relocates death and destruction not in the nightmares of the disturbed but in the daydreams of the all-American kid. It may be a film about killing but it is stylish, intelligent and bloody funny.

But then faced with 'the end' you have to laugh, don't you? It's certainly a great deal easier than facing Kieslowski's painful and choking realism which shows that every death is a violent death and every death sentence an act of even greater violence.

Electric shocks

When Jane Campion walked into a press conference at the Venice Film Festival, the assembled mob of journalists rose to their feet and cheered this young director from New Zealand. Her film *An Angel at My Table* swept up eight prizes at Venice and also won the Critics Award at Toronto. This is vindication, if any were needed, that Campion, who also directed *Sweetie*, is more than just another offbeat and arty film-maker.

Sweetie, a disturbed and disturbing film, is certainly a hard act to follow. While some welcomed Campion's quirky framing and dark humour, others dismissed it as mere film-school posing, thus writing off the content of the film alongside the style. And though, as Campion says herself, *An Angel at My Table* is a 'gentler, kinder — a humanist piece', it shares many of the preoccupations of *Sweetie*.

Made in three parts for television, it is based on the autobiographies of New Zealand writer Janet Frame — *To the Is-Land, An Angel at My Table* and *The Envoy from Mirror City*. Despite her many literary awards, Frame is still known as New Zealand's 'mad writer', her work inspired by her experience of insanity. What Frame did in her autobiographies, and what Campion does in the film, is to take apart piece by piece her supposed schizophrenia, to separate the myth from the madness, and to release Janet from her own legend.

Starting out as a fat, frizzy-haired little girl, the world of Janet's childhood is already dominated by the power of storytelling — lies, fairytales and secrets. Campion still frames each shot with a powerful precision but uses it to evoke the perfect *seriousness* of childhood. When Janet's sister drowns, she retreats further into her world of poetry and the pain of adolescence. At university, these feelings of shyness and inadequacy come to a head. She bungles a suicide and ends up in a mental hospital. Already she is an 'interesting case'. When she makes a desperate attempt to get help because of her rotting teeth, she is viewed only as a potential genius. It is as though those around her would prefer her pain to be the spiritual misery of a writer rather than the real agony of toothache. This is the familiar 'madness as the price of creativity' scenario.

In hospital she undergoes systematic torture in the form of two hundred shock treatments over eight years, 'each one equivalent in fear to an execution.' There were no drugs to take the edge off the terror and these scenes are truly harrowing. It is only her writing that saves her from having her mind hacked to pieces in the name of medical science as she is 'offered' a leucotomy. Eventually she leaves, publishes her first novel, and, with a travel grant, goes to Europe. After a romance with a selfish American poet in Spain and after suffering a miscarriage, Janet once more puts herself into psychiatric hospital. She is diagnosed as never having been schizophrenic in the first place and is told by a down-to-earth therapist: 'If you don't feel like mixing, then don't.'

As with *Sweetie*, Campion makes us ask questions about the conjunction of madness with femininity. Sweetie's behaviour — monstrous, aggressive, self-destructive — also had its own perverse appeal. You couldn't help liking her. And somehow Campion does the same with Janet Frame. Awkward and unattractive, you also care about this woman. This is helped by a breathtaking performance by Kerry Fox.

Both *Sweetie* and Janet disobey or disrupt the myriad rules of feminine behaviour — Sweetie deliberately, Janet disingenuously. Sweetie always goes too far, Janet is paralysed into inaction. The people around them can cope with neither. Madness in Campion's work does not have the lunatic excitement of David Lynch, rather it is a reaction to those everyday codes. And when Janet is finally released from having to understand herself as mad, the whole idea of madness is itself undermined.

For, in the end, what could be more insane than locking up a talented young woman for eight years simply because she is cripplingly shy? Only perhaps believing that electric shocks can take the place of human contact.

████████████

Fag ends

Whoever it was who said that it was their ambition to die without ever having been to California has my deepest sympathy. For these days you don't even have to get on a plane to get a dose of sickly Californian imperialism. You just need to go to the movies and you are in a strange land where everyone emotes endlessly, the sun always shines, no one smokes and the language is a peculiar kind of therapy-speak. This world is peopled by *individuals* who believe that the root of all evil is simply that we don't know how to 'relate' to each other. The goal of these saccharine-coated characters is to 'come to terms' with everything it is impossible to come to terms with, like sex, death or growing up.

So in this sanitised, anti-smoking atmosphere of user-friendly smiles, it is a pleasure to see two films which blow smoke in the face of clean living. The first looks as if it was sponsored by the tobacco industry and the other examines the fag end of a marriage.

The Fabulous Baker Boys stars Jeff Bridges as Jack Baker, a man who has 'had a cigarette in his mouth for five years.' He and his older brother Frank, played by real-life sibling Beau Bridges, are the fabulous Baker boys: a low-key cocktail lounge act whose dire repertoire includes the dreadful song 'Feelings' as well as a lot of schmaltzy patter. Early on in the film, written and directed by Steve Kloves, Jack is established as the epitome of cool: i.e., besides chain-smoking, he fucks waitresses and doesn't really talk to anyone except children (the little girl upstairs) and animals (his dog).

His brother holds the whole thing together with the help of spray-on hair and smarmy small talk. He has to for the sake of his wife and kids, but even he realises, 'Things have changed. Two pianos aren't enough any more.' So they recruit a singer and end up with ex-call girl Susie (Michelle Pfeiffer), whose breathy renditions and horrible outfits go down a storm with audiences. Predictably enough she falls for Mr Cool who, surprise, surprise, actually wants to be a black jazz pianist.

But the centre of the film is not so much this affair but the relationship between the two brothers. This is played out beautifully, as is the portrait of life on the road, so that despite the clichés (strong, silent type meets tart with heart of gold), this is a film that is consistently watchable. But Pfeiffer — touted as the new sex goddess — wiggles so obviously on the top of a piano that it makes you long for the likes of Bette Davis who could suggest more by smoking a cigarette than any amount of bump'n'grind. The days when screen idols had a cigarette *instead* of having sex rather than *after* having sex are long gone. In the era of New Prohibition no one has either any more, they're too busy air-brushing those unhealthy urges and flossing their feelings to meet the exacting standards of moral hygiene currently required by Hollywood.

At least some of the baser emotions are allowed to emerge in Danny DeVito's *The War of the Roses*. DeVito, better known as an actor, showed considerable flair for directing black comedy in *Throw Momma from the Train* and here he brings together his old pals Michael Douglas and Kathleen Turner in a film which looks at that increasingly popular activity, divorce.

They star as Oliver and Barbara Rose, a couple who on the surface of it have everything: success, kids and a beautiful home. But after seventeen years of wedded bliss, Barbara realises what she hasn't got — an identity beyond being Oliver's wife. She asks for a divorce and Oliver is stunned, though the tell-tale signs have been there for a while.

Oliver cannot understand why she wants to end the marriage after all he has given her. But she cannot put a name to the problem ('I can't give you specifics'). All she wants is the house, which is the one thing Oliver won't concede, so full-scale war breaks out between them. The house and its contents symbolise their different investments. Oliver believes that it should be his, as he has paid for everything in it. Barbara believes it should be hers because she has chosen and maintained all their precious possessions. Their home is the fruit of her invisible labour and she won't part with it.

The result is a domestic horror film which echoes many of the 40s 'battle of the sexes' films. Only instead of poisonous repartee, the Roses actually slug it out physically with both partners going to extraordinary lengths to make each other leave. They kill each other's pets, he pisses on her gourmet food, she drives over his car.

This is domestic violence of a highly unusual kind, because Barbara with her background as a gymnast is more than able to meet every physical challenge. However nasty things get, this is still comedy and not real life, so he doesn't beat the shit out of her and instead admires the lengths to which she will go to destroy him. The laughs are always double-edged, deriving from a fantasy of equality (she is as strong as he is), and a sense of unease that she might not be.

Yet the most striking aspect of this modern morality tale is the house itself. It starts off as a perfect expression of a coveted lifestyle and ends up literally as a prison — the Roses have barricaded themselves in. It metamorphoses during the course of the movie from a light and spacious dream home to a strangely threatening and unfamiliar place full of dark nooks and crannies.

Turner once more proves her abilities as a comic actress, but we rarely get more than a glimpse of what has driven her character this far. Like the work she has put into the house, the source of her anger remains hidden. The film never allows her to reply to the question that DeVito, the cynical narrator of the film, says that men ask all women eventually: 'What the hell is wrong with you?' But then rhetorical questions are always the most difficult to answer.

Soft soap

Does David Lynch have a problem with women? I'm not referring to his split with Isabella Rossellini, rumoured to have taken place because of his obsession with not having any hot food in his house. I'm not referring to much-reported canoodlings with his very own Laura (Dern, not Palmer). I'm talking about the women he creates in his fictions. And five episodes into *Twin Peaks*, I'm rapidly coming to the conclusion that they may be weird but that doesn't mean they are wonderful.

I know this is trendy telly *par excellence* but does that mean we are so overcome by the dreamy music and dreamier script that we suspend all critical judgement, as most of the male reviewers have done? Fascinated by Sherilyn Fenn's very own twin peaks and tight sweaters, the main question that seems to have arisen is: When is a soap not a soap? Answer: When it's by David Lynch, in which case this thoroughly derided feminine genre suddenly becomes a revolutionary televisual form.

I can get off on postmodernism along with the best of the boys but I don't know if I want to any more because the bottom line is that postmodern irony means never having to say you are sorry. Or that you are serious. To complain or even to raise questions about Lynch's treatment of women means you have been caught in the Lynch mob's favourite noose. 'Oh God, you didn't take it seriously, did you? How frightfully unhip to think a scene about torturing women is really *about* torturing women.'

This was my own position a few years back when I went to see *Blue Velvet*. At the time it was being picketed by feminists who of course hadn't seen the film but just knew it was appalling. I think that is ridiculous and still do. And I would defend Lynch's right to make whatever images he wants but after *Wild at Heart* and now *Twin Peaks*, I am getting a little bored by his variations on a theme. The theme being female masochism. From Dorothy begging, 'Hit me, hit me,' to the powerful 'rape' scene between Dern and Dafoe in *Wild at Heart* to Laura Palmer's taped admission in the last episode of *Twin Peaks*, 'A couple of times he's tried to kill me and I really got off on it,' the Lynch oeuvre is packed with beautiful but deadly women. Some of whom might just end up dead, like Laura herself.

There is no doubt about it, Lynch is very good at sex, and violence. Nobody does it better. And what is so seductive about this enigmatic director is the urbane spaceman persona he adopts. Beneath this charming man's ordered exterior lurks the genuinely strange stuff that spills out into his films. I wouldn't ask him for sanitised sexual politics, yet he constantly refuses to analyse what he is doing, presenting himself as a medium through which the deep, dark forces of the American unconscious can express themselves. Thus he pulls off the remarkable feat of being both the ultimate auteur and yet somehow not responsible for the content of his work.

So who is responsible? If I hear the phrase 'the underbelly of American society' once more in connection with Lynch, I shall scream. The underbelly of American society has been exposed so many times now, by so many writers, it must be permanently naked. What bothers me about Lynch, and especially about *Twin Peaks*, is that the innate deathwish of the American Dream is carried out literally on the bodies of women.

Rape as a metaphor is nothing new and many avant-garde directors use corrupt sexual relations to explore corruption in general. Think of Godard and his tired obsession with prostitution or Almodavar and his 'bonds of love' in *Tie Me Up, Tie Me Down*. Lynch is indeed correct in tracing his lineage back to the surrealists. Their notions of *l'amour fou* and 'convulsive beauty' have all found a place in his work, again largely through his female characters.

Like the surrealists, however, he uses women to represent the unconscious itself. They are emotional, irrational beings, often little more than a bundle of sexual drives. The younger ones are often femme fatale or complete innocent types, while in *Wild at Heart* and *Twin Peaks* the older ones — the log lady, the drape woman — are good old-fashioned hysterics.

Underneath Audrey Horne's repressed plaid skirts and saddle shoes, we know there beats something truly Wild at Heart. In contrast, Agent Cooper may have a line direct to his subconscious but we never doubt he is fully in control of himself. For he is the hero trying to penetrate the mystery of Laura's death. Just as it has upset the little community, so has it upset ours. The nation — well, some of it — is in the grip of a necrophiliac obsession with Laura Palmer's body, and this is *sexual* obsession. Imagine if she had been Larry Palmer — swell highschool jock. Would the series have the same allure?

No. We're talking serial sex murder here — the stuff of a thousand exploitation films. But we're talking arty serial sex murder and don't we just love it to death? What once looked like a critique of the sexual relations between men and women now looks more and more like a superbly constructed reinforcement of them. Sadism and masochism may underlie all our relationships but Lynch is not interested in asking why. Evil is not explained socially but in morally vague terms as a presence 'out there in the woods'.

Loony psychiatrist Dr Jacoby may be right when he says, 'The problems of our entire society are of a sexual nature' but the dapper Agent Cooper will not be drawn. He is a proponent of the 'Funny chaps, women' school of philosophy: 'In the grand design. women were drawn from a different set of blueprints,' he says smugly.

So that's it then. No questions asked. And while Laura's

sexual history and her violated body became public property, both he and Lynch get to have their cherry pie and eat it.

FLESH

Good vibrations

It was an offer I couldn't refuse. The holly-trimmed party invite was offering me the 'splendid chance to examine and try a wide selection from the Ann Summers range of sexy garments and marital aids'. At last something more titillating than tupperware. At last an all women 'do' that would put the sex back into parties. A place where aids meant erotic and exotic sex toys instead of a depressing disease. What more could a girl ask for?

So armed with a bottle of Piat d'Or, I set off to boldly buy where lots of other women had bought before. I recited the phrase that Cilla uses every Saturday . . . 'You will not be disappointed.'

By the time I got to my friend's house our 'local demonstrator' had arrived and was sitting demurely with her bulging suitcase. The other women arrived in various states of embarrassment, a certain tension filled the air until we settled into our places in the bedroom. As we began to relax, the foreplay began. The naughty nighties and tacky under-wear were pulled out of the suitcase and passed around, an attempt I suppose to get us in the mood. Paula, our travelling saleslady produced item after unremarkable item. Cheap nylon bodystockings and corselettes, French knickers trimmed with something described as 'Love you' lace seemed to do little for most of the guests. Their names were just as uninspiring — things like Kitten, Sabrina and Hustler. All this stuff is available in better quality materials in the chain stores anyway.

What was remarkable though, was the sales patter accompanying all these 'sexy garments'. Paula emphasised which garments had 'easy access' for the nights 'you've decided to let him in'. Some allowed him 'entry' while you were 'getting on with the hoovering', while others were for the 'No-No nights' which involved elasticated ankles which were apparently to stop him 'getting up the leg'. One's body began to feel like a receptacle under siege. Sex was clearly something 'he' did to you. Forget any notion of autonomous female sexuality — the woman's only activity appeared to be indicating through your choice of nightie whether you were giving him permission or not.

'Clothing as Language' has got nothing on this. I imagined whole relationships being conducted without ever needing to speak. There was even a pillowcase which said 'Yes' on one side and 'No' on the other in order 'to give him the message'. Yet the Ann Summers vocabulary is frighteningly monosyllabic, even retarded — the anchoring of all sexual possibilities to the only one that really counts — yes or no. Multiple refers to orgasms, not meanings. In the Ann Summers linear and limited scheme of things, men are continually seeking sex everywhere and women are just there waiting . . .

But the women at the party began to get impatient — I mean, just how many pairs of naughty knickers are you expected to ooh and aah over? Paula moved on to the 'novelties'. From the downright offensive to the inane and infantile — these items all shared a worrying obsession with the phallus. We saw the penis ashtray, the penis mug, the plastic penis and glasses set to wear on your face, the sperm soap, the willy care kit and the wind up willy. Needless to say all these little pricks that popped out from cups, purses and aprons were erect. The catalogue describes 'Lipdick': 'Surprise! Surprise! Go to use the lipstick and a little penis pops out.'

As the room became littered with dismembered pricks which the guests passed around distastefully, the term phallocentrism took on a more concrete meaning. We are used to seeing the fragmentation of the female body, but to witness this overt fetishisation of the phallus was strange. Clearly we were supposed to find the concept of an erect penis hysterically funny (a real novelty?) at one minute, yet desire it the next. The vision of legions of jolly peckers and wind-up willies ('Watch his frantic pitter-patter!') taking over the world is one I prefer not to think about.

Just as obnoxious were the 'flasher pouches' which caused one woman to leave the room, though she did return a little later explaining she was only there for the 'gadgets'. These of course are always saved for the climax of the evening. In fact apart from the dildos and devices, the rest of the merchandise could be bought elsewhere. They certainly inspired most interest, although our demonstrator seemed unwilling to go into much detail about the pros and cons of each model. Vibrators that lit up and ones with leprechaun faces were discussed for their lack of aesthetic appeal, while others were recommended. One woman, a 3D Design student, commented on the Bauhaus qualities of one particular vibrator. I managed to drop the Duo Balls in my wine as I was trying to get Paula to explain one particularly mystifying item that involved a lot of wires.

Then it was out with the order forms and catalogues — never mind 'How was it for you?' The lager-flavoured Booby Drops (make mine a Grolsch) were a hit. And then there was the interesting sounding Maximus Big Man Cream — a five to eight week course in 'penis development'. How's that for your penis-envy, girls? As we were making our choices our hostess with the mostest modelled some of the underwear for us, which she thoughtfully accessorised with rubber gloves. A couple of other brave souls put on the nighties and were instantly transformed into something from *Revenge of the Stepford Wives*. Amongst the laughter, a lot of intense form-filling went on, Paula collected our orders and then was off into the night promising to deliver within a few days.

Of course it's a brilliant move for Ann Summers to go into the home selling business. Women who feel too embarrassed or intimidated to go into one of their many sex shops can be persuaded to part with their cash in the privacy of a friend's house. And if you tried hard enough you could feel the probing and penetrative thrust of capital — more repulsive than any veined and throbbing dildo. You could feel it come right into your living room, ejaculating pathetic little replicas of itself in the form of Bully Boy vibrators and Flasher Gonks. But you could also feel something else . . .

For once the reactionary ideology that sells these products to lone men in sex shops is put in the feminised space of the home, something different happens. Consumption becomes a collective activity — women talk about, laugh at and discuss what's on sale. Just because they buy part of the deal doesn't mean they have to buy all of it. To view them as passive consumers is as idiotic as the Ann Summers view of passive female sexuality. Consumer research and testing — that staple of soft porn was much in evidence at the party I went to.

And that completely undermined the sales pitch. Women who obviously knew about their desires were being offered a view of femininity which oscillated between hanging around in a nightie and being thrust at with a Grafenberg Rouser. Our demonstrator's telling phrase for sexual arousal was 'getting het up'.

Though no one believes any longer that the recognition of the clitoral orgasm will bring about the collapse of Western civilisation, there is something valuable in women having the space to find out about what they like or don't like. That this should be tied to a ludicrously phallicised view of female desire is a shame. It's obviously time to really 'Take the toys from the boys'.

———

Deviant Laws

'If a man wants his scrotum sandpapered in the privacy of his own home, is it anyone else's business?' asked Nick Cohen in *The Independent*. He was referring to the jailing of eight men for what the appropriately named Judge Rant described as 'degrading and vicious' sexual activities.

In other words, if a precedent is set by this case then the answer to the question posed by Nick Cohen is 'Yes'. What may at first appear to be an entirely private if peculiar activity is in fact subject to public jurisdiction — the law. This particular case was disturbing, not for the shock-horror headlines about a sadomasochistic torture group which dominated the headlines but for the implications it has as a civil liberties issue.

I would not actively encourage grown men to go around nailing each other's genitals to bits of wood. Yet I would defend their right to do so. Indeed many of the details of this case are so unpleasant to so many people that they have clouded the political issues that such a prosecution throws up. It is doubly important therefore to get the details right, to be sure what these men were and were not doing.

A group of men met regularly to engage in sadomasochistic sex sessions. This involved beatings, genital torture, sex with animals as well as the use of drugs. Fifteen men were given sentences ranging from conditional discharges to four and a half years imprisonment. Eight of them were jailed for what the judge deemed to be beyond the limit of 'acceptable behaviour in civilised society'.

But the point is they were not forcing or coercing people into doing things they didn't want to do, nor were they making a profit from their activities. No harm was caused to anyone but themselves and none of the injuries inflicted resulted in hospital treatment. The average boxing match would be far more likely to result in long-term injury than anything that happened here.

So why was the case brought in the first place? No member of the public had complained. What had gone on happened in private. It was only because the police had got hold of a video the group had made that the case went to court. The hackneyed phrase 'even hardened detectives were sickened by what they saw' was trawled up once more. Have you ever heard of a case where these mythological creatures, these anonymous hardened detectives, are not sickened by evidence of one kind or another?

Usually, though, these unelected arbiters of morals are not allowed to go forward with such completely unnecessary prosecutions. It is only because the behaviour that occurred here was between homosexuals that such a case could even be considered. Clearly the law in this area is inconsistent.

Now your idea of a quiet night in may not involve inviting a few friends around and cutting their penises with surgical scalpels, but the issue here is one of *consent*. Although this may well be distasteful to the average person, it didn't cause harm to anyone else. Is it any more disgusting than deriving pleasure from dressing up in stupid outfits and riding around the countryside in order to encourage a pack of dogs to rip apart a wild animal? And more mundanely, is sending any of these men to prison really going to stop them or anyone else doing this kind of thing?

It's like a sick joke. Question: where do you send a bunch of homosexual sadomasochists for punishment? Answer: to an all male enivoronment where s&m relationships have been institutionalised to a sublime degree. More seriously though, this case where private and consenting behaviour between adult homosexuals has become an imprisonable offence, makes a mockery of what passes for consent in many rape cases. Only a few weeks ago a rape case was dismissed because a fifteen-year-old girl had agreed to go for a walk with a man. He violently raped her, but saying 'yes' to going for a walk was, according to the judge, tantamount to saying 'yes' to sexual intercourse.

In other words when a heterosexual woman says, 'no' she really means 'yes', but when a homosexual man says 'yes', the law says that is just not good enough. Homosexual men are not allowed to perform acts of violence on each other, even when both parties consent, while the law repeatedly stands by as heterosexual men beat the shit out of women in a definitely non-consensual way.

If the law is to start being used, as it is increasingly, to prosecute individual and private activities, all of us have cause for concern. Spanking, whipping, scratching, biting, piercing can all be construed as acts of violence, yet they are all sexual activities that many people have indulged in. That harmless love-bite could easily count as an assault, you know.

Most (heterosexual) people assume that the law has no right to poke its nose behind the bedroom door, that their sexuality is somehow beyond public discussion. Unfortunately homosexuals have always known different and would quite sensibly prefer public money to be spent on prosecuting 'queer-bashers' rather than cases such as these. Yet such cases depend on a clustering of moral outrage — homosexuality equals perversion equals paedophilia equals murder — that may start in the tabloids but in this instance was reinforced by the judiciary.

The organisation Liberty (formerly NCCL) has suggested

that part of the problem is that we don't have a bill of rights, which in some ways would give a less confusing account of freedom of expression and principles of privacy. Instead we have the likes of Judge Rant rattling on about 'brute homosexual activity' and literally making it up as he goes along. These days you don't have to be a sadomasochist to know that there may be a thin line between pleasure and pain; but it's not as dangerously thin as the one between private lives and public morality.

Everyday eroticism

That obscure object of desire, the male body, has been a long time theme of photographer Bruce Weber's work. His stylish black and white fashion photographs manage a lucrative combination of classiness and eroticism that has been much imitated. A few years ago you might have seen Weber's fashion spreads in magazines like *The Face* but now they're more likely to adorn the ad pages of *Arena*. For both Calvin Klein and Ralph Lauren have used him in their advertising campaigns.

Weber himself has always claimed that some of the beautiful men that he has photographed were not models but real people that he just came across — life guards and construction workers and farmers. Certainly the idea that these hunks are 'found objects' enhances the homo-erotic appeal of his work, allowing the viewers' fantasies to run free. His first film, *Broken Noses*, does the same.

Ostensibly *Broken Noses* is a documentary about a charming young boxer named Andy Minsker, a lightweight fighter who loves to talk about himself. Better still, in Weber's terms, he has a face like the young Chet Baker and a body that never seems to be clothed. Minsker's life is in many ways unexceptional. Having failed to make the big time on the boxing circuit he now coaches the local boxing team. We watch him ironing at home, horsing around with the boys or arguing with his father.

All of this is shot in either the ravishing grainy black and white style that Weber has made his own or the blue velvety hallucinogenic technicolour of Super 8. The movie is long on stylish and stylised images and short on just about everything else. This might be called minimalism but it verges on self-indulgence for much of the time. Even those who share Weber's intoxication with little boys' bodies and the ritualistic pampering and preening that the boxing world allows, may find the whole exercise wearing.

There are moments though when the mask of masculinity slips. Andy's vulnerability is exposed both in discussions of his unhappy childhood and when, for a hundred dollars, he takes down his trousers. He is wearing underpants, the crotch of which has an illustration of his girlfriend's face. As touching as these scenes are, they tend to be overpowered by the sculptural quality of the images and the reluctant realisation that the sophisticated Weber is exploiting an unknowing innocent.

The deliberate homo-erotic imagery is everywhere. A scene where Andy uncomfortably reads some Shakespeare in a rose garden was, one can't help feeling, a suggestion made by the director rather than Andy himself. Like Weber's stills, *Broken Noses* is interesting in its blurring of homosexuality and heterosexuality, of homo-eroticism and 'straight' narcissism. His influence in aestheticising, or indeed creating a new aesthetic around the male body, is politically and historically exciting. Yet Weber seems almost coy about explicit homosexual imagery, preferring instead a selfconscious style that sexualises that most unselfconscious of states

155

— masculinity itself, producing a kind of eroticisation of the everyday.

Weber's black and white photography is amazingly tactile but somehow always just out of reach. This distancing also has the effect of making everything look artily timeless. *Broken Noses* has the timeless feel and obsession with Americana of a jeans commercial. It could be the 50s but is in fact the 80s; history becomes a dressing-up box for the fashionable to rummage around in. And this matters. Having a beautiful torso doesn't free you from the forces of history and repressed longing is still, when all is said and done, *repressed*.

Isaac Julien's *Looking for Langston* is superficially similar to *Broken Noses* in that it, too, is shot in black and white and it is about gay identity. But they couldn't be more different. Julien's film kicks down the closet door to provide a lush testimony to the power of understanding your own history. A meditation on the work of the black American poet Langston Hughes, the film glides between the 20s and the present-day to examine what it meant and what it means to 'sin against one's race', to be both black and gay.

Archive footage of the Harlem Renaissance, when black artists and writers were taken up by white society only to be dropped when they refused to play the primitive, blends with dreamlike sequences to make a sensually visual poem. The contribution that black artists have made to modernism is rarely talked about in the selective tradition of literature and art. And to even mention homosexuality is taboo in many versions of black history. Julien plunders this history, not just to make pretty pictures (although he does this brilliantly), but to also find a continuity that gives a resonance to the present.

Instead of being submerged in the depths of earnest worthiness that so much 'history from below' suffers from, Julien floats through it unanchored by the need for realism.

His previous work with Sankofa is also part of a renaissance amongst young black film-makers whose interest in formal experimentation has led to accusations of inaccessibility. But there seems to me no better way of making your films accessible than by making them visually beautiful — *Looking for Langston* achieves this.

It ends with last year's acid chant *Can you feel it?* Unlike *Broken Noses*, where one simply admires the physiques of the bodies Weber photographs and the techniques with which he does so, *Looking for Langston* does make you *feel*. Desire drips through the words and images, as bodies touch, police truncheons are wielded. Even in the velvety darkness fear of AIDS leads to fear of intimacy. Neither desire nor anger is repressed. Often pleasure and politics chafe against each other, resulting in little more than mutual irritation; here they rub up against one another showing what can happen when each arouses the other.

One big act

Rehearsed pleasure lies at the core of Juliet Bashore's extraordinary *Kamikaze Hearts*. Featuring the tabloid trinity of lesbians, junkies and porn stars, *Kamikaze Hearts* is underground film-making of the highest order, complete with Warholesque, self-obsessed starlets. Does this mean in twenty years from now Bashore will be also producing slick Hollywood fodder? I sincerely hope not.

The film looks like a documentary based on the lives of two women who work in the porn industry. But soon it becomes clear that some scenes have been set up for the camera. In fact the camera is no objective observer but an integral part of the central character Mitch's life. She is a tough, streetwise veteran of sex shows and porn movies who seems to live only to be filmed — 'I don't know whether I'm more truth or fiction.' Mitch is constantly performing — 'I am permanently a personality', continually camping and vamping to the camera. This both frustrates and fascinates her lover Tigr, who wants to find out whether their 'porno-romance' is real. The first time the two women made love was as part of a porn film.

Kamikaze Hearts is ostensibly about their affair, the difficulty of trying to work out their lives in the midst of the sex industry. This is further complicated by their regular drug use. Tigr was first attracted to Mitch's sophistication — she knew how to use a needle — and now both women are dependent on drugs. Yet Bashore never moralises. And though the hot subjects of pornography and lesbianism are the backdrops to the film, *Kamikaze Hearts* isn't really about them.

Unsurprisingly, it has already upset the positive images brigade. Mitch and Tigr are certainly not sharing, caring, successful, woman-identified-women. For god's sake, they work in the porn industry! But nor are they victims. It's obvious that they work for the money but then who hasn't done a shitty job just for the money?

The scenes shot on the set of a sleazy porn flick are notionally funny but also disturbing. There is the make-up artist busy covering pimples on arses who says nochalantly, 'I have never seen anything erotic in the four hundred films I've worked on.' There is the actress who refuses to do a scene in the presence of the obnoxious, medallioned producer. And there is the actor who refuses to be fellated twice when he has only been paid for one cum shot.

Halfway through all this Mitch has to do a rape scene which is as horrible and sordid as you might imagine. Yet somehow Tigr strives to maintain a relationship with her, to get to know the real Mitch, though she worries: 'She fucks off camera the same way she fucks on camera — you don't know what's real.'

What Tigr wants from Mitch is some kind of truth, something more than an image. In the last scene, which is an emotional showdown, one expects to see them actually making love instead of performing. Instead they shoot up together and ramble incoherently. Like pornography itself, the film promises the one big act, the one scene that will make the whole thing right, but never delivers it. Juliet Bashore makes us painfully aware of our voyeurism.

She plays on our confusion about sexual honesty. Mitch is constantly naked but totally self-possessed. We know nothing of her though she talks about herself all the time. What Bashore shows us is not intrinsic to pornography but rather part of our whole sexual ideology. She overturns the idea that sexuality is a magical essence that is somehow the truest part of our beings — that we are most ourselves when we are having sex. Here sex is a game, a performance, a way of earning a living. There is nothing natural about it. Despite what we might like to think, it has nothing to do with the notion of an essential self.

Sex offers no guarantees, no truth, no reality separate from its image. And, least of all, love.

<hr>

A screw of convenience?

Christine Keeler, naked, long legs astride a chair; Christine Keeler clutching her patent leather handbag, coyly pushing the hair out of her dark glasses as she leaves the courtroom; Christine Keeler 'model' and 'show-girl' cavorting with lords and cabinet ministers in country houses. Keeler, the impassive icon of the early 60s, now lives in a council flat and is broken, many say, by the strain of always having to be Christine Keeler.

John Profumo, the then minister for war with whom she had an affair, is still rich, still happily married and was awarded an MBE in 1975 for his work for charity. Stephen Ward, the society osteopath who introduced them and the only man Christine says she loved, took his own life during the trial which followed what came to be known as 'the Profumo affair' in 1963.

The affair which Christine now more aptly describes as a 'very, very, well-mannered screw of convenience' is the subject of the film *Scandal*.

Starring John Hurt in another quintessential victim role as Ward and Joanne Whalley as Keeler, the film belongs to the growing number of movies which re-examine and re-assess recent British history. *Scandal*, with its commercially viable mix of sex, hypocrisy and breaches of security, strikes an oddly contemporary note in the light of the *Spycatcher* episode.

Though adultery, as Lord Hailsham spluttered out in an interview at the time, was neither the prerogative of the Tory party or even the rich, this particular scandal came at a watershed in British history and was, and still is, perceived to have brought down the Tory government. In reality it was simply one factor, but a factor that nonetheless fleshed out a growing sense of anxiety: the economy was in deep trouble, Britain no longer had an empire. And, more crucially, as regards the Profumo affair, its defence and foreign affairs policies were crumbling. Instead of the nuclear independence that Macmillan had promised, there was complete dependence on the Americans.

Supermac, who in his diaries describes himself as 'old, incompetent and worn-out', handled the Profumo affair disastrously by simply refusing to handle it at all and expressing an aristocratic disdain for matters involving 'personal affairs'. In contrast, Wilson cleverly homed in not on matters of personal morality but on the more politically damaging question of national security — Keeler had been sleeping with a cabinet minister and a Russian called Ivanov — who was thought by M15 to be a spy — at the same time.

To Wilson, who was busy presenting the Labour Party as a party of modernisation, the whole affair was a gift. He was able to exploit the Rachman connection (Rachman, the notorious slum landlord was Mandy Rice-Davies's boyfriend, and sometime lover of Keeler) to suggest that under the Tory party the top echelons of society were decadent beyond belief, while the ordinary people were bullied and cheated by thugs like Rachman.

The film, like so many fictionalised documentaries, prefers to personalise the story into the relationship between Keeler and Ward, keeping the historical context to a few headlines. In capturing the hypocrisy of the British establishment closing rank and baying for blood this works well, but in trying to portray Keeler and Ward as 'class rebels', as producer Stephen Wooley describes them, it definitely fails. Using sex to cross class barriers is, after all, hardly new and if it is a revolutionary act, Cindrella would be the greatest class rebel of them all.

Perhaps it's fairer to say that Ward was a great pretender and his crime, like that of Profumo's, was not what he did but the fact he got found out. Voyeuristic, charming and a connoisseur of the perverse, Hurt plays him sympathetically. He discovers Keeler working in a nightclub and, like Pygmalion, he takes her over, introduces her to his upmarket friends with their downmarket sexual preferences.

For my money, Joanne Whalley just doesn't have Keeler's stunning indifference; the enigmatic coolness that stares out from all those black and white photos. Ludovic Kennedy says of her at the trial that she had 'a terrifying little face, vacant yet knowing'. This may have been helped by the fact that she was doped up to her eyeballs on phenobarbitone — the valium of its day. Nor was she so *ingenue* as the film makes out; she had already had a horribly botched abortion and had stolen a car to get to London.

After Profumo admitted that he had lied in the Commons, Ward was sacrificed, prosecuted for living off immoral earnings. The trial and Denning's whitewashed report, which cleared the security forces and vilified Ward, were little more than a device to make it look as if after all the government was at least doing *something*.

Ward couldn't take it. The film's cry of 'It's not fair' is moving, but then the insidiousness of class has never depended on fairness — despite its protestations to the contrary.

Scandal revels in this hypocrisy and is as voyeuristic in its filming of Keeler and Rice-Davies as the lecherous old men they slept with. To think that their beauty could ever be as powerful as the shabby goings on of the men is naive. The girls were very young: their ambition was to be in a Camay commercial, not to bring down a government.

The real interest of this film lies in the unanswered questions. Did M15 set the whole thing up with Ward working for them? Were they trying to get Ivanov to defect? Did they murder Ward as some have suggested? And the biggest question of all, what happens when politicians lose control of their own security services? What happens when 'British Intelligence' is responsible to no one but itself?

I'll leave the last word to Mandy Rice-Davies, as astute now as she was then. Those that suppressed the truth about the Profumo affair still hold power in this country. 'That group still exists in the shadows. The people who pressed the buttons remain a shadowy group who inhabit the labyrinths of Whitehall. The sheer ego of it drives me crazy.'

Well, she would say that, wouldn't she?

———

Missionary sex

Now that *The Last Temptation of Christ* has been officially declared Art with a capital A, we can all relax. Well everyone that is except a few senile bishops and the picketing nuns from the Evangelical Sisterhood of Mary who still want a film that they have never seen banned. Unfortunately though, calls for censorship come in all shapes and sizes and another kind of evangelical sisterhood has been at work protesting at Sheila McLaughlin's film *She Must Be Seeing Things*. This has already caused quite a stir: because when it was shown at a lesbian summer school a group of women tried to smash the projector and destroy the film.

A film that explores sexual jealousy, voyeurism, dominance and submission — all within the context of a lesbian relationship — certainly sounds like hot stuff, doesn't it? But as so often happens the issues surrounding *She Must Be Seeing Things* are far hotter than the film itself.

The 'story', such as it is, centres on Agatha, a black civil rights lawyer who finds a diary detailing her lover Jo's previous relationships with men. She becomes obsessively jealous, imagining that Jo is having affairs with men left, right and centre. Jo, a flirty blonde, is oblivious to all this as she is absorbed in directing a film about Catalina, a seventeenth-century nun who spent her life disguised as a man. If you think this sounds pretty naff you would be right.

The main problem is that nothing really happens and what does happen is rather charmless and lacking in wit. This may be because the film self-consciously foregrounds certain ideas derived from a psychoanalytically informed brand of film studies. 'Screen theory' has been successful in asking fundamental questions of cinema that many other kinds of criticism simply cannot tackle: Why do we get pleasure from watching films? How is that pleasure structured? And, most significantly, what is the role of gender and fantasy in that pleasure?

She Must Be Seeing Things, however, highlights the failures and absences of such theories by focusing on the pleasures of voyeurism, and by questioning the relations of activity and passivity between women. Can women be voyeurs too? What does it mean to turn yourself into an object for another woman? Is it really different for girls? So the film is stuffed full of mirrors, windows, cameras and, if you get aroused by a bit of theory made flesh, this is the film for you. But I couldn't help feeling that you will actually find just as complicated a relay of looks, *mise-en-scène* and playfulness in the average Madonna video. If, on the other hand, you were hoping to get aroused by seeing what lesbians do in bed you may be disappointed. There is a line in the film that goes 'clichés can be sexy too'. Yes, but they still remain clichés.

Nonetheless, this rather mild film has aroused violent emotions in some women. The scenes which are clearly Agatha's fantasies have been denounced as 'pornographic'. She imagines Jo being killed in what looks like a series of rejected Cindy Sherman stills; and worse, she imagines Jo making love with men. It seems that to suggest that lesbian relationships are shot through with heterosexual imagery and conditioning and that all sexuality is bound up with power, dependency, dominance and submission is anathema to some radical feminists. They would prefer to believe in an essential femininity somehow sealed off in a vacuum and untainted by the nasty old male libido. Sex should be soft-focus, sentimental and loving devoid of vulgarity, aggression, messiness or any of the things that actually make sex sexy. But the trouble with this new 'missionary position' is that, as Eileen

Willis has said, the concept of sex and eroticism is not feminist but *feminine*. It ends up as an equally repressive fantasy and, if we cannot explore female sexuality in what is clearly a feminist film, where can we?

Fantasy, however, is exactly what the anti-porn 'sex-cops' will not deal with. Yet *She Must Be Seeing Things* is too calculated to be successful on this score — it is *about* fantasy rather than being in any way fantastic.

If you want something quite fantastic and totally un-inhibited by any notions of taste — political or personal — go and see *Hold Me While I'm Naked: The Perverse Comedies of George Kuchar*. The work of this underground film-maker has to be seen to be believed. Lurid, amateurish and unashamedly voyeuristic, Kuchar's method is like watching Douglas Sirk on speed. It dispenses with all the boring bits of B movie melodrama and goes for a gang bang of climaxes. Mad, deliriously funny, full of lust and self-disgust, these short films are strangely moving, and because Kuchar does not censor himself they do have the disturbing power of a private fantasy.

It is this ability to disturb, to excite and to make uncomfortable, that has to be defended in the face of the 'ban it and burn it' brigade. The arguments about censorship flare up regularly and yet the feminist case against censorship is rarely heard. I'm not crazy about pornography or about lots of the images of women that I see around me, nor am I some sort of time-warped libertarian. But I agree with Ruby Rich who said that: 'In the fight against pornography what gets lost is as important as what gets won.' Much of the anti-porn lobby relies on emotion rather than analysis, on simplistic, almost Victorian, ideologies about the innate differences between men and women, and a self-righteous moral superiority.

Some feminists in the US have organised themselves to fight censorship particularly the Dworkin-inspired legislation which allows a person to claim damages if they are offended by pornographic publications on public display. Perhaps it's time we did the same? But let's not kid ourselves and couch our arguments about censorship in hypothetical terms asking whether censorship should exist. It *already* does — ask the Terrence Higgins Trust who cannot import the safe sex videos they need for their educational work on AIDS.

The women who tried to stop *She Must Be Seeing Things* from being shown (and the protesting nuns) may be extreme cases but perhaps they need reminding of George Bernard Shaw's saying — 'that the extreme form of censorship is assassination'.

The struggle for safe endings

Recently, when speaking about the effects of the AIDS epidemic, Derek Jarman used the analogy of the first world war's lost generation of young men. In the US such metaphors have already become reality. More Americans have died of AIDS than died in Vietnam. As Michael Bronski has said, 'There is no need — as they used to say — to bring the war home: it is already here.' Yet, in the absence of a governmental response to the crisis (Reagan couldn't bring himself to say the word AIDS until 1985), the most political response has come from cultural quarters. The day-to-day work of informing, counselling and caring taken on by the gay community has been inextricably bound to an activist cultural politics manifested in organisations such as ACTUP and Out Rage.

Documentation of the struggle simply to put AIDS on the public agenda has often been like reportage from a battlefield, moving in its urgency, its need to tell it as it happens. And the war analogies certainly apply to the tapes by AIDS activists Voices from the Frontlines. Often shot quickly and cheaply on video, the raw material of these films has been strikingly overlaid with a sophisticated understanding of how media imagery works. Many of these film-makers haven't learnt about 'the politics of representation' in a seminar room, but organically, in the actual process of trying to represent their politics.

A decade into the crisis comes a couple of more mainstream efforts — *Longtime Companion*, billed as 'Hollywood's first feature film to tell the historical story of how AIDS devastates and how it has transformed the gay community', and the documentary *Common Threads: Stories from the Quilt*.

Longtime Companion is aiming for a wide audience, with its profits going to various AIDS organisations. Indeed, it owes far more to the conventions of the Hollywood liberal *Angst* movie than to the more vibrant work that has emerged in response to the epidemic. Undoubtedly well intentioned, at least it escapes the trap of portraying AIDS solely as an individual tragedy, while capturing the changing relations of the gay community.

Charting the lives of a number of white, affluent gay men, the film picks up their various stories each year from 1981 to the present day. Starting on the beach at Fire Island, where hedonism rules, it seems nothing could go wrong. Rumours of a strange cancer found increasingly in gay men are laughed off. Suggestions that it is linked to the use of 'poppers' or other drugs mean that it can be dismissed by many. These characters don't do that many drugs, they don't sleep around that much.

A year later, of course, the disease has already entered their lives. *Longtime Companion* is good on all the denial mechanisms that come into play around AIDS, one character explaining that only self-destructive people get it and that the

167

answer is to think positively. A film like this, however, can only really work if one cares about the individual characters, and Fuzzy, Howard, Bob, David, Paul, Sean, John and the token woman, Lisa, are so undifferentiated that it it's difficult to do so. They are all so unremittingly 'nice', all have stable monogamous relationships and, as the years go by, are so endlessly supportive that it doesn't ring true.

Sure enough there is a gradual politicisation but it's all very *thirtysomething*. Indeed, the classy soap feel is built into the film which, after all, contains the basic elements for a soap — 'a closed community in crisis'. Of course the gay community, like any other, is never closed in this way — it just acts as a dramatic device. The lives of the characters in the film revolve around a daytime soap tellingly called *Other People*, which Sean writes and Paul stars in.

Yet the limitations of using the soap format are nowhere more apparent than in the bizarre ending of the film. Judith Williamson has written perceptively, in *Taking Liberties*, about how the horror, melodrama and detective genres have been used repeatedly not just in fictional accounts of the AIDS virus but also in our 'common sense' understanding of the disease. Slotting the incomprehensible into familiar narratives is one way we try to make sense of it, but it also precludes other, more political, reactions. *Longtime Companion* can make the disease accessible through this soap opera structure but then cannot cope with the demands that the structure makes on it.

Soaps may never have overall resolutions but they do have mini-ones. Here, death is the only closure. And it is repeated over and over again. Yet the demand for the happy ending persists and is granted in a fantasy sequence in which all the dead come alive again as a cure for AIDS is found. Sure we have to have hope, but such a crass scene is insulting.

I couldn't help wondering what Vito Russo, the New York writer who appears in *Common Threads*, would have made of it. He lost his lover and now has the disease himself but remains admirably angry, honest and unsentimental. 'Intellectually I believe that when you're dead, you're dead — that's it.' Nevertheless he made a panel in the AIDS Memorial Quilt for Jeffrey as part of the Names Project. The quilt, with its connotations of tradition and domesticity, grows bigger each day as more panels are added to it. It serves not just as a reminder of those who are gone but brings together those who have lost their friends, lovers and relatives.

Common Threads picks out five stories from the quilt, straight and gay, black and white, including David Mandell, a haemophiliac who died at eleven. It is a real tearjerker, as it should be. But it also reveals the criminal negligence of governments who still talk about 'the general population' as if gay people were not part of it. It exposes our inability to deal not only with deaths from AIDS but with death in general. Michael Bronski's plea that having politicised sex by linking the personal with the political, we need also 'to politicise death', is more relevant now than ever. Death is not a metaphor for anything, no matter how hard we try to make it one. Though we are continually told that we don't know how to talk about death or AIDS, *Common Threads*, through the stunning eloquence of ordinary people, shows that we not only can, but we have to.

FAITH

Kidnapped by the counter-culture

While Patty Hearst was in prison serving a sentence for armed robbery, she wore a T-shirt that said: 'Being kidnapped means always having to say you're sorry.' It's a kind of sick joke, but then much about her life must have seemed that way . . . Brought up to be 'supremely self-confident' in the midst of the Hearst dynasty, she appears, even in her own autobiography, to be fabulously bland in the way that the fabulously wealthy often are. Uninterested in politics but studying at one of the most politicised American campuses, Berkeley, the most radical act of this Californian heiress before her kidnapping was voting for McGovern rather than Nixon.

Yet, suddenly, this granddaughter of one of the first newspaper magnates — immortalised in *Citizen Kane* — was herself headline news. In 1974 she was kidnapped by the Symbionese Liberation Army (SLA), a little-known terrorist organisation. She was to spend the next five years in captivity, two with the SLA and the rest in jail for the crimes she committed with them.

She is not an easy subject for a film, but Paul Schrader, who directs *Patty Hearst*, has never been interested in making 'easy' films. More often than not, his characters are people who are propelled into increasingly desperate situations and somehow have to make their own sense of them. De Niro in *Taxi Driver*, Richard Gere in *American Gigolo* and George C Scott in *Hardcore* all follow their chosen paths to the end — to the point where they no longer have a choice. Whether this is some kind of working through of Schrader's strict Calvinist upbringing is a matter of debate. What is without doubt, though, is that his films are uncomfortable in their insistence on looking at questions that are normally swept under the secular carpet — questions of individual morality, of free will and of truth.

Certainly the fascination of the Patty Hearst story centres on these issues. Why did she *choose* to stay with her captors? What kind of *choice* was it? Did she do it of her own free will or was she brainwashed? As the film makes clear, she was blindfolded and kept in a cupboard for fifty-seven days before she made this 'choice'. She was raped and abused. Schrader captures her torment, her disorientation and depression through strange camera angles, cutting shots as the cupboard door swings open and shut. As she comes to depend on her captors, we see more of this strange underground organisation.

Led by Cinque Mtume (meaning fifth prophet), the SLA is revealed to be a ridiculous sect whose revolutionary rhetoric masks a bizarre collection of misfits. Despising most other radical groups — including the Weather Underground and the Black Panthers — for selling out, they believe in armed struggle and third world leadership and are happy to die for these causes. The film is relentless in its portrayal of them as not only inept, but stupidly hypocritical. They are desperate both to be black and to give up all bourgeois behaviour, yet their sexism was disguised as comradely free love and their fantasies about black people amounted to the worst kind of inverse racism. But if we are to believe Hearst's book, on which the film is based, they were even worse than Schrader paints them.

Hearst drifts into this new life and identity wanting only to survive. She studies their texts, learns to use their weapons, trains to be a soldier until, as she says: 'Reality for them was different from all that I had known before, and by this time their reality was my reality.' What starts off as 'communist claptrap' becomes second nature. She robs a bank and fires a sub-machine gun to enable her comrades to escape from the police. Her former life fades further and further away until the visions she sees of herself blindfolded with her family no longer appear.

The 'fascist pig media' move from sympathy to horror as this all-American girl turns urban guerilla. A poll conducted just before her arrest showed that 68 per cent of those questioned thought she should be sent to prison, and more than two-thirds thought she had joined the SLA voluntarily. Half of them actually believed she had planned her own kidnapping. As one of the lawyers hints in the film, she became a symbol for a generation who felt that their children had all been kidnapped by the counter-culture.

Once arrested and tried, she seems to move passively from one hell to the next. The media and the courts voyeuristically questioned her about whether she had slept with blacks, women and hippies. Her crime was not so much robbing a bank but turning against middle-class morality — the press wrote obsessively about the question of whether she was brainwashed.

Her case disturbs all that we hold precious. She did, in many ways, become another person. Her true identity, her true self, was subsumed during the two years she was with the SLA. If it could happen to her, it could happen to any of us. What can we hold up as fundamentally true and right if, in order to survive, we have to reverse our whole value system?

Worst of all, how was it that she was so good at it? The absurd ravings of her captors may have degraded all she held dear and glorified all she had been taught to fear, but were the ideals really that different? What first seemed nonsense became her sense. One ideology replaced another and she was, after her release from jail, able to swing back once more — she is now apparently a staunch Republican.

Hearst's story and the film are both filled with a sense of loss, of the precariousness of what we presume identity to be. As the anaesthesia of ideology wears off, we are left only with a disturbing numbness that represents the most supreme loss of faith that we can imagine — the loss of faith in what is sacred to our modern 'religion' — we can no longer believe in our supposed freedom to choose. Our individuality can be kidnapped at any time.

Sculpting in time

The films of Russian director Andrei Tarkovsky epitomise all that is right or wrong (depending on your point of view) with 'art' cinema. It's certainly true that apart from being very long, slow and subtitled, it's not everyone's idea of a good night out to spend two and a half hours watching obscure characters endlessly discussing the meaning of life, love and the universe, however beautifully bleak the settings are. Yet for fans of Tarkovsky's films, *Solaris, Mirror, Nostalgia, Stalker, The Sacrifice*, it is precisely the depth and purity of his work that marks him out as one of the cinema's great directors. His total disdain for commercial cinema — the celluloid strip as commodity, as he refers to it — and his absolute insistence on cinema as one of the highest art forms, produced films that were not afraid to deal with deeply unfashionable spiritual questions.

Tarkovsky's questioning of the nature of faith, of prayer, of sacrifice in the modern world, alongside his elevation of personal experience eventually lead to his exile from the Soviet Union. By the mid-60s the liberal attitude to cultural affairs was hardening. Cuts were demanded by the authorities on *Andrei Roubleuv*, his film about the life of a medieval icon painter. Tarkovsky's work was increasingly denounced as 'élitist' and his continued emphasis on the profundity rather than the reactionary nature of Christian faith was taken as a subtle critique of communism and indeed of the Soviet state.

These issues are alluded to but not explored in *Directed by Andrei Tarkovskij*, a Swedish documentary by Michal Leszczylowski. From the opening shot of Tarkovsky himself, face screwed up in intense concentration, you know that this is going to be very much in the portrait-of-the-artist-as-god genre. And you would be right. Filmed during the making of *The Sacrifice*, it is given extra significance as Tarkovsky died of cancer shortly after editing the film from his hospital bed.

Despite the over-reverent attitude and moving interviews with his widow, Larissa, the film almost inadvertently allows an occasional critical edge to poke through. These surface not in the interviews with Tarkovsky or his wife, or in the scenes where he is describing his theories of cinema to adoring students, but when we see him on set actually working. While the respectful voice-over describes Tarkovsky's meticulous attention to detail, to every aspect of the film from set-design to make-up, we see before us a tyrant, interfering everywhere, refusing to let anyone else make decisions. This may be a little harsh because without a doubt his charm, brilliance and sheer determination to find the exact image inspired enormous admiration in those working with him.

Nonetheless, the documentary unwittingly highlights the problems of *auteur*-theory, of looking at films as the product of a single mind. While Tarkovsky is an *auteur* if ever there was one — every film uncompromisingly his own — the process of making a film involves hundreds of other individual talents as this documentary graphically illustrates.

He is at his most impressive when expounding his ideas on what films should do, on 'sculpting in time'. Seeing himself as a poet rather than a cinematographer, his films are mosaics of memory and time. The past is always a resource and cinema, he says, is the only medium that can take an impression of time. At his best his films excel in doing what film should do — they show things visually rather than saying them narratively. For Tarkovsky is not interested in the intellectual response of an audience but in its spiritual illumination — in a pure moment of what he calls 'aesthetic acceptance of the beautiful on an emotional level'. This is the truth he strives for through creating his own world, directly perceiving it, not by commenting on or imitating reality.

His absolute faith expressed time and time again in his book is the ability of the right image to communicate directly. He dislikes metaphors and searches for images that are 'innocent of symbolism': that in the beloved style of the Japanese haiku expresses a 'specific, unique, actual, fact' — a precise observation of life. Fittingly, he doesn't like Freud or Eisenstein both of whom, in different ways, elevate the ambiguity of images and facts, their potential for multiple meanings. Eisenstein's use of the third meaning — that derives from the interplay of two images — is for Tarkovsky incompatible with the nature of cinema: he believes the image exists within time, within the frame, for the spectator to make of it what she or he will. Editing, he insists, is to bring out the essential nature of the filmed material rather than to tell the audience how to read the imagery. Indeed, he is famous for the rhymes and rhythms of his films, his single takes, scenes lasting five or six minutes and shot in real time such as the house burning down in *The Sacrifice*.

What is fascinating about Tarkovsky, regardless of whether or not you like his films, is the way that both thematically and stylistically his work runs counter to nearly everything that could be called 'contemporary'.

His almost Zen-like characters are strong because they are weak, their passivity and humility is valued above all. We need to return to the time before we lost the ability to pray, to believe, to offer ourselves to the 'greater good'. Some find this visionary, fluid quality in his films full as they are of water, fire and wind. Others have described his work as cold, sanctimonious, egotistical, over-intellectual and lacking in warmth or humanity.

Above all, as Mark Le Fanu points out in his excellent book *The Cinema of Andrei Tarkovsky*, Tarkovsky stands in opposition to most modern atheistic directors such as Bergman and Bresson whom he admires. Tarkovsky believes in the power of 'the word' and in the reality of 'the self' — two concepts that have been undermined with equally religious zeal by many modern western theorists. Tarkovsky clearly believes that there is a correlation between truth and language and that inner experience proves the existence of the individual, of the soul. Thus, it is possible both to believe and to tell the 'truth', to have faith even in the modern world.

As we all know Tarkovsky's sadness at the secularisation of society both in the east and the west is a view strongly held by many people. Whether you find the films of this 'poet of memory' radical or irritatingly anachronistic, his visions of the time we have lost or are yet to have remain real and heartful and unique. They are quite unlike anything else: disturbingly beautiful and evocative and always too strangely lucid to be dismissed as mere nostalgia.

Playing Jesus by night

Jesus Christ may have had a lot of press but not enough to stop my nagging doubts. Two vital questions have been left hanging. Was Jesus an old hippy and was he the sort of bloke you could have a laugh with? Having seen Denys Arcand's film *Jesus of Montreal* the answer must be both yes and no. Yes, he was into peace and love and intense staring, and no, he didn't seem to have much of a sense of humour.

Nonetheless, this Canadian film comes heaped with prizes and critical praise. Obviously there is nothing like an old-fashioned morality tale to make us feel good about ourselves — look at the acclaim *The Cook, The Thief, His Wife and Her Lover* received. And Arcand is not a director afraid to tackle big issues. His film *The Decline of the American Empire* focused on a group of academics discussing little else but sex. This time he is dealing with religion so perhaps we can hope that his next film will break another dinner-party taboo and talk about politics.

The director says that *Jesus of Montreal* was inspired by a real life encounter with a young actor who was playing Jesus by night and auditioned for beer commercials by day. So in the film we have Daniel, a skinny young actor who is invited by the local priest to play Christ in the *Passion Play* that is performed nightly on the mountain overlooking Montreal. Assembling an unknown but dedicated cast, he starts researching the life of Christ.

His preparation for the role makes Robert De Niro's indulgences look amateurish. Sifting through recent archaeological evidence he starts to realise that, in historical terms, Christ remains a shadowy figure. Was he the illegitimate son of a Roman soldier, a violent revolutionary or just one of the many wandering magicians of the middle east?

When the play is finally performed, it is a great success and Arcand takes the risky step of using up twenty or so minutes

177

of the film by showing us the performance. This works largely because it is moving and because we get to see the effect it is having both on actors and audience. After ecstatic write-ups by the critics Daniel himself is hailed as a saviour of sorts, a kind of Messiah of fringe theatre. But he is to be tempted in the wilderness of corporate media by being offered production deals, promotions, sponsorship, ghosted autobiographies and that most sickening temptation of all — a chance to appear on chat shows.

This clearly is not *his* plan and Daniel, getting more self-righteous by the minute, turns it all down and at an exploitative ad audition throws a temper tantrum, smashing up a few cameras. Daniel, you see, is turning decidedly Christ-like. Arcand cleverly uses this device to express moral outrage at the commerciality and spiritual bankruptcy of the modern world from porn films to aftershave advertising. He hits his targets on the nose but they are rather easy targets. Who couldn't satirise the pretentious scumbags who make up the media or the inefficiency of hospital casualty departments?

As Daniel goes further into his psychic transfiguration, he starts looking and behaving more like a 60s drop-out. But he has the continuing support of the two actresses who play the Virgin Mary and Mary Magdalene. They take care of the practicalities, trailing around after Daniel who is 'other-wordly' in the way that Christian ideology only allows men to be.

The loose analogies between the life of Christ and Daniel's experience seem at times rather trite. And the worst is the crucifixion/resurrection theme which is handled by Daniel going into a coma and his organs being given for transplant. Many a cheap horror film has explored the idea of eternal life or possession through donor transplant with considerably more verve than we get here. But then this is an art film so we shouldn't expect anything so gross or so intelligent.

This is part of the problem. There is no doubt that *Jesus of*

Montreal is a quality product: it is well made, well filmed and well performed. But, if it is to sell itself (which it does) on its cleverness or the strength of the themes with which it engages, these ideas should be sharper. Saying that capitalism is nasty and that Christ was a closet Marxist seems a little obvious. Likewise, the suggestion that if He came back today He would be given just as hard a time as He was then. Arcand tells us, just as Greenaway did, all the things we knew anyway. Their skill and our pleasure is in the stylish way in which they dress them up. While Greenaway may score intellectual points and Arcand moral ones, the problems they point to, such as greed and exploitation, are fundamentally of a political rather than spiritual nature.

Yet there is still a spiritual promise that draws us to films such as these. We still want to believe in the possibility of a deeper meaning, a moment in which it all becomes clear. Arcand, though, is too knowing ever to provide it. The story he tells is not of Christ's return, but of a life that has many parallels with Christ's. Like most of us who live in secular society, he prefers a degree of ambiguity to a fixed meaning. The modern aesthetic, after all, is one of openness. Or doubt. Certainty requires faith and this is why some of the most spiritually powerful cinema — whether by Tarkovsky, Kenneth Anger or Sergei Paradjanov (*The Colour of Pomegranates*) — is made by *believers*. Believing passionately must be better than believing that Jesus was a social worker.

Nothing but the truth

Truth, it has to be said, is a rather outmoded concept. What matters is not whether the truth is told but the ways of telling for, in the end, that is all there is. Our obsession with style has left a vacuum where there used to be things like truth and reality and the good old real thing.

Films have never told the truth; but they have been great pretenders. And sometimes they have got as near to truth as you could hope to get. Images on a screen, pictures of reality, have had the unsettling power to seem more real than life itself. Day to day existence pales in comparison with the intensity of a screen kiss or a screen tear — so much so that people say, 'It was just like being in a film,' to describe the most precious moments of their lives. In fact, we no longer need to go to the movies since, sooner or later, we all feel like an extra in someone else's badly-scripted film. This feeling can be called reality or unreality or even hyper-reality — it doesn't really matter any more.

Well it doesn't until you see a film like Errol Morris's *The Thin Blue Line*, which throws all those questions about truth — the image of truth and the truth of images — back in your face. This film, which the director calls an 'epistemological thriller' is not some impenetrable and élitist show reel. Instead it is a documentary, albeit an unusual one, about a man sentenced for a murder he has always denied.

This murder took place in 1976 when a Dallas policeman was shot during a routine car check. There appeared to be no motive and no clues. Then, a few weeks later, sixteen-year-old David Harris was arrested in Texas. He had apparently been boasting to his friends that he had 'offed the Dallas pig'. Once in custody he admitted to having stolen the car and driven to Dallas, and to having been in the car when the murder was committed But he denied shooting the police officer, swearing that it was Randall Adams, a hitch hiker he had picked up earlier, who was guilty.

Despite the fact that Harris already had a lengthy criminal record and Adams had none, the court chose to believe Harris and sentenced twenty-seven-year-old Adams to death. In 1979 he was reprieved. He is now serving a life sentence.

The Thin Blue Line opens up the case again by interviewing Adams, Harris, the witnesses and attorneys. Gradually a picture very different from the original one emerges. But what makes Morris's film so unusual is its break with the documentary conventions. Forsaking the usual cinéma vérité or fly-on-the-wall approach that normally signals an objective stance by an impartial observer, Morris instead shoots all the interviews using techniques normally reserved for fiction. Interviewees are carefully lit and speak straight to camera for long periods, their testimonies backed by a doomy Philip Glass score. It is this self-conscious and obviously subjective account which gives the feeling that these people are actors rather than real people. For in real 'true story' style these people are more all-Americanly weird than even David Byrne's bizarre collection of case histories.

Morris intercuts these interviews with clips from detective films and re-creations of the crime, all from slightly different angles and perspectives. What emerges, alongside the mounting evidence in favour of Adams, is Morris's almost obsessive interest in the myriad forms of documentation that surround the mystery. Each of these forms claims in some way to represent the truth: from Morris's own film-noirish shots of the murder weapon to the grainy newspaper photos to the carefully typed police reports.

So we, like Morris, are forced to become detectives, sifting through all these accounts and shifting perspectives, deciding who to believe and who to doubt. And how do we make those decisions except by recourse to all the other crime films and detective stories that have become part of our collective unconsciousness? Adams, described as 'a drifter', is edgy and ironic, while Harris is goofy and affable. Which one is the psychopath?

The judge decided it was Adams and this was corroborated

by a report from the 'killer shrink' Dr Death, a psychiatrist who, after a cursory twenty-minute interview, decided that Adams was a violent man. Then there were the surprise witnesses suddenly produced by the prosecution, who turned up later in order to identify Adams. Yet, as the film progresses, it becomes clear that what seemed to matter most to the courts was convicting someone old enough to receive the death sentence, which Harris wasn't; and what mattered to the prosecution was to win rather than to convict the right man.

Strangest of all though, is the way that most of the people in *The Thin Blue Line* express themselves in cinematic clichés and constantly allude to fictional detectives. Through their own experience they derive narrative via the language of cinema: for Harris 'Time just stopped'; one witness tells how she always fantasised about being a detective; and the judge says his eyes well up at the idea of the thin blue line of the police that separates order from anarchy.

In the midst of all these fascinating layers of fact and fantasy, representation and reality, one fact remains. A man's life has been destroyed and Morris, despite his elegant preoccupation with the construction of truth, becomes involved in solving the murder. In the interviews he has given it is almost as if he has been drawn reluctantly in to campaigning for Adams's release. This was not his original intention and it points awkwardly to something 'real' jabbing its way into his measured philosophical investigations. It is appropriate that all this takes place in Dallas. The setting of a world famous soap, a city of eerily postmodern buildings, a place of nightmare violence, Adams describes it as hell on earth.

And he might be right. Because if you believe, as politicians and postmodernists do, that the truth is something with which you can be economical — that there is nothing outside the endless spirals of images and words except more images and more words — then what do you do when you are faced, as Randall Adams was, with the electric chair?

■■■■■■

Always a love story

It may not be possible to be too thin or too rich, but is it possible, I wonder, to be too popular? Take Steven Spielberg. He is the most popular film-maker ever: he has directed half of the ten most successful films of all time. So it's strange that he has never won an Oscar and is not revered in the way that Scorcese or even Woody Allen is. Spielberg's films are still generally thought to be manipulative entertainment rather than anything else. How could something this popular ever be regarded as art, let alone great art?

The cynical dismissal of his work is littered with the well-worn put downs that are always summoned in the presence of truly popular culture: it is banal, sentimental, predictable and shallow, say the critics. But, even the critics have to admit grudgingly that somewhere along the line Spielberg manages to key into something that makes his movies a success from La Paz to Leeds. And though *Always* opened to mixed reaction in the States, I think he's done it again.

Always, a love story, has been widely represented as Spielberg's first grown-up film. In fact, he has already made a love story. What else was *ET* but the tale of a little boy's romance with an alien? *Always* is perhaps more conventional in that it does feature a man and a woman. On the cards for some ten years, it is essentially an adaptation of the 1943 Spencer Tracy film *A Guy Named Joe*, though at moments it has flashes of Powell's *A Matter of Life and Death*. Like the Indiana Jones films it is full of knowing nostalgia for an age of purity and faith and a hankering for a kind of security that is no longer possible either in modern life or in modern movies.

The love story of Dorinda (Holly Hunter) and Pete (Richard Dreyfuss) is set amongst fire-fighting pilots. He is, of course, a courageous flier while she is a dispatcher who waits patiently on the ground while he does his derring-do. All this gives Spielberg the chance to inject some spectacular flying scenes using old war planes without the intrusion of anything so morally suspect as real war. Instead, Dreyfuss is a positively green hero risking his neck for the sake of a few trees and his best friend Al — the ubiquitous John Goodman of *Roseanne* fame, whom, you might like to know, has just been voted the sexiest man in America.

Dorinda, though tough on the outside (she wears boiler suits) is actually soft on the inside — she's worried sick about her man. Their relationship, outlined in a long opening sequence, is somewhat overstretched. It even includes a musical number in which Pete gives Dorinda 'girl-clothes' in the form of a horrid dress that only some retard like Diana Spencer would consider wearing. Needless to say, Dorinda is immediately transformed from spunky tomboy to drippy female and waltzes around the canteen with a set of fighter pilots.

The whole thing gets a lot better when, in one too many feats of bravery, Pete pops off and finds himself in a field of daisies with none other than Audrey Hepburn. She plays Hap — a kind of New Age angel in white slacks and sweater who sends him back to earth to be a young man's guiding spirit. The young man just happens to be Ted Baker, a young pilot who is himself in the process of falling in love with Dorinda. Here the gears begin to shift and Pete has to come to terms with giving up his 'girl' to Ted.

True love, the movie suggests, means letting go. And Hap mouths a lot of New Age/hippy platitudes in a thoroughly convincing way: 'To gain your freedom you have to give it', and 'The love that we hold back is the only thing that follows us here,' and, best of all, 'Time's funny stuff, Pete.' The 'here' she refers to might be heaven (if your idea of heaven is a meadow) or it might just mean death. This is the heaven of an agnostic. But Spielberg manages to play out his personal themes — around love, belief and sacrifice — in a way that mixes naivety with profundity.

This is Spielberg's forte because, whether you feel his philosophising is cosmic or comic, you cannot deny the way he taps into concerns that everybody has. Normally, we only refer to them in an off-hand kind of way, like the embarrassing area of spirituality. It is evident in all those action adventure movies that he can make with his eyes closed, but comes to the fore in his more personal work such as *ET, Close Encounters* and *Empire of the Sun*. In this context you can see why he was drawn to the transcendental humanism of Alice Walker's *The Color Purple*.

There is a consistent refusal to accept death as the end (even *ET* comes alive again) and a continuing emphasis on communication and connections that cannot be explained rationally — the telepathic messages of *Close Encounters* feature again in *Always* — that is both enormously attractive and resonant for audiences everywhere. Such popular mysticism is routinely dismissed by the left whether in the guise of intellectual anti-humanism or morbidly literal readings of materialism.

In the real world, however, we read our horoscopes, consult psychics and bore our friends with everyday instances of synchronicity. This world remains completely outside the realms of politics, mainly because it is continually belittled by it.

Spielberg does just the opposite. He elevates these concerns and integrates them into the most traditional of genres, whether it's the love story or the adventure movie. Some have read his preoccupation with loss and separation as a result of the childhood trauma of his parents' divorce. Yet this doesn't explain his universal appeal to all age groups. Officially, Steven Spielberg is now more successful than Disney. And for someone who provides 'mere entertainment', he has an instinctive grasp of one of modernity's deepest secrets: that underneath we just want to believe. We really do.

Jazz junkie

The day in March 1955 when Charlie Parker failed to turn up for one of his gigs, everyone said 'Bird goofed again.' And he had. At thirty-four he was dead — ulcers, pneumonia, advanced cirrhosis of the liver, a bleeding-heart jazz junkie. The doctor who examined his body estimated that he was aged between fifty and sixty.

This man who could never just say no — to drugs, drink, food, women — to life, might seem a strange choice for the upright Mayor of Carmel, Clint Eastwood to make a film about. But he has and *Bird* is a tasteful unsentimental journey through the latter half of Parker's life. Starting with his attempted suicide brought about by his daughter's death, it charts his decline and his addiction. Forest Whitaker is terrific as Bird, this great bear of a man, as is Diane Venora as his wife, Chan Parker. From sassy, sharp jazz enthusiast she moves to sardonic, but supportive life-line, a jazz widow long before he died.

Structured mainly through flashbacks, the film starts when Parker had musically at least 'made it'. He had already proved himself a genius, a virtuoso player, a true saxophone colossus. Yet we don't really see how he got to be those things and what exactly made him so special. It is as though he was born a fully-formed sax player who just so happened to invent bebop along the way, rather than a musician who practised, jammed, listened and struggled in order to create a new musical vocabulary — a 'language in motion'. But then Parker, a shambling, cryptic, inaccessible man, is ripe for the classic treatment of portrait of the artist as tragically fucked-up genius.

Originally called Bird because of the vast quantities of fried chicken he could consume, the name became synonymous with his ability to take off on the saxophone, soar, hover, swoop — to fly. In some ways his whole life was an attempted flight from the reality of being black at a time when Eldridge Cleaver talked of black people living 'in an atmosphere of novocain'. The need to numb oneself in the margins of society, to escape and be insulated from fear and oppression meant that novocain became more than a metaphor. Heroin could give you that emotional distance, that medium cool confidence to cope with the hassles and the hustles of getting by. In the hip circles of the jazz community with its ritualistic drug abuse, its fraternity of junkies, alienation from white culture could be turned into a virtue.

Junk made you feel in control and, more importantly, while alcohol made musicians sloppy, you could still play on heroin. Parker's speed, accuracy and unfailing ear was legendary. Art Blakey has observed: 'You do not play better with heroin, but you do hear better. Bird said he wanted to kick the habit so that he could tell people what he heard . . .' In the end though, the question was not whether Parker could play better on junk, he was simply too sick without it to play at all.

Predictably, Eastwood underlines both the anti-drugs message and the myth of the self-destructive artist with scenes of a disintegrating Parker stumbling around in back streets or stoned in squalid hotel rooms. His addiction is shown mainly as both a physical and mental painkiller. And younger musicians such as Red Rodney, a young Jewish trumpet player — who thought that to play like Bird you had to do like Bird — are firmly admonished by the man himself 'doing that shit — it don't help man, it don't help.' As Harry Shapiro says in *Waiting for the Man*, if heroin symbolised the flight from white society for blacks, for young white musicians it symbolised the flight towards black society.

Being the good Republican he is, Eastwood, though obviously a passionate jazz buff, tinges *Bird* with a straight anti-drugs message rather than examining the connections between drug abuse and racial oppression — those famed old social conditions. Parker's story is individualised into the stereotypical addictive personality who had carried a death-wish since the age of fifteen.

Parker is seen somehow to dance around the racism of the time setting up Red Rodney to score liquor while he hides in the car. In the documentary *Bird Now* directed by Marc Huraux, the real Chan Parker recalls the difficulties of a mixed marriage and of finding an apartment. In some archive footage we see Parker and Gillespie awkwardly receiving an award from an incredibly patronising white television host. The most telling moment of Eastwood's film however, is a conversation on a beach between Gillespie and Parker. A drunken Bird asks Gillespie his secret, Dizzy replies that to be reliable, to be on time, to be in control is a living defiance of the white man's idea of a nigger.

Perhaps Eastwood is not so interested in Parker's origins — we don't see his early life, or where all that anger and pain came from, because he is interested in reclaiming him as an essentially *American* hero. Hence the Scott Fitgerald quote at the start of the film: 'There are no second acts in American lives.' Clint, instead, wants to universalise a specifically black music into something more general: 'Americans don't have any original art except Western movies and jazz.' And so even in *Bird*, Clint's tall-in-the-saddle warped patriotism shines through. He finds him 'interesting as a representative of something very special creatively, something uniquely American'.

But what did it mean in the 40s to be a *black* American? To be a black 'evolutionary' musician? To find the solutions to the problems that had been occupying avant-garde European composers for years? And to do it in a *uniquely* black American musical form?

What's missing from Eastwood's film is this sense of what made Bird so stunning, so ahead of his time. Because whatever else he was — and psychiatrists' reports describe him as a psychopath living only for the pleasure principle — he had the discipline to learn twelve keys when most musicians learn two or three. He listened to Schoenberg, Stravinsky, Bartok and Varèse. He spent years apprenticed to big bands, disappeared for months woodshedding, jammed after gigs until he was ready to pare down the big band to just two horns that played off, and against, each other. This new music, bebop, with its speed, its edge, its intricasies, its reorganisation of sound was decried as 'anti-jazz', yet jazz has never been the same since.

The documentary *Bird Now*, though made with typically French reverence for all things to do with jazz, succeeds where Eastwood's film doesn't in placing Parker's music as part of a continuum. Abstract, impressionistic with odd dramatic episodes, the film features many people close to Bird — his wives Doris and Chan, Dizzy Gillespie and Earl Coleman among others. It is as much a homage to New York as to Bird with its emphasis on the urbanity of the music. Through the words of musicians who knew him, it manages to convey what he did, what made him fly. A saxophone is unlike any other instrument in that each individual note can be bent or coloured and, as Dizzy Gillespie says, what made Bird truly special in the end was 'the way he got from note to note — how he hooked 'em up'. You can't say more than that.

3 POWER

PLEASURE

Understimulation

You have to make an awful lot of effort to relax these days. You can't just *do nothing* when you do nothing, and I should know. I've spent the past few days desperately trying to relax to the New Age ambient videos that I've been sent, but something has gone very wrong. I understand how Michael Ryan felt when he ventured out on the streets of Hungerford. I know why Charlie Manson did what he had to do. And all as a result of watching *The Art of Landscape* and an hour of a tape called *Basil the Parrot*. If you want something that expresses the sheer bloody futility of life, the utter pointlessness of existence, forget Beckett and tune into *Over the Dark Cloud, A Lingering Look at Disused Aircraft* or, better still, *The Aquarium.*

Obviously this is not the desired effect, but perhaps I never had the right attitude in the first place. The whole idea, after all, of ambient videos, is that, like muzak, they provide an unobtrusive background. You are not meant to think about them. Instead, they provide 'an enjoyable visual stimulus'.

The series that I watched — *At the Fireside, The Aquarium, The Water Wheel* and *Basil the Parrot* — is marketed by Jettisoundz, which is quite explicit about its modest aims. 'Modern folk need their senses stimulating.' All of them. So when you put on a record, tape or CD, switch on the TV. Turn the sound down . . . But it's too distracting. You want to know what's happening — what President Bush had to say about disarmament. And so on.

The answer, of course, is a New Age ambient video — 'They allow you to relax, listen to your favourite music without staring at the furniture. They introduce a new dynamic to your living room without being too obtrusive.' The videos themselves are a model of simplicity — a single, hour-long, shot of a not particularly interesting fire, a modest aquarium, a rather frantic water wheel and a bored parrot.

What is New Age, or even new about this is open to question, though such videos use a New Age tag to cash in on the booming market of semi-mystical, self-improvement tapes. These are an amazing range of videos that promise everything from 'out of body experiences' within a few days, to 'subliminal' tapes with titles like *I Can do Anything, The Mastery of Money* and *How to Radiate Sensual Poise*.

No longer do you need to go to Nepal to achieve altered states of consciousness. Meditation tapes promise to send you into a deep trance that normally only yogis or people in flotation tanks in Hampstead claim to achieve. The tape apparently consists of a metronome signal that is supposed to correspond to theta brain-waves.

I'm not sure about theta waves, but I recommend altered states of consciousness, chemical or cosmic, to anyone who has to spend even five minutes watching the *Art of Lanscape*. This video of 'the most requested titles from the popular Channel 4 series' consists of a series of tracks of deliberately unstimulating footage with drippy classical/New Agey music over the top. Thus we have Canal Longboat Crossing an Aqueduct in Wales accompanied by New World symphony, or a film of penguins walking excruciatingly slowly about the Antarctic. This doesn't work as ambient background because there is just enough happening to make you wait for something else to follow. And this is fatal. Will the longboat explode mid-aqueduct? Will the penguins keel over and die? Will someone turn off that awful music? As you can see, these things make me very tense.

I'd had these feelings before when confronted with all the avant-garde films in which nothing ever happens: one is supposed to suddenly grasp the 'materiality of film itself'. All those viciously anti-narrative, structuralist films were just a forerunner for this cinematic equivalent of muzak. Yet those films, with their rigorously radical aims, were to make you think. So it's a paradox that these methods can be used to make you not think at all.

And they run into the same problems. The drive to create a narrative is so strong that people will make up stories in their heads, whether it's a film of a swinging lightbulb or a windmill in West Sussex. This destroys the very ambience of an ambient video just as it destroys the austere formalism of an avant-garde film. In both cases, the desire to be entertained is a rather base need that you have to train yourself out of.

The other strange effect of all this overwhelming under-stimulation is that it flips over into the same zonked-out feeling you get from, say, the over-stimulation of *Total Recall*. In fact, *Total Recall* is actually more relaxing than any of this lot — though not very New Age, I guess. But then it's a thin line between love and hate, pleasure and pain. Or, as Roland Barthes said, between boredom and bliss.

Perhaps the most sinister aspect of all this is that it makes ordinary TV look so wonderful. Two hours of this stuff, and Jeremy Beadle looks like God. Adverts are almost too brilliant to comprehend. The news is simply unbelievable. The air of excitement contained in *Blockbusters* explodes out of the screen. Images change. Things happen. People talk. At last, you can relax.

And Now The News

What I am about to say is not very important. It just feels like it is. Because this is what 'the media' is so good at — self-importance. The media is all-powerful and all-seeing. We know it is. Because the media tells us that this is the case. And despite the recession, newspapers, magazines and TV programmes breed like there was no tomorrow. Even if there isn't you can be sure that the next series of *Tomorrow's World* is already in the can anyway.

There are more TV channels, more adverts, more print than anyone could ever hope for. Only connect — to BSB/Sky or Astra. Bank with First Direct but only because of the ads. Video *Twin Peaks* and watch it while you are reading the *Independent on Saturday* on Sunday afternoon. Pile up the *Sunday Times, Correspondent* and *News of the World* until Monday. Give up your job so that you can stay at home for the repeat of *Knott's Landing* and *Take the High Road*. Rob a bank so that you can afford to see *Total Recall, Flatliners* and the re-released Bresson film. Kill your partner so that you have time to read all the novels on the Booker shortlist as well as *Viz* on a regular basis.

Does all this make you feel better? More alive? More at the centre of things? If it does you are suffering from *media anxiety*. Information saturation is taking its toll. There is only one cure. Switch off. And thank God that seems to be what a lot of us are doing. After decades of predictions concerning the unlimited power of the mass media, even television — always held up triumphantly as the most influential medium of all — is starting to lose its grip.

We have more choice than ever before, with the result that both here and in the States we are viewing less and less, as BSB knows to its cost. Reports from the Henley Centre for Forecasting and the Policy Studies Institute show an overall decrease in the average number of hours we spend watching TV.

Instead we are hiring more videos and going to the cinema

more often or maybe, just maybe, participating in leisure activities that have nothing to do with the media at all. BBC chiefs may blame the decline on a hot summer rather than admitting that the revival of *The Generation Game* is hardly the stuff to get the nation's adrenalin racing. But is it really possible that television will go the way of radio and become either a quaint and reassuring medium or simply an ambient visual prop? Imagine no more telly — I wonder if you can.

Yet one of the simple facts ignored by media men from McLuhan to Michael Grade is that we only have so many hours in a day. Am I the only person to find it reassuring that as the Sunday papers continue to reproduce and mutate into more and more sections that the general response has been mass apathy? Nobody with the semblance of a life could possibly read all this stuff. Which is why if you meet anyone who claims they do, you can be sure that they already work in the media.

Whether this is the kind of implosion into the meaningless babble of self-referential signs that postmodern theorists love to wallow in, is debatable. What is certain is that they usually link this condition with consumer passivity. Yesterday's couch potatoes don the Emperor's new clothes to become Baudrillard's 'Silent Majorities'. The model for all this is America. Not America the Real — a place of startling diversity — but America the Imaginary, a place where a giant hypodermic regularly injects the population with endless Big Macs, MTV and Oral Roberts. What such snobbery ignores is not only the way that we produce our own disposable culture — one of the few manufacturing bases left unscathed — but also the way we consume it.

The pessimism inherent in such work on the media often assumes its unlimited power as well as underestimating our ability to make choices. We may be offered simply more of the same but does that mean that we always take it? Ask the sales reps for BSB who had so much trouble flogging a dish a day. Yet for those in the grip of media anxiety, more choice also means more chance of missing something relevant. This is actually a strain of industrial illness that affects journalists and TV folk alike. It may feel real but it is actually a psychosomatic disease that eventually paralyses the ability to distinguish between what is important and what is not.

As it reaches epidemic proportions the result right across the board is that TV stations, newspapers and advertisers are spending an awful lot of money trying to brand their particular identity on to our consciousness. It may all look the same but we are meant to believe that one satellite channel is vastly different from another. Hence all the logos, vague commercials for corporations that you have never heard of and the trend in advertising that pretends it is actually anti-advertising: the First Direct campaign is a prime example, or the ads for Molson lager which tell you *not* to drink it.

Out of the phenomenal number of advertising messages each of us receives daily, it is only the unusual or unexpected that stand out. Likewise it is important that we remember what channel that programme we saw last night was on. If we don't, the corporate image is just not coming on strong enough. The money that could go into making great television programmes goes instead into making brilliant graphics that fill in the slots between the programmes or ads for Sky. Which is precisely the reason why so many of us can look at the paper and say quite casually: 'there is nothing on telly tonight. Nothing at all.'

Film slobs

People who take films seriously go to the cinema, those who don't watch them on video at home. Or, at least, that is the unspoken cultural snobbery surrounding the subject of film and video. When it comes down to it, most of us are film slobs. We are quite happy to nip down to the local video shop to select the movies we want to watch at home. We all like the fact that you can have a drink or make a cup of tea in the middle of the film. We know it's cheaper than going to the cinema, and besides it's a damn sight easier to hire a video than it is to hire a babysitter.

But the film snobs say, quite rightly, that film is a different medium from television; that films are made for, and therefore should be watched on, a big screen. This is usually accompanied by some diatribe about how the lack of a true cinema culture in this country contributes to its intellectual barrenness. They fear for the future of British cinema, and indeed Britain, and then tell you about some wonderful little art deco cinema that is threatened with closure.

While I share some of these concerns, I can't help feeling that these are the same kind of people who would defend theatre whilst deriding television. For implicit in many of these arguments is the notion of cinema as high culture, as art rather than entertainment. But technology changes things, and the advent of video recorders and video libraries has, it could be argued, put film back at the heart of *popular culture*. So much so in fact that most films (97 per cent) are not seen in the cinema but at home — either broadcast on TV or as hired cassettes.

But if video has been responsible for a *democratisation* of film culture, it has also been hampered by the kind of moral panics that surround the introduction of any new mass cultural form. Indeed, there is nothing like a bit of choice to bring out the most reactionary elements in critics from all shades of the political spectrum. If people were, God forbid, actually allowed to go and choose their own viewing for consumption in their own homes, civilisation might crumble from the VCR outwards. Three-year-olds would be fed a diet of the *Texas Chainsaw Massacre* and hardcore porn loops — this is the view you might have got from reading the papers leading up to the 1984 Video Recordings Act.

However, in the light of the increasingly confused and confusing discussion around deregulated television, it might be worth looking at what people do watch once given the relative freedom and more selective viewing habits that the 'video revolution' has brought.

And surprise, surprise the biggest selling video in this country is that well known video nasty *Pinocchio*. The cassettes that people buy tend to be a mixture of children's stuff, sports videos (Greavesie's *Six of the Best: Manchester United* is currently at number 11 in the top 30) and Jane Fonda-style workout tapes. The most popular feature films such as *The Terminator, The Jazz Singer, 9½ Weeks* and *Amadeus* represent an equally eclectic mix.

The video rental charts, on the other hand, although reflecting a wide range of movies, tend to be dominated by films that have already been box office successes. *Wall Street*, with its recent ad campaign 'It's better than sex', is currently number 1. A glance at both charts, however, suggests that you cannot regard the audience as a homogeneous lump that sits on the couch watching whatever is put before it. Instead, there is a massive and massively diverse audience that is highly selective in its viewing. Family films may prevail, but there is a place for both Bertolucci (*The Last Emperor*) and John Waters (*Hairspray*) in the top thirty.

This new kind of audience, with its new kinds of pleasure, power and knowledge, is one that most writing about film either ignores or patronises. Yet many of the video magazines wear their populist colours on their sleeves while addressing their readers as already movie literate, precisely as *critical* viewers in a way that most contemporary criticism fails to do. Thus *Video Times*, for instance, can castigate Barry Norman for his 'distaste with most forms of popular cinema' because he slagged off *Phantasm 2* without realising that there had even been a *Phantasm 1* which had been a major international success.

Yet, like any popular leisure form, video viewing takes its place within already structured relations of power. Once brought into the home, all sorts of minor decisions such as who chooses the films, who can work the machine, and even who is allowed the remote control become important. Looking at the context in which films are watched has been a sorely neglected part of media analysis. Research by writers such as Dave Morley and Ann Gray indicates how gender difference pokes its way into the most cosy and intimate picture of the family gathered around the glowing hearth of the TV screen.

According to their research, video libraries tend in themselves to be very male, the films categorised into what are traditionally male genres; war, action, adventure, horror and porn. That doesn't mean other films aren't there, but they are certainly harder to find. The choice of film is often made by the man, though negotiated by the woman who often expresses distaste at the violence of some of these types of movies. For many of the families that were interviewed in Gray's research, watching a video was an event in the way that ordinary TV wasn't. But for women who work in the home as well as out of it, it is often much more difficult to clear a space where they can sit for two hours without feeling guilty. This, combined with many women's alienation from the actual VCRs themselves — the number of women who don't know how to work the timer switch for instance, means that the undoubted 'freedom' that video offers may benefit men far more than it does women.

Nevertheless, video culture has become as much a part of our lives as going to the pub. It promises to make film buffs of us all, it takes us further into trends towards privatised consumption and it undermines old notions of mass taste and mass audience. Above all, it offers those precious commodities of choice and control something that I've heard rumoured the left was also once interested in . . .

The metal age

It was the first proper gig I ever went to see, a heavy metal band. I was fourteen and had come up to London to see Black Sabbath. I'm not sure about the head-banging but I went home covered in lovebites, having had a brilliant time. I remember even as a fan thinking there was something faintly ridiculous about the whole enterprise. Ozzy Osborne (the lead singer) had longer fringes on his jacket than anyone else, and he swung them about like a mad thing. But he seemed not so much satanic as just plain frantic. If the performance didn't electrify me, the stuff of their songs did. They had all the elements that any serious teenager requires — they seemed to be dark, druggy and dangerous and, for me anyway, symbolised a big 'fuck-off' to the world of Donny and Marie Osmond, to civilisation as we knew it then.

I have an excuse for liking heavy metal. This was five years before punk after all. What the hell were we supposed to do in the meantime? But it's difficult not to be defensive about it, for heavy metal, despite its phenomenal success, is regarded as the soundtrack of the mentally retarded, emotionally stunted and grossly sexist members of our community. Which may be why it is very big business both here and in the United States.

The fact, then, that one of the very few female directors working in Hollywood should choose to make a film about heavy metal is interesting in itself. But, when you know that the director is Penelope Spheeris who made *The Decline of Western Civilisation: Part 1*, a brilliant documentary about the hardcore punk scene in Los Angeles, you know it makes sense. Spheeris's empathetic explorations of various American sub-sub-cultures in *Suburbia, The Boys Next Door* and *Dudes* have been equally hard-edged, never shying away from covering the violence or boredom of these lifestyles.

In her new film, *The Decline of Western Civilisation Part II:*

The Metal Years, Spheeris once again walks the fine line between condemnation and celebration and gets it just right. Basically a series of interviews with bands, fans and wanna-bes involved in the LA scene, the 'Mecca of current American metal', she proves herself not only an astute social commentator but also a first-class documentary maker. A lesser film-maker would have gone for *Spinal Tap* parody or overplayed concern. Spheeris instead has made a movie that is both funny and desperately sad, whose displays of self-deception are as shocking as its honesty. And like all good documentaries, this one was made in the editing room.

Cutting between live footage and interviewees from deservedly unknown bands like Faster Pussycat, Odin and the dire London to old timers like Alice Cooper, Kiss and Aerosmith, the movie soon establishes that heavy metal is everything that people say it is. It is loud, repetitive, aggressive, sexist and racist. (*Glasnost* is evidently not big in LA. During their song, *Russian Winter*, the lead singer of London, Nadir D'Priest, burns a Russian flag.) It is also obsessed with images of death and destruction, whether it's images of skulls or songs about air crashes. Yet none of these things is as simple as they first appear.

Sure many of these disciples of sex, drugs and rock'n'roll lifestyle think with their crotches and treat women like objects but, as the film shows, some women play a very *active* part in turning themselves into objects. It requires an awful lot of determination to be *that* passive. Ultimately, however, the sexual bravado of heavy metal culture is pathetic, not because it is not right-on but because it doesn't *work*. The endless promises of 'doing it all night long' may be wishful thinking for the boys, but don't seem to have much effect on the girls, which is why it remains such a male domain. Soul music, which contains just as much sexual boasting and is just as explicit, is far more seductive because it pretends a dialogue. For, when male sexuality becomes nothing more than an aggressive expression of self-assertion, as it has with much hip-hop and rap, it becomes just as unappealing as any heavy metal thrash.

Some of the worst offenders are the prettiest boys. Faces carefully made up, their narcissism is strictly heterosexual. They may have long hair and lipstick, but these are many props for the much needed 'attitude' and, as they repeatedly assure us, they know how to 'kick ass' and 'rock'n'roll'. They are the would-be stars, convinced against all odds they are going to make it. They have no choice, many of them say: having dropped out from school, they don't know how to do anything else. Their belt buckles may say rebel, but more than anything they want to be rich and famous. After all they are not punks, they don't even bother paying lip service to the notion that the music business might stink.

Finally, though, there are the rich and famous — casualties of the lifestyle these kids aspire to. Apart from the eminently sensible Lemmy of Motorhead, most of the stars reminded me of nothing more than Vietnam vets. Fresh out of rehab clinics ('I must have snorted up the whole of Peru') they have the air of the terminally bored, they have done it all — the girls, the drugs, the compulsory hotel-trashing — and there is nothing left, no edge, no point.

They are a far better warning for kids than the bizarre demetalling programmes organised by paranoid probation officers. Chris Holmes of WASP floats out of his brain in a swimming pool watched by his mother. As he tips bottles of Smirnoff into himself, he seems to have regressed completely into an infantile, incoherent wreck. In comparison Megadeath's interest in death, destruction and frenzy seems positively healthy.

Then there is my old friend Ozzy Osborne, puffy faced in a leopard-print dressing-gown, stumbling around his LA mansion trying to make breakfast. I was right when I was fourteen. He is completely ridiculous. For someone who has bitten the head off a bat, he has a great deal of trouble with the bacon. His grip on things is decidedly hazy, his spell in the Betty Ford clinic dismissed as boring. He can't seem to remember what happened to all the money they made, or indeed much of the time they were making it.

Is this the satanic majesty so feared by religious fundamentalists? As he spills the orange juice into the scrambled-eggs he says he was attracted to the outlaw image of rock'n'roll. Weren't we all? But then what do you do after the thrill has gone?

All night long

When most of us go to the cinema, we usually see one film or, at the most, a double bill. But for those who demand more there is always the all-nighter where you can sit up all night watching four or five films. The only other people who watch so many movies at one sitting are, I suspect, film critics, who let me assure you are usually snoring loudly by the second film. In contrast, all-nighter audiences are usually just starting to warm up at this point.

The whole experience of watching films in this way is quite different mainly because it is a *whole* experience and the audience is as important — if not more important — as the films. For a start you can drink, smoke, wander in and out as you please — in other words behave normally. As John, one of the programmers at the Scala (the only cinema in the country to have weekly all-nighters), explained: 'This is not a church. We wanted to create an atmosphere where people can use the place freely. Watching films at all-nighters, you're not removed, you can enjoy them subjectively.'

The Scala's audience varies from eighteen-year-old punks

for whom staying up all night is some sort of revoluntionary act, to old people who find it the cheapest, warmest place to spend the night. But as with most all-nighters the kind of audience depends on the kind of films shown. The most popular and repeated programmes are either the heroic action movies — Schwarzenegger is a big favourite — and the kind of cheap schlock horror movies that Joe Bob Briggs would definitely check out. Other cinemas have run highly successful women-only nights with themes such as lesbian vampire movies.

A recent Troma (an American company which promotes low budget horror films) all-nighter — featuring Toxic Avenger and Rabid Grannies — was a sell-out, the audience ranging from trendies to train-spotters. They don't *like* these films in spite of them being cheap and trashy, they like them *because* they are cheap and trasy.

Yet for many serious film buffs, the behaviour and style of all-nighters would be anathema. However, these same people will write long and complicated papers in journals about how classic realist film texts serve only to keep the spectator passive and unthinking.

This is the last thing that all-nighter audiences are. But it's only fair to admit that not everyone goes to see the films. A friend, a regular all-nighter, can recall little of what she has seen. 'Well, you don't really go for the films do you? It's the snogging I go for.' Which, is of course, one of the remaining great unspoken joys of cinema.

The money game

According to a poll conducted during the last war, the thing that the majority of Americans most wanted when the war was over was a new car. Yes, a shiny new car, a roadworthy symbol of modernity, a future that you could get inside and steer.

Preston Tucker, automobile designer and part-time visionary, was determined to build that car — no matter what it took. Francis Ford Coppola's film *Tucker* sets out to tell of his efforts. Jeff Bridges plays Tucker as a grin-happy, big-hearted, family man whose dream of building 'the car of tomorrow — today' brings him into conflict with the industrial and political power brokers of the time.

The film itself is fuelled by a swaggering big-band score and a skilfully lush evocation of forties style — all sharp suits, walnut interiors and factories that are just crying out to be turned into film sets. It's also full of Coppola's irrepressible artful quirkiness: clever cuts that melt one scene into another and telephone conversations that do away with the usual split-screen convention, using instead a camera pan from one room to the next, even though in narrative terms the callers are supposed to be miles apart.

Despite such mechanisms, *Tucker* is basically a simple story, simply told. Self-conscious as ever of the mythical status of movies, Coppola uninhibitedly idealises Tucker, his car, his friends and his family so that we are always entirely sympathetic to this little man with the big idea. As Tucker's revolutionary new car design captured the public imagination, Tucker, a born self-publicist, is shown almost inadvertently stumbling into the world of advertising rather than as being very good at manipulating the medium. When his dream eventually goes into production he becomes a real threat to the big Detroit car manufacturers who, through their political contacts, conspire to take him to court for fraud. Naturally enough he makes the classically patriotic and impassioned speech and gets off. However, only fifty of his cars were ever made, and he died six years after the court case.

Many people have been tempted to see *Tucker* as a mirror of Coppola's own career — the rebellious genius up against the impenetrable system. But it takes more than one person to make a car or a movie. Tucker's wife and children are portrayed, as always, as cheerfully supportive while the cars themselves are lovingly put together by his loyal team of friends. And, although it was that other more famous car manufacturer, Henry Ford, who helped to pioneer the techniques of mass production, we never see this in the film.

What we get instead is an incredibly romantic version of inspired creativity. These cars are not built by robots, but by human beings. The cars are somehow wrenched out of the dirty work of the manufacturing process and into the realm of the pure object. They become the proverbial collectors' item — a work of art. Coppola, incidentally, owns two of them. It's this very collectability that gives them status well above both the cruelty and crudity of the commodity cycle. They are about refined things such as the dignity of labour and as a labour of love they glide through the film like handmade pieces of an imagined future.

Eventually, though, Coppola's *Tucker* sits uneasily as a critique of the way that corporate capital stifles individual imagination mostly because it operates so completely within its own terms. It actually ends up reinforcing one of capitalism's cosiest bedtime stories — that of the heroic entrepreneur struggling against the bureaucracy. As we know, at its most radical, free enterprise is never quite so cosy and dreams are not enough when they can be bought and sold alongside everything else.

From Japan comes a much more interesting film about materialism — Juzo Itami's *A Taxing Woman*. We have already seen his previous films *Tampopo* and *Death Japanese Style* and this, his third feature, has been phenomenally successful in Japan.

Nobuko Miyamoto plays Ryoto — one of the most unlikely heroines to hit our screens for a long time. Ryoto is a workaholic tax inspector who graduates from exposing minor fiddles to the major frauds, investigating big-time tax evaders, gang bosses, crooked businessmen. Her main target becomes Hideki Gondo, owner of a chain of 'adult motels'. Becoming both spy and detective, she obsessively uncovers all his scams — the multiple bank accounts, the illegal property deals, the mistresses.

Though we discover that she is divorced and has a son, the film is notable in the way it hardly touches on her personal life. Apart from a telephone call where she is instructing her five-year-old on how to microwave Chinese dumplings, we see her always at work.

This unglamorised portrayal of a woman who simply does her job very well, who likes video games and computers, who is not somehow humiliated or shown to be a psychological disaster area is highly unusual. Though there is an attraction between the hunter and her prey we are never in doubt that her job comes first. Unusual, too, is the way that the film never moralises. We are never made to feel that Ryoko thinks that tax evasion is a particularly terrible sin — it's just that she loves her work of making visible this most invisible of crimes.

While *Tucker* relishes the fetishisation of the perfect commodity, *A Taxing Woman* hones in on money itself. Money as an abstract, mobile, ultimately meaningless sign. Tax evasion is just one part of the shifting of money from one account to the next in the game of pure appearances. Finally, money is not used to buy things, but simply transferred and exchanged into stolen receipts, false accounts, gold bars. *A Taxing Woman* paints a picture of wealthy Japanese society where materialism is almost a spiritual pursuit. While the film doesn't always work and the action is far too drawn out in places, Itami manages to conjure up the sexiness both of crime and of money. Ryoko gasps when at last she finds

Gondo's illicit stash. As with Bresson's *Pickpocket* there is something implicitly erotic about crime and its detection.

It makes Coppola's efforts to embody dreams into an obscure object of desire — a car — look rather dated. For, if anything, it is the immateriality and the endlessly circular movement of money that comes closest to the quality of dreams. Money no longer makes things — in the highest forms of capitalism it reproduces itself like some mutant amoeba. As it speeds through from Wall Street to Tokyo, flashing on screens for a brief second, it achieves a purity that only a few recognise. Money may make the world go round but those who make it know that its true value is that it has none.

Mall-content

Heaven, we are reliably informed, is a place where nothing ever happens. It is a place where everything you've ever wanted is under the same roof and within easy reach. It has perfect weather, there is always a parking space, and no one ever has any problems. It's blissful and bland in the way that only paradise can be. I think heaven must be like a shopping centre.

But even heaven can be improved, remodelled and updated. And shopping centres, our gardens of earthly delights are moving into the next phase. Every high street having been Nextified — nice shops, shame about the clothes — people are apparently demanding that peculiar thing known in the trade as 'individuality'.

The trade being, of course, marketing. Wally Olins of the design company Wolff Olins has remarked that 'marketing is to the 1980s what sociology was to the 1960s'. The difference though is that while many a sociologist dreamed of changing the world, marketing men have actually done it. And they have done it in the most breath-takingly banal of ways, by asking people what they want and then giving them more of it than they ever thought possible — at a price. Just how many shops can you go to in a day? How many times a week can you eat out? How many daft pairs of socks from Sock Shop can you take?

Now it seems the marketeers have decided that the way forward is not simply bigger, brighter shopping centres, but what is described as a 'retail-leisure mix'. This can mean anything from Metroland in Gatehead's Metrocentre — a vast, themed leisure complex that is linked to the main shopping mall by a food court — to local shopping centres with quality dining facilities. So far London doesn't have anything like Metroland's Kingdom of King Wizz (sic) where kids can speed through roller coasters and video games while their parents stroll through these muzaked, weatherless environments described in the semi-mystical language of marketing as 'ambient spaces'.

But the signs are there. London's shopping centres are diversifying. Carl Gardner and Julie Sheppard, authors of the excellent *Consuming Passions*, quote Ron McCarthy, a prime mover in this area: 'The traditional mall no longer has a competitive edge. As north American experience shows, the retail environment must provide more than just shopping. It must be a dramatic celebratory space . . .'

Perhaps this was the idea behind 'The Food Theatre' in Walthamstow's Selborne Walk shopping centre. God only knows. The bizarrely named Food Theatre is in fact a rather ordinarily bad food court in a rather mediocre shopping centre whose only remarkable feature is 'the rear half of a beautifully restored 1953 pink Cadillac (the equivalent front half is located in the Cardiff Food Theatre).' Food courts combine a number of franchised food operations around a central eating space. Often they are themed. Ideally they are a place to be and be seen that increases 'dwell-time' in the centre. They rely on capturing some of that free-floating desire that shopping centres are supposed to stimulate. If you're going to buy a new dress why not have some pasta along the way?

Though Walthamstow's Food Theatre is run by Custombetter Foodservice Ltd, which also created food courts in Cardiff and the Oxford Street Shopping Plaza, unfortunately, it seems to combine all that is wrong with these sorts of places. Tucked away at the top of the building it is a lifeless area patrolled by bored security guards. The choice of food — despite nine outlets — is basically hamburgers, pizzas, chips, baguettes and semi-defrosted doughnuts. You can't get a decent cappuccino or even a bacon sandwich. Its theme is, I suppose, 'America' if you can call half a car and a hamburger stand a theme.

Robert Brophy of Custombetter explained that, 'Food-courts are inevitably an American concept now that shopping is more of a *leisure experience*.' His company is essentially 'adapting an American idea to British culture'. The American idea is one of 'grazing', snacking throughout the day on whatever takes your fancy rather than the traditional English sit-down meal. It democratises the experience of eating out. Anyone can do it. Anywhere.

What the Walthamstow experience provides — *experience* along with *concept*, and *leisure* are the words that these businesses continually use — is fuel for those who view the rise of the shopping centre not so much as the building of heaven on earth but as the ultimate signifier of the barren hell of consumer culture. You only have to move from the dead zone of the Food Theatre outside into the bustle of one of the biggest street markets in Europe to ask yourself a simple question. Why?

There are two ways to look at it, neither of which provides the complete picture. You can denounce it all completely, drone on about the lack of civic space, bemoan the eroding of genuine cultural amenities in favour of numbing commerciality. Why didn't they build a crèche? A youth club? What happens at night when the centre closes down? What about the local community? What about those disenfranchised from new-found consumer power — the old, the unemployed, the great underclass who can't afford electricity, never mind electrical goods?

Or you can denounce the fuddy-duddy, puritans of the old left and the new left and become Next Left. Postmodernism means being post-guilt and these glittering palaces are not bad, consumerism isn't bad. How can it be when it's the only thing that we have got left that means anything at all? What could be better than these 'total environments' where we can drift deliriously in a world where reality intrudes only when there is a fault in the air-conditioning system? This is it, the cool, organless, modern world beloved of the theorists of hyper-reality. I want to believe. I really do. But we're not talking about the big fantasy malls of America or Australia here. There is the home-grown variety and the reality somehow never matches up to mooted hyper-reality. The irony is that we can only celebrate postmodernism pastiche when it *works*, otherwise it's just plain depressing.

Food Street works. Food Street in the Trocadero Centre in Piccadilly bills itself as 'A stunning re-creation of an Oriental market'. It is the only Oriental food court of its kind outside of Hong Kong — a place 'where you can travel many countries in your lunch-hour'. We're talking Concept with a capital C. In the basement of the Trocadero you can eat sushi, dim sum, satay, drink exotic cocktails and sample food from India, Singapore and Thailand. It services over 12,000 people a week. It's cheap, fast and the food is good. 'This,' says Food Street's commercial manager Paul Kavanagh, 'is the real thing.' Real Japanese people work in the sushi bar, Malaysians cook the satay. 'We're not trying to *imitate* the experience,' he says, 'but to *relive* it.'

The feel of the place is important. They have touts — 'Little Thai men and Chinese women running round selling food' — to give it that extra air of authenticity. Tourists apparently love it. But then who isn't a tourist in a place like this? And who am I to say it doesn't *quite* have the atmosphere of an Oriental Street Market? So successful is this 'special and unique concept' that the company is opening an Edwardian food court in Blackpool. 'The theme is of utmost importance,' Kavanagh confides, 'and it must be stuck to, or you don't get that special atmosphere.'

The retail-leisure mix is also coming on strong at Whiteley's, the recently opened shopping centre in Queensway, which houses London's first purpose-built multiplex cinema. Eight screens. A video wall. 'A pick 'n' mix operation,' and, of course, food courts and shops. The old department store of Whiteleys has been gutted, leaving its façade. Inside it's airy and bright and feels suitably upmarket.

The multiplex will no doubt benefit from the closure of two local cinemas due, they say, to 'trouble'. Trouble, you see, is not something you get in shopping malls with their high-tech methods of surveillance. UCI, which opened the first multiplex in Milton Keynes in 1985, sees itself as part of a cinema renaissance which has pushed attendance figures up from 53 million in 1984 to a predicted 90 million in 1990. This is all well and good but the programming looks predictably dull and why do they have to refer to films as 'presentations'?

Soon, Whiteleys and the Trocadero will both be places you never have to leave. They will provide food, entertainment and shops all in the same building and unlike so many shopping centres they will stay open at night. Their creators claim they offer endless choice; but is this our choice? These places occupy a strange territory that is both public and private, and that is why viewing them as simply postmodern pleasure palaces or miserable temples to consumption is inadequate. They cut across the private and the public in an entirely new way. These are public spaces for private experiences. Postmodern theorists, who can never imagine any kind of collectivity, neglect this public aspect while the critics of shopping centres won't accept the pleasures of the individual consumer or the differences between different kinds of shopping centres.

In the end though, internal rather than external demands will dictate the future. The grinding down of the credit boom, high interest rates, enormous ground rents will take their toll. But one other factor seems to be significant: consumers themselves are now demanding better and more knowledge-able service, and analysts are predicting that service, not marketing, will be the keyword of the future. Clearly, self-service is not enough. We want personal as well as financial interaction when we go shopping. Stores like Ikea which provides créches are leading the way — another example of an all-in-one shopping/eating/recreational space.

Whatever happens, the dream of plenitude 'everything under one roof' will continue. Yet what architectural historian Margaret Crawford refers to as 'the ecology of fantasy' that these mall/centres/multiplexes cater for has to be maintained just like real ecology. We have to put back as well as take for the fantasy to work. Nothing is free, least of all 'leisure'.

Years ago in the States I was hooked on one of the daytime soaps. In it a young couple who were desperately in love but whose parents were against the romance ran away. This modern day Romeo and Juliet hid for weeks in a department store. They had everything they wanted and owned none of it. Their imitation of life was more perfect than life itself. Eventually though they were found and taken away by security guards.

Maybe it wasn't a soap opera after all. Just another premonition of the future.

Mini-Politics: saying no in public

Pretty Polly, manufacturers of stockings and tights, have managed to run some Pretty Pathetic advertising campaigns in their time. Do you remember one a few years back — huge posters of women's legs with the caption 'For girls who don't want to wear the trousers?' It implied a return to an 'authentic' feminine identity against an artificial and butch notion of liberation. It might as well have read, 'For girls who want to be treated as complete bimbos.' Yet the glossing over of real questions of female access to power was as transparent as the stockings themselves. The image of feminism could be 'retouched', even if real feminists couldn't.

Nowadays, judging by the masses of young women striding around in mini-skirts, it seems that there are many of us who may not literally want to 'wear the trousers'. However, I doubt if most of us feel that exposing our legs automatically disenfranchises us from the power that goes with them. Mini-skirts are no longer only worn by the extreme or the ultra-trendy — even Marks and Spencer are doing it: 'This season we are offering an extra short length twenty-one inches — two inches above the knee'. Wow!

At the American collections, full of Calvin Klein 'slips' and the 'Shortest, Briefest Dresses of Them All', we saw what New Yorkers mean by High Rise. International buyers rushed back home 'to get all their existing stock chopped into minis'.

So what does all this mean? Indeed, does it have to mean

anything? Maybe not, but unlike many items of fashion, the mini-skirt is generally perceived to signify *something* — whatever it may be, the '60s, sex or success. It now acts almost as a vacuum, pulling every and any potential meaning into itself. People who denounce fashion, and particularly women's clothes, as superficial or regard it as merely decorative, have poured into this insignificant garment so many meanings that it brims over with possible clues to modern behaviour.

This iconic status allows it to be taken outside the closed world of fashion and read against the economic and political climate. Desmond Morris, who should really stick to talking to monkeys, has a go at this in *Elle* magazine, telling us that while short skirts signal liberation, long ones mean 'female subjugation and peasant toil'. The only thing, he says, that has delayed the return of the mini has been the uncertainty in the FT index. Such glib determinism ignores the variety of styles available at the moment and fails to explain how they change so rapidly.

To put it crudely, as Julie Burchill always does, 'You cannot take the temperature of a culture by measuring a hemline, the collective whim of fifteen French fag [sic] dressmakers says absolutely nothing about the shift in status and sensibilities of western womanhood'.

Yet fashion isn't just about designers. Some styles filter down and become acceptable to the mass market. Others don't. Short skirts have cropped up regularly in the designer shows of the last few years with clothes inspired by physical activity, dance and sport. We've had the tutu and the skating skirt, among others. On the streets the adoption of the mini-skirt in PVC or rubber by female punks was a deliberate rejection of the long, floaty and 'natural' skirts of the late 70s. It was all very synthetic, suggestive and full of shockability.

Now it's no longer just smarties or punks who want to wear

mini-skirts. Which is why it's also tempting to read them as a sign of a post-feminist consciousness. Is this perhaps why there is a difference between the flimsy and skimpy clothes of the catwalk and the way that short skirts are actually being worn? In the collections the clothes were all little girlish, on the streets they are far more businesslike and practical and worn with black tights against the cold wind.

Further, it seems that power dressing can now incorporate the short skirt into its corporate identity. The boss as well as her secretary can wear it. Looking like she means business in a mini-skirt and tailored jacket, she can now display her perfectly-toned body and sexual confidence. It's no longer a distraction, but a 'tangible asset'. This may be anathema to some feminists who feel that this mythical world of women 'having it all' is still far away for most of us, and that the tyranny of fashion still excludes all but the adolescent and the anorexic. But fashion is about pleasure as well as pain. About playing with the boundaries of the body. About the constant negotiation between what is public and what is private.

For women, these are always political as well as aesthetic decisions. Can I wear that to work, on the bus, in the pub? We might think that we are signalling sexual autonomy in our 'look, but don't touch' outfit, but for every sophisticated Tom and Harry who understands the rules of the game there's a Dick that doesn't. For some men autonomy dressed up is remarkably like availability. Like all those snarling models in the ads — defiance is just another kind of provocation.

The move towards more blatantly sexualised women's clothes, which provides an overall context for the shorter hemlines, is also seen by some as an imaginary working through of some of the dilemmas posed by AIDS. For women — and men — taking refuge in monogamous relationships in these days of safe sex, the message is 'Look erotic, but don't deliver'; as designer Antony Price says, 'If the product is the same then the packaging had better look thrilling.'

Yet of all the meanings we attach to the mini, its 60s connotations are the most powerful. Many contemporary fashion shows have a strong 60s feel. Katherine Hamnett's is completely derived from 60s styles, right down to the psychedelic colours. But it's all very knowing — a million miles away from innocence. For how we perceive the 60s has largely been influenced by Thatcherite discourse; the 60s is what has been repressed in the 80s. Thatcherites talk of the 60s as the time when everything started to go wrong; so it's interesting that designers should visually reclaim the era. But the 60s refracted through 80s sensibilities meant something quite different, especially for women. The freedom the mini-skirt symbolised in the swinging 60s was the freedom to say 'Yes'. In the late 80s, it symbolises the freedom to say 'No'.

Belushi's last high

Nothing in the world makes me feel more like taking drugs than the combined spectacle of Lady Diana and Nancy Reagan telling me to 'just say no'. I accept that this unhealthy attitude may indicate some severe personality disorder and, believe me, I've tried to get over it. This week, for instance, I went to yet another anti-drug movie in the hope that somehow I would see the light. Instead I saw *Wired*, the film based on the life (and death) of American comedian, John Belushi.

Belushi, star of *Saturday Night Live*, *Animal House* and *The Blues Brothers*, died in 1982 from a drug overdose. A mixture of cocaine and heroin known as a speedball finally did him in. His death — neither the first nor last in Hollywood — seemed to reverberate around the community. Even Belushi, famed for his excesses, had finally proved to be mortal. And worse, he died doing what so many of them enjoyed doing.

It's an unlikely story for Bob Woodward, the journalist who broke the Watergate scandal and author of *All the Presidents Men*, to pursue. But the result of relentless investigation produced not just a series of articles but a book — *Wired: The Short Life and Times of John Belushi*. The book — scrupulously researched, every source authenticated, every chance conversation documented — is a major indictment of the 'Hollywood system'.

Belushi may have been responsible for his own death but it certainly would not have been possible without the lavish care and attention of a cast of Hollywood hangers-on. These varied from the pathetic Cathy Smith, the woman who supplied drugs to many of the inner circle (and who fixed Belushi his final high) to the big names such as Robert De Niro, Hugh Hefner and Chevy Chase.

Because so many people were implicated in Woodward's book, *Wired*, the film, has taken years to get off the ground. Legal action and threatened libel suits have meant that, though now completed, the film is completely devoid of what made the book worth reading: there are no intimate tales of Hollywood Babylon here. Instead we get a clumsily banal portrait of a minor talent bent of self-destruction. Anything that might be worth saying about drugs/addiction/the star system/fame/the tacit agreement between producers, managers and agents that keeps people like Belushi well supplied with drugs, cannot be said.

Belushi himself is presented as comic genius. Certainly he was emblematic for a generation of Americans who considered themselves 'alternative'. The height of his fame was in the late seventies as *Saturday Night Live* peaked and he made *Animal House*. It's difficult now to understand the significance of *Saturday Night Live*, but in the context of American TV, it continually pushed the boundaries of what was considered acceptable. Its knowing, in-joke humour made constant references to drug use which thrilled its young audience. You had to be stoned to laugh at most of the jokes. Veering between political satire and infantile humour it may now seem unwatchable and unfunny but it was unlike anything else on TV and made stars of Belushi, Chevy Chase and Dan Ackroyd.

Wired makes the awful mistake of trying to duplicate the 'classic' sketches which made Belushi such a cult. Despite Michael Chiklis's careful impersonation, they just look embarrassing. The biggest laugh to be had in the film is from the dubious comparison of Belushi to the brilliant Lenny Bruce. Apart from their drug habits they couldn't be further apart. Belushi's appeal lay in his physicality, almost Neander-thal at times, his ability to appeal to the lowest common denominator. Playing the slobbish Bluto in *Animal House*, he takes the logic of consumption to the extreme — eating, drinking, farting and belching excessively.

Belushi lived up to the image. A friend remarked, 'he wants to grab the world and snort it.' Cocaine seemed the ideal drug and it was in plentiful supply. Cocaine didn't fuck you up — quite the opposite. It made you work better, feel clear-headed and clever. Just what a comic under pressure needed to get the edge, the sharpness necessary for a great performance. Drugs, Belushi maintained, helped him to stay alert to the comic possibilities of every situation. It's a pity then, that, often by the time he got on stage, he could barely stand.

As the film shows through two very awkward scenes using flashbacks, Belushi soon deteriorated into a selfish junkie. The fact that he was famous didn't make this process any more interesting. The fact that he was always given enough cash to buy drugs by producers, concerned that without them he might have fucked up a recording deal, is glossed over.

Belushi's story is of pre-clean and sober Hollywood. Today everyone is now busy polishing their own detox stories. Not a day goes by without some star confessing an addiction of one sort or another. Belushi once said that shooting up was 'like kissing God'. But who needs God when you can be born again at the Betty Ford clinic? The most unfortunate part of this spiritual conversion is that you have to spend the rest of your life mouthing anti-drug slogans which are about as helpful as they are inane.

Mind you, some of them seemed just as stupid before they gave up the chemicals. Robert De Niro, apparently so steeped in The Method, thought it was a good idea to use real heroin when Belushi was shooting a drug-taking scene so that the emotions expressed would be truthful. It's just as well the script didn't require a road accident. *Wired* doesn't go into such details though it remains voyeuristically fascinated with the paraphernalia of drug abuse. The camera is as fixated on the needle and spoon as any addict and, as usual, heroin is treated with a special awe.

It's almost as if you can take cocaine till your brain is falling out through your nostrils but look once at smack and you die instantly. The media seem to need the bogeyman of drugs at a time when the old enemies like 'reds under the beds' are fading away. Drug dealers represent the ultimate evil that figure in every major contemporary thriller. As Schwarzenegger and James Bond fight the international drug trade, so will George Bush who, like his predecessor, knows that life always imitates art. Drug dealing may be one of the most enterprising and efficient forms of capitalism, creating insatiable demands and wrecking lives, but it is not the root of *all* evil.

The 'war against drugs' cannot be won by simplistic moralising. Legalisation is now being mooted in the most unlikely places (Judge Pickles has even cottoned on) as it is realised that current policies don't have a hope of succeeding. People working day to day with drug users are now discussing drug addiction in new ways. Rather than the usual 'addiction as disease' syndrome, they are talking about patterns of drug use with many people spending a few years taking drugs and then coming off them by their mid-thirties as their lifestyle changes.

Hollywood, like most governments, would still prefer to deal with the drug problem with repressive methods. This repression leads to hysteria: it leads to bad movies like *Wired* and bad moves like the police raid on Broadwater Farm. No one is arguing that drugs are a 'good thing' but when 'just saying no' clearly doesn't work, perhaps we should have the courage to 'just say yes'.

Something to stay home about

You know that you are well and truly past your sell-by date when you would rather stay at home on a Saturday night to watch *thirtysomething* than paint the town red. Please don't give me excuses about baby-sitting problems. Please don't try to pretend you are cocooning or whatever the latest media buzz-word for being boring is. Please don't hint you are writing a thesis on Capra's influence on modern American soaps. Just tell the truth. That somehow watching a load of smug Americans lead their lives is better than leading your own.

Because who wants real life when you can have something this true to life? Actually *thirtysomething* is about as true to my life as *Dallas* is. But that's not the point. It pretends it is. Just like it pretends that its very specific world view — white, American, middle-class — is in fact universal, *thirtysomething* makes us believe that all over the world people live in big houses with wooden porches and colour co-ordinated

Venetian blinds. That everywhere men wear thoroughly tasteless shirts and women horribly casual cardigans. That everyone thinks the ideal woman is Carly Simon, the ideal man James Taylor.

Worst of all, it pretends that we can 'work it out'. There is no problem that can't be talked through, no difficulty that can't be resolved by people relating to each other. 'How are you?' is not asked out of politeness but as an invitation to a monologue on our deepest hopes and fears. For if the structure of so many soap operas is that of 'the closed community in crisis', the crises in *thirtysomething* are entirely personal. Forget the wicked oil barons and adulterous wives of the Dallasty era, forget the Victorian obsession with illegitimacy that dogs every English soap, the problems of the *thirtysomething* crowd are what make the series so compulsive or repulsive, depending on your point of view.

But these people don't have real problems, say many of the programme's critics, revealing themselves suddenly as closet Marxists. They are not starving or homeless. The *Evening Standard* called it 'self-indulgent garbage'; the *Daily Mail* said, 'If this is reality, please spare me from it.' Nothing ever happens, they complain, as though a drama without a car chase is automatically inferior.

Of course it's true that, judged in these terms, *thirty-something* manages to make *Neighbours* look like nonstop, action-packed adventure. But why must it be judged in these terms? If you want a model for this kind of classy, multi-narrative playing, look to *Hill Street Blues, LA Law* or any film by Robert Altman.

Because, despite its ability to annoy, the programme has a devoted audience both here and in the United States and appeals particularly to women. Indeed, it is the female characters who form the backbone of the series. Of the seven regular characters, four are women, any one of whom might become the subject of a whole episode.

The central couple are undoubtedly Hope and Michael, their house the focus of the eternal dinner parties. Hope is the perfect wife and mother. She worries about Michael. She worries about her daughter. She worries about her friends. She worries about the planet. And, in between walking round her huge house with endless piles of beautifully laundered towels, she does a bit of investigative journalism. And everyone I know hates Hope with the kind of passion usually saved for child molesters. In fact, unbeknown to the uninitiated, hating Hope is one of the main pleasures of the programme.

While the men are often peripheral to the storylines, it is through Hope and Nancy, Ellen and Melissa that the ethos of the series is worked through. The constant foregrounding of feeling, the urge to confess, to reveal the most intimate emotions, is all played out between the female characters. OK, so the men talk and get personal, but this is usually awkward and jokey, and emotional contact can only really be achieved when they are playing basketball. It is the women who are experts, amateur therapists, continually treating each other for minor ailments. Except that now Nancy, married to the infantile Elliot, has got the big C, nobody knows how to treat her at all. Naturally she has just gone to a cancer counselling group.

And, this being *thirtysomething*, counselling *will* help. Because in this strange land if you say to someone, 'I want more space' they say, 'Why, of course, you should have told me,' whereas in the real world they would probably scream in your face and throw you out of the house.

For *thirtysomething does* deal with real problems. It's the way it treats them that is unreal. The programme asks that most simple of questions, 'How do I grow up?' and we can all relate to that. Just as we can relate to Ellen and Melissa, the single women of the series.

Ellen is the archetypal single working woman. A success at

work, a mess at home. We are supposed to believe that giggly, flaky Ellen has some high-powered job, though I've never understood what it is that she is supposed to do. All I know is that it must be important as she gets long enough lunch hours to have sex with the revolting Jeffrey in hotel rooms. We are supposed to be worried for her because he is married. Personally I think that's a minor problem compared with his beard.

Forget the expense accounts and the dinner party caterers, the most unbelievable thing about *thirtysomething* is the idea that all these attractive women go for men with beards. Even the holy Hope nearly had an affair with a man with a beard. Elliot has got red stuff growing on his face. And Melissa even went to bed with Gary, the failed Bjorn Borg lookalike, despite his disgusting facial growth.

But then Melissa can do no wrong. Everyone loves Melissa. To the point that a spin-off Melissa series is being mooted in the States. Melissa, unlike Ellen, is not so obviously desperate for a relationship which is why she was able to knock off her decorator instead of agonising about it for months. Melissa has fun. She wears wacky clothes and lives in a loft. So I don't want to spoil it for you and tell you that in the next series she goes on a date with the evil Miles (head of the ad agency and another beard) and he tries to rape her. No doubt she will go into some kind of therapy and it will all be sorted out. Because after all, the promise of *thirtysomething* is that not only will it make a drama out of every crisis, but that it will almost make it worth staying in for.

Reach for the stars

Imagine a group of middle-aged women in a circle in a darkened-room. They are swaying from side to side — each holding candles. Two of them are holding a life size effigy of a man on their shoulders. Some have their eyes closed and some are crying — what's going on? Is it a coven? A weird religious gathering? No it's a 'Barrynight' — a meeting of Barry Manilow fans held in a suburban semi. Apparently Barrynights are frowned upon by the official Barry Manilow fanclub. Why I found myself wondering — is it that they might somehow go too far? What would too far be?

I guess we are all fans in some way or another but this fascinating programme showed that for some of us adoration is uncomfortably close to obsession. Interviews showed fans such as fifty-four-year-old Patricia, an American who came to England just to be nearer her idol — David Bowie. Then there was Sandra who had written 'please' 77,000 times (that's four hours a night for three and a half months if you are considering it) in order to meet Shakin' Stevens. The actual encounter appeared too much for Sandra who when confronted with the dreadful ordinariness of the man could only mumble 'How's your golf?' It was worth every minute — I'll always remember it,' she sobbed afterwards.

Mary, also afflicted with unrequited longing for Shaky, was perhaps the saddest figure of all. 'What have I got?' she asked. 'Two kids and Shaky.' He is simply the only man that she has ever loved — having dreamt of him when she was four. She thoughtfully sends him shirts — 'to save the washing.' 'I've given up trying to understand it myself,' she said wistfully.

Throughout the programme we also saw Cheryl's letters to Nick (Nick Kamen? Nick Heyward? Does it really matter?). When the letters were not answered she attempted suicide. Patricia also spoke eerily of death, 'I've thought of killing him

227

at times — at least then our two names would be linked together forever.'

Many of the women interviewed described their 'first time' — when they had first seen Bowie/Barry or Ben from Curiosity Killed the Cat. They somehow knew that this was it — the moment that would give meaning to their lives. The conversations were reminiscent of the worst kind of religious fundamentalism, but you couldn't help feeling that these women had actually experienced some kind of 'rapture' here on earth. God save us from Born-Again Barry Manilow fans!

But after all isn't this the ultimate in transcendental 'consumer mysticism'? It matters not which star/product you choose — the important thing is to be a fan/consumer. The star is really, as one fan put it, just the 'mailing box'. Fred and Judy Vermorel, who worked on this programme, suggest in their book *Starlust*, that there is a potentially subversive value in taking publicity as literally as fans do. Though fans may re-interpret what stars give them, they do it in such a way that it cannot be effectively 'absorbed, normalised and recycled' back into the system. In a star-obsessed culture steeped in 'celebrity values' — it is perhaps the overwhelming passions of the fans that trouble the very values that sustain it.

This seems to be all the more troubling when it is female desire that we are talking about. Are women's lives so empty that they need filling with impossible dreams? Or is this just the flipside of romance which is after all equally unobtainable. Romance as it is sold to women depends upon a suspension of time — the perfect moment frozen in fantasy until the next ... What goes on in between for most of us, as Angela McRobbie points out, are long stretches of the mundane and the monotonous. For fans, time also appears to stand still — they live from one concert to the next with maybe — as Mary said — years in between.

Now wonder then that what fills in these empty periods are in fact fetish objects — a poster, a ticket stub, a video, a doll, an exact replica of the jacket, HE wore. The artist Mary Kelly working in a different context shows how as babies grow away from their mothers, the mother tries to hold on to the child by keeping objects — a lock of hair, toys, first drawings, clothes and so on. This strikes me as a peculiarly female kind of fetishisation.

As Ros Coward writes: 'Female dissatisfaction is constantly recast as desire . . . dissatisfaction displaced into desire for the ideal.' Many of the fans interviewed seemed to have achieved just this — a way at least to cope with dissatisfaction. And by deliberately over-consuming their objects of desire they unwittingly show how fragile the myths and mechanisms that try to stem that dissatisfaction are. A lesson for anyone interested in the politics of consumption — sometimes to believe *too* much undermines the system more than not believing at all . . .

Starship stories

Captain's Log: Stardate 191089.

My battle with the Federation continues. After all these years of tucking my trousers into my boots and boldly going where no man has gone before, I feel I've earned a rest. Shore leave at least. I just don't feel the same about interstellar travel these days. I look back at all the old episodes when the galaxy was my oyster and life seemed to be an endless adventure and I wonder what happened to us all. Me, Spock, Bones and the rest — what a crew. There was no mission too dangerous, no warp factor high enough, no alien more ludicrous than the ones we encountered.

Now I wonder what happened to all that time, all that

optimism. I guess we got kind of institutionalised up there on the Enterprise. It's funny if I'm not lost in space. I don't kow what to do with myself. Well, I was saying all this to the Admiral, feeling that it was time to lay down my transporter for good when he came up with an offer I just couldn't refuse. 'Jim,' he said, 'how about if we give you a new Starship Enterprise, a new wig and a chance to direct? Will you do just one more movie?'

I talked it over with Spock — after all he directed the last film and for a Vulcan he didn't make a bad job of it — and we decided to get the old mob together and make *The Final Frontier*. At first I didn't have much of a story and then I had the brilliant idea of the Star Trek crew meeting God. Back home I've been watching some of those TV evangelists and, you know, we've always prided ourselves on the way we deal with metaphysical questions as well as being socially relevant.

So, in this movie, we have this half-Vulcan, Sybok, a charismatic kind of prophet who persuades his followers and half the crew of the Enterprise to go into the centre of the galaxy to find Sha Ka Ree, which is a kind of multicultural concept — Eden, paradise, Shangri-la or something like that.

As you know, up here in the twenty-third century we like to keep ahead of the times so I encourage my crew to talk a lot of New Age twaddle. Sybok derives his power from getting people to 'share their pain'. This is a 'cleansing experience' that helps one 'draw strength from within'. Even Bones tries to get us to 'open up' and I have to explain my personal theory about fear being The Great Barrier. But if this cosmic encounter group gets too much for you there is always the running battle with the Klingons.

To be frank, though, the one problem that no special effect could solve was the fact that we've all aged. I mean it was 1966 when we first started the whole damned enterprise. I don't see why a little middle-aged spread should stop me, though. In *The Final Frontier* I prove what an action man I am by a spot of rock climbing. It's a pity about the huffing and wheezing, but it's the others I'm worried about: Spock, bless him, has always looked half-dead; but Bones looks decidedly unwell. Uhuru is rather matronly so I thought I'd help her recapture her youth by getting her to take her clothes off and express a long-repressed desire for Scottie.

I had thought of renaming the movie 'fifty-something' after I realised that we've been doing for years what these yuppie upstarts aspire to. After all, in our self-enclosed world we explore personal crises with the same verve as we explore new planets.

For years now I've realised the final frontier is the human soul, space is merely the arena in which we investigate it. Yet the great mysteries of the universe remain unsolved. I've never told this to anyone before but, after all this time, I still can't figure out why Uhuru has a screw-driver in her ear, how Scottie can mend the whole of the Enterprise with a pocket torch and a spanner and why we always have to drink blue drinks. Maybe it really is time I retired.

POLITICS

Political poison

'Because there's one thing I know, I'd live long enough to savour/That's when they finally put you in the ground/I'll stand on your grave and tramp the dirt down.'

This is one of our most respected songwriter's view of Margaret Thatcher. It's from Elvis Costello's 1989 album *Spike*. Morrissey wanted to see Margaret on the guillotine. 'When will you die? When will you die?' he wailed plaintively in an acute piece of political analysis. Hanif Kureishi's reaction on Thatcher's resignation was: 'I just feel sorry she didn't suffer long at the end.'

Howard Brenton in *The Guardian* wrote of the Thatcher decade: 'It may seem exaggerated but it was as if some kind of evil was abroad in our society.' At the battle of Trafalgar, the chant went up among anti-poll tax demonstrators 'Ceaucescu's gone, Thatcher's next'. The woman was clearly inspirational. It takes more than a few unpopular policies to bring out this level of vitriol. And now she is gone, who will we hate?

Can you imagine anyone working themselves up like this over John Major? The man with no upper lip, who, as someone pointed out, ran away from the circus to join a firm of accountants, who is described even by fellow Tory MP

Julian Critchley as having 'all the excitement of a provincial bank manager'.

Will right-on pop stars be baying for the blood of Mr Major? Will he be compared to Hitler or even Winston Churchill? Will he present himself as the Tin Man in contrast to the Iron Lady? I hardly think so. For after a decade of personality politics — Thatcher here and Reagan in the States — we have ended up with a prime minister who appears to have had his personality surgically removed. Kinnock too has been so busy of late repressing any traces of individuality that he is now rivalling the Tories in the bland-leading-the-bland stakes.

But whether you like it or not, the politics of hate has been important for the Left in the Thatcher era. For a long time it has been enough to hate what she stood for, to hate what was happening to Britain, but above all to hate *her*. And I can't help feeling that the depths of hatred, and conversely loyalty, that Thatcher inspired, were tied to the fact that she is a woman.

After eleven and a half years, we should have come to terms with the centrality of gender to her reign; but reading her political obituaries it seems in many ways we are just as much in the dark as ever. She was a woman, but she did nothing for women. She destroyed once and for all the idea that being a woman necessarily meant you were softer, more caring, more sympathetic than a man. Yet she didn't disturb gender relations enough to ensure there would be more women in the cabinet or even in parliament.

And less than two weeks after she had gone the veil was being lifted. Teresa Gorman will squat the front benches, Edwina Currie has murmured her discontent, 'the woman problem' is being debated publicly in the most right-wing papers. It is as if the figure of Thatcher herself blocked any discussion of gender. Now finally it is being talked about.

The 'Thatcher factor' was thought, like the woman herself,

to be somehow above gender. More manly than any man, and yet a housewife who like baking cakes as much as international politics. While we on the left talked endlessly about the fluidity of subjectivity, sexuality and identity, here was a woman who slid effortlessly from one identity to another. A woman who instinctively knew that femininity was a masquerade and that contradiction was not a flaw but a fact of life.

But culturally and politically there has been a failure to deal with that. Anti-Thatcher imagery has always been at base crude, even in its most sophisticated guise. *Spitting Image* took away the handbag, the ultimate and for some disturbing symbol of mysterious femininity (What do they keep in there?). It was replaced with the obvious signifier of masculinity, the big cigar. Thatcher was (surprise, surprise) really a man, right down to wearing a shirt and tie. The woman with power can only ever be seen in terms of masculinity — the phallic woman — never on her own terms. But her great strength, surely was that she changed those terms.

Alternatively, Maggie was arch-dominatrix or nanny, the nation and her colleagues finding their thrills in some strange sado-masochistic relationship that exploited the innate British desire for punishment. Trying to get to the bottom of this in a ludicrously literal application of Freud, Leo Abse attempted a psychobiography of the woman.

She had, he told us, despised her mother, glorified her father, had a peculiar time on the potty and a bad time on the breast. That's why one of her first public acts was withdrawing free school milk, geddit? Germaine Greer gave us an analysis of the Thatcher bosom. Was its appeal asexually matronly or invitingly motherly? Meanwhile, Mitterrand drooled at the woman 'with the eyes of Caligula and the mouth of Marilyn Monroe', while a couple of drunken Tory MPs had the audacity to make passes at her.

Yet the Left has always denied her sex appeal. Its stock reaction has always been that she is not a 'real woman'. However you view her, Maggie was enough of a woman for misogyny disguised as political analysis to rule the day. Remember Labour's cries of 'ditch the bitch'. Sure enough, I hate her too. Always will. But now we have to face up to the business of dealing with Thatcherism without Thatcher, maybe we have to realise that it wasn't all Her.

There is something pure about the politics of hate. It doesn't even feel like politics any more, just good old-fashioned morality. I think she understood that. But without her as the target I wonder what is to become of all that venom, all that hatred, all that righteous anger? After all, it's far too good to waste.

Junk culture

Somewhere in the blank drawing board of the Australian desert, modern design has achieved its brilliant apotheosis. Line, colour and material come together to provide the ultimate design solution for society's ultimate problem — a colour-coded maximum security prison. All is not well however at this New Generation facility and Central Industrial Prison is on 'lockdown': a state of emergency has been declared, following continued outbreaks of violence and all the inmates are indefinitely confined to their cells, deprived of their former 'privileges'.

This is where *Ghosts of the Civil Dead* starts and where it ends as it retraces the events that have led to the lockdown. The first feature film of director John Hillcoat and producer Evan English, this independent Australian movie is one of the

235

most powerful films of the year. It is ostensibly about prison — the events in it are based on fact (the lockdown since 1983 at Marion, Illinois, where prisoners are confined to their cells for twenty-three hours a day) which make it even more disturbing. But it is actually about control, repression and fear; about the way we voluntarily imprison ourselves; about living in the modern world.

Shot in documentary style, the film connects the various incidents that led to the lockdown and intersperses them with series of computer print-outs that are the official explanation of what has happened. These reports of an anonymous committee provide the background to the more personal testimony of the inmates. The interaction between technology and people is integral to the film. For New Generation prisons (the kind of prisons that are currently being built in America and Europe) rely almost entirely on computerised security and surveillance systems.

In 'Central Industrial Prison', guards sit behind central observation booths, reducing guard/inmate contact to a minimum. Announcements are made over the speakers by a disembodied female voice. In 'General Population', a self-contained 'housing unit' for the less dangerous inmates, prisoners move relatively freely. Drugs, sex, tattoos and electrical goods are the currency in this numbing environment. Shooting up junk and junk culture in equal quantities, nothing much ever happens. When a new, and naive, inmate, Wenzil, steals a radio, he is dealt with by the other prisoners brutally and bloodily. Under the fluorescent lights, the muzak plays on as the word 'cunt' is cut into his face. The guards do nothing. They don't need to. 'Humane containment' has reached its finest hour.

But the prison administration start to change things. In the high risk unit of the prison — Administrative Segregation — where the most dangerous men are kept, privileges and personal property are taken away and 'the psychos' are brought in. Yale, a prison officer, can't understand what's happening. It's almost as if the prison administration is trying to provoke the inmates.

And this seems to be confirmed when the drug supply is cut off in 'General Population'. The prisoners turn inevitably on each other, on the guards, on themselves. The prison is put on lockdown — a new 'super-maximum security' prison is being built.

Ghosts of the Civil Dead is fundamentally about the self-policing nature of society. We need criminals and we need them bad, very bad, to justify the increasing methods of surveillance, repression and control that are woven into our social structure in the name of safety and security. Control, like William Burroughs says, is a living organism. It gets into your system and you can't get it out. You don't even realise that once it's in your body, it can continually reproduce itself. It lives on fear. And fear of all these dangerous 'others' and, even more terrifyingly, of the 'enemy within', requires a paranoid creation of boundaries (both physical and mental) of electric fences and locked down minds.

Michel Foucault — who might have been a consultant on this film if he were still around — understood this. The methods of social control, of discipline and punishment, that he described so well in institutions of every kind from prisons to hospitals have permeated everyday life to an amazing degree. It's hard to find an environment that hasn't been reshaped to make things 'easier', 'cleaner', 'safer'. From open plan offices to shopping centres, we behave ourselves as if we were being watched and we watch ourselves behaving until we can't tell the difference anymore.

Yet the problem with viewing power/control as a fine web, a mesh in which we are all caught, rather than simply repression from the top down, is that it still leaves you with a rather hazy and conspiratorial conception of who 'they' are. In the film it is clearly not the guards who benefit from the

237

new regime — they are as much victims of it as are the prisoners. It is only the prison administration which issues instructions that is actually in control.

If there is in *Ghosts of the Civil Dead* a slight tendency towards conspiracy theory, it is a minor flaw in a major film. It gets you in the gut and not simply because of the graphic violence. As the blood is smeared across the prison wall, the boundary between self-policing and self-mutilation dissolves; your stomach knotting up tightly as recognition of one of the hidden mechanisms by which we all live is strip searched before our very eyes.

_____

Never really at home

The beliefs and practices of voodoo have long fascinated film-makers. Its rituals are, after all, eminently filmable. But, as David Byrne's documentary *The House of Life* with its intriguing footage showed, this fascination is almost inseparable from plain voyeurism. Byrne's film deliberately avoided a commentary, presumably because he was trying to get away from the position of a white expert, the knowledgeable outsider. In so doing, however, we were left with little more than holiday snaps, albeit unusual ones, of this most 'other' of other cultures.

Wes Craven's *The Serpent and the Rainbow* also manages to avoid anything that could be called a sensitive examination of voodoo. Which is a shame because Craven's work as a horror director (*Nightmare on Elm Street* and *The Hills Have Eyes*) has been as consistently interesting and subtle as the genre would allow, in exploring the nether worlds of nightmares and dreams.

The film is adapted from a non-fiction book by Wade Davis — a real-life anthropologist who went to Haiti to look for the drug that voodoo priests used to simulate death and turn people into zombies — but Craven never seems sure of what kind of movie he is trying to make. So we get part horror, part love story and part political commentary in an unsatisfying mix held together by appalling dialogue.

Dennis Alan (Bill Pulan) is the American hero in search of the drug; Cathy Tyson, an unlikely Haitian psychiatrist is the 'love interest'. As they try to uncover the drug they become embroiled in the political confusion surrounding the end of the Duvalier regime. The villain of the piece (Zakes Mokae) is not only an evil voodoo priest but head of Duvalier's dreaded secret police — the Ton Ton Macoute.

Apart from a penchant for keeping souls in bottles, he also hammers a nail into Alan's groin. In true swashbuckling fashion our hero carries on — 'It's nothing, it only went through the scrotum.' While Alan staggers about the island half-dead through the effects of the drug, revolution is in the air and there are some rather glib points about the battle being 'not in the streets but in the mind'.

As you would expect from Craven, there are some good set pieces but, given the material, they seem highly inappropriate. It is telling that one of the most chilling scenes is when the screen is completely black and we hear nothing but the sound of Alan being buried alive. The horror of nothingness is far more disturbing than the villain who, by the end, has deteriorated into Freddy Krueger's poor relation.

Ostensibly this is a film about a black religion and a black culture that is full of good liberal intention. Yet, as usual, it is through the female character that the racist stereotypes come to the fore. Cathy Tyson, hair scraped back and sensibly dressed, is a dedicated doctor one minute and the next whirling about 'ridden' by the spirits. She has access both to the 'white' world of science and the other world of faith and of the unknown. She is the bridge through which our intrepid hero can cross over, and it is notable that in the ridiculous sex scene her body is lit to emphasise its blackness, her otherness. Like Lisa Bonet's character in *Angel Heart*, another inadequate film around voodoo and possession, the black woman is supposed to represent some kind of unrepressed sexuality.

Yet voodoo is interesting precisely in the power that it grants women, the way it is used in many communities for women to express their dissatisfactions and the way that it makes a space to step outside traditional female roles. To reduce this to a semi-titillating spectacle undermines what is *actually* different and disturbing about these beliefs. Incidentally, generations before the current trendy preoccupation with other cultures, avant-garde film-maker Maya Deren went to Haiti and studied voodoo for several years before becoming a priestess herself. Her films of the ceremonies are shot through with an understanding of the power of ritual that is completely lacking in these contemporary investigations.

Chocolat, a quietly self-assured film by Clare Denis is also an investigation into other cultures and about being an outsider. Set in the Cameroons of the 50s, its flashback structure takes a young Frenchwoman back to her colonial childhood. Through her eyes we see racism, not in some monolithic form but in all its complicated nuances, through the relationships between the little girl, her family, the black servants and some white visitors. Understated, and at times ambiguous, *Chocolat* never gives us the answers or questions on a plate. It simply observes the strangeness and pain of a colonial past and the impossibility of being truly at home in a culture that is not your own. There is a sadness and emptiness about the film which avoids right-on political statements and instead concentrates on the minute gestures and expressions that constitute racism. This sparseness is in marked contrast to the lavishness and nostalgia for Africa and India that we have lately seen so much of in the cinema, and shows that, as they say in the beer adverts, less is sometimes more.

———

A problem of identities

A film-maker for whom the whole question of identity has never been simple or unproblematic is David Cronenberg. His relentlessly intelligent horror films, from *Videodrome* to *The Fly*, have continually probed and prodded at the psychological membranes that enable us to live as individual and independent beings — at the things that both separate us from one another and the things that separate humans from non-humans.

It's fitting then that his brilliant film *Dead Ringers* should concern twin gynaecologists whose whole business involves probing into the insides of women's bodies and whose whole problem involves their inability to separate from each other and construct separate identities.

Jeremy Irons, in an astonishingly clever performance, plays both Beverly and Elliot Mantle, successful gynaecologists who have a completely symbiotic relationship. They share their apartment, their work, their women often doubling up for each other in difficult situations.

The harmony between the suave Elliot and the more insecure Bev, is shattered by Clare Niveau, an actress played by Genevieve Bujold. She is a gynaecological freak with a trifurcate womb, a uterus with three entrances. But for the brothers she is even more unusual as she and Bev form an emotional attachment that excludes Elliot.

The pain of the separation both from her and from Elliot causes Bev to decline in a mixture of drug addiction and paranoid delusion. There are some wonderful scenes which both expose and play upon medical attitudes to the female body. In his madness, which is in many respects so frightening because it is totally rational, Bev invents some bizarrely beautiful but horrific 'gynaecological instruments for operating on mutant women'. Garbed in red surgical gowns, he becomes the high priest of this radical technology complaining that it is not the instruments that are the wrong shape but the increasingly internally deformed women he has to deal with.

There is little outright horror though. This being Cronenberg, even a shaving scene is tinged with a nerve-wracking suspense. I guarantee, however, that most women in the audience will sit with their legs tightly crossed throughout. Much more than a horror movie or indeed any of his previous films, *Dead Ringers* is a highly unusual mix of entertainment with intellect combining the visceral with the cerebral.

By the time the film has progressed to its haunting conclusion, Cronenberg has made us think about the dissolution of boundaries between bodies, between souls, between individual wills. About the differences between inside and outside, between men and women, between animal and human. In short, about the binary logic that underpins all of our thinking. It is the woman with her trinity of cervixes who makes this logic fold in on itself causing death and destruction. As the twins find out that two into one won't go, that they literally cannot be different from each other, it is this mutant woman that survives. Not only because she is a different kind of woman but because she is different *as* a woman. Cronenberg seems to suggest that the twins' refusal to accept both her and their own differences is what makes the ultimate difference — the difference between life and death.

Brand loyalty

Would you vote for Arnold Schwarzenegger? The man whose most famous line is probably 'Fuck you, asshole' (from 1984's *The Terminator*) has recently vigorously denied any political ambition. But after campaigning for George Bush in 1988, he made a speech introducing him at the Inaugural Ball and has been made chairman of the President's Council on Physical Fitness and Sports. Well, I guess if the bumbling Reagan could invoke the spirit of Rambo, then the wimpish, waspish Bush could do worse than have this real-life superhero on his side.

And Arnold is a big man in more ways than one. Big muscles, even bigger box office. Few stars wield such power in Hollywood. It took one phone call to get the $50 million that his film *Total Recall* needed to get off the ground. His films have enormous international clout. And apart from the contacts with Bush and his cronies, his marriage to journalist and Kennedy clan member Maria Schriver means that he knows all the right people.

For the body-building Austrian who only arrived in the US in the late sixties, this is cultural assimilation *par excellence*. The man who is now a naturalised American citizen may not have lost his accent but he epitomises the (white) American Dream at a time when it is falling apart. Arnie has recreated his identity as carefully as he has built up his body, slowly and methodically until the past has been erased and there exists only America. But the land of the free comes at a price. And the price is that you forgo your original culture, your original community, in the race for vicious over-achievement. Would that all immigrants behaved as Arnie has. Things would be a lot easier.

They could take a lesson from Arnold. First, change whatever you can — your body, your nationality, your personality. What you can't change, turn into a registered trademark. So Arnold has the accent and the face. The great slavic slab, sculpted out of granite resting on that huge neck. That impassive expression that breaks out into an almost crazed smile revealing teeth that are just too straight and too white to be true.

The next step, as they say in business (and Arnold is a supreme businessman), is to turn your defects into assets. So people say you can't act. Don't even try anything fancy. You're not Robert de Niro. Just play yourself in every single film. Build up a brand loyalty to Arnold Schwarzenegger, never mind the movie. Whether it's *Conan the Barbarian* or *The Running Man*, the public likes to know what it's getting. It can rely on a Schwarzenegger film to deliver unadulterated Arnie. And cleverest of all, if people say you act like a machine, then act a machine in *The Terminator*.

Finally, when you can make action films until they come out of your ears, surprise everyone with a comedy — *Twins*. But remember to exploit those Arnoldisms that the public knows and loves. So play a flawed superman this time — a product of genetic experiment. A charming innocent who is forced to resort to violence to protect lovable Danny DeVito. Take it from me, the formula works — *Twins* was Arnie's biggest film to date, grossing more than $110 million dollars.

Total Recall looks as if it will be even bigger. As befits its star's status, this is a giant film. Massive sets. Extraordinary special effects. Non-stop violence and a soundtrack loud enough to blast you out of your cinema seat. Based on a Philip K Dick short story, *We Can Remember it for You Wholesale* (Dick's work was also the inspiration for *Blade Runner*), *Total Recall* is directed by Paul Verhoeven, the Dutchman whose *Robocop* was such a success.

2084 AD. Schwarzenegger is Doug Quaid, a construction worker with a beautiful wife and a beautiful home. Or is he? Haunted by dreams of Mars, he visits Rekall Inc. It specialises in fantasy holidays, 'ego-trips', by implanting devices into the brains of its customers. Quaid opts for life on Mars but it all comes unstuck when another personality that has been blocked from his mind comes back to life. Pursued by unknown men, he finds a video image of his former self, complete with instructions of what he must do once he gets to Mars. Up till then, his whole life has been a sham, simply a memory implanted into his mind. 'If I'm not me,' he asks, 'then who am I?' 'You're not you, you're me,' comes the reply.

The film builds and twists this multi-layered reality all the way through, maintaining a sophistication unusual these days in either action or sci-fi movies. Yet how does Arnie cope with the self-doubt and paranoia induced by having had your mind stolen and your reality adjusted? You've guessed it. He blasts his way out of it. This is the most violent film I've seen for a long time, bodies torn apart and corpses riddled with bullet holes every ten seconds. Verhoeven likes splatter. He puts this down to having been in Holland during the German occupation.

The combination of Verhoeven and Schwarzenegger is a strange one. Super-normal Arnie and this bearded, lefty Dutchman who likes to talk about conspiracy theories and psychosis: 'The element of psychosis is basically what interested me in the movie, because philosophically I have a strong feeling that something like that might be possible.' *Robocop*'s theme of the evil of corporate power is replayed here too. In many ways, Verhoeven's preoccupations, identity, reality, authenticity, control, find an echo not just in the roles Schwarzenegger has chosen to play but in his own life.

While these themes are also debated in the intellectual arena, is it not appropriate that popular cinema — that cherished medium of identification — should be addressing them with greater panache? Somewhere in this confusion between reality and image, Schwarzenegger has become the modern hero. He represents pure will, pure power unfettered by memory of a past. These Nietzschean overtones were spelt out to comic effect in *Twins*: the scientist who has genetically engineered him tells him that while he contained all that was 'purity and strength', his twin brother Danny DeVito was made up of all the crap.

Arnold may not be able to shoulder the burden of authenticity, because he is not authentic. Who is these days? He may be the ultimate insider but he will always remain the outsider. Besides, he simply does not look real. He instinctively understands the power and the paradox of this particular fantasy. While critics complain that his films contain only the infantile fantasy of complete destruction and uncontrolled violence, Arnold manages to inject humour in a way that always says, 'Hang on a minute, this is only a film.' There is a brilliant line in *Twins* where he turns to Danny DeVito and says, 'I hate violence.' DeVito just looks up and says, 'Yes, but you're so good at it.'

With his new baby and the interest in Culture with a capital C, Arnold has been described as 'socially gifted'. Whatever that means. But don't forget, this is the man who in *Pumping Iron* said that working out in the gym was 'as satisfying to me as coming is . . . So I am coming day and night.' He clearly doesn't need anyone else. Why should he? He is, after all, the ultimate in self-made men.

Sun rises in the east

Is it really fair to compare a film made in one of the poorest countries in the world with a $37 million production by one of Hollywood's flashiest directors? No of course not. But

Yaaba, made in Burkina Faso, a country with no film-making infrastructure will have to compete with Ridley Scott's *Black Rain*. Such is the democracy of the marketplace.

Yaaba, directed by Idrissa Ouedraogo, with its clear images, its wide open spaces and faith in storytelling is a million miles away from the cluttered frames of Hollywood. *Yaaba* means grandmother and the plot concerns the relationship between an old woman and a young boy. But underneath the deceptive simplicity of the film we see a complex portrait of village existence. Though these people have nothing — no electricity, few possessions — Ouedraogo never simplifies their emotional life.

One wonders what Ridley Scott would have done in the brilliant light of this red desert landscape. Could he bear one frame of a film not to be stuffed with *things* and reflections of things? How could he even contemplate a movie without smokey light filtering though grey-blue venetian blinds? For Ridley is a former ad man, the designer director par excellence. This obsession with surface has produced some of the best and most influential movies of the last ten years. Both *Blade Runner* and *Alien* looked fantastic and had the added extra of exciting plots. *Black Rain* simply looks fantastic.

It is set largely is Osaka, which will no doubt interest those who are in the business of constructing the cyberpunk canon. *Blade Runner*'s vision of a future American city was swarming with Asiatic influence and Chiba City, one of the locations of William Gibson's seminal novel *Neuromancer*, was also in Osaka. Yet Scott's explanation for choosing Osaka over Tokyo is based on practicalities — it was an easier place to film in. Here, in this empire of neon signs, the previous influences of his films can be foregrounded and you can't help feeling that, like so many of us, he is far happier dealing with Japan as *the future* rather than dealing with it in the present.

The plot itself is as old as they come. Two New York cops witness a murder and are assigned to take the killer back to the

Japanese police in Osaka. It's another cop-out-of-water scenario with the culture clash played for all it's worth. Michael Douglas plays the hard cop Nick, an unlikeable macho bore who watches his partner, the soft cop, get disembowelled by a gang of Japanese maniacs on motorbikes. They are all members of the Yakusa, 'the Jap mob', which is crudely portrayed here as a more exotic version of the Mafia. After the death of his buddy, Nick reluctantly teams up with his Japanese counterpart, the cautious and honest Masahiro and ends up teaching him a thing or two about American philosophy summed up here as 'sometimes you have to go for it'.

As dubious and racist as this film is, full of lines like 'Isn't there a nip in this building who speaks fucking English?' (which hasn't stopped it being acclaimed in Japan itself), it is undeniably first-class entertainment. It is slick, loud and full of thoroughly enjoyable, mindless violence. Every frame is crammed with surface and superficial detail, steam and light. Every puddle is spotlit, every pair of sunglasses dazzling.

Yet underneath all these shining surfaces there is an emptiness that is not just the emptiness of a formula plot but a sense of foreboding. America doesn't know how to deal with Japan. It cannot accept that it is no longer itself the centre of the world. And it cannot begin to accept that it has been beaten at its own game, rather than by some commie plot. Japan has made capitalism *work*.

The central relationship of *Black Rain*, between Nick and Masahiro, is a crumbling assertion of American superiority. Nick cannot come to terms with the Japanese code — the stereotype of membership of a group being more important than individual desires. Nick sees Japan as a mere imitator, a country full of repression and with no originality. There is nothing more alien to the American ethos than the idea of a voluntary rather than an enforced collectivity. Nick's is the desperate voice of rugged individualism, a man who refuses 'to play by the rules'. Japan is full of rules that are incomprehensible to him. And then we have the Yakusa who are actually fighting over counterfeit money. It is almost an admission that Japan cannot only produce goods more efficiently than the west, but that it can now make its own dollars. America is redundant which is why this movie makes such a conspicuous and botched effort to turn us back to the American way.

Outside the fiction of the film, Japan is buying into the fiction-making machine of Hollywood in a big way. Sony now owns some of the major studios. As the sun rises in the east, the American debt crisis grows. The only female character in the film, naturally enough a glamorous American bargirl on the make, describes her relationship with the country as a love-hate one.

But *Black Rain* is full of very little love for Japan. It is fear that drives it, and the Japanese themselves are portrayed as the ultimate *Aliens*. Instead the film mouths its T-shirt slogan, 'Sometimes you have to go for it', as jingoistic compensation for what even the American government is having to come to terms with: that sometimes it's too late. Someone else has already gone for it and is winning.

You can't do the right thing all the time

Spike Lee's film *Do the Right Thing*, ended with quotes from Martin Luther King and Malcolm X. His *Mo' Better Blues* ends with a quote from John Coltrane from *A Love Supreme*, as if to underline the fact that this is a very different kind of film. 'I don't want to be thought of as a man who's only capable of making one kind of movie, and that's it,' Lee explains.

Yet whatever kind of film Lee made, it would not be the right thing as far as some people are concerned. His unprecedented position as a black director whom Hollywood takes seriously also means that he is under enormous pressure to be all things to all men. Since *Do the Right Thing*, he has been accused of heightening racial tensions at a very difficult time. He has been criticised for refusing to denounce Farrakhan, slagged off for promoting Nike trainers and chided for being too middle-class. None of this is helped by the fact that Lee himself obviously takes great pleasure in stirring it. He is a brilliant self-publicist, and public feuds like the one with Eddie Murphy only add to his bolshie image.

Mo' Better Blues, although superficially a far mellower film than *Do the Right Thing*, is already the subject of controversy in the US, where it has been accused of being anti-Semitic in articles in the *New York Times*, the *New York Post* and the *Village Voice*. A recent piece in the *Voice* was accompanied by a blank space instead of the usual film still. The caption read, 'The reason that this space is blank is that the Spike Lee organisation refused to allow the use of a photograph of the two greedy Jewish club owners in *Mo' Better Blues* to illustrate this column.' This one looks like it will run and run . . .

In the meantime we have the film. Neither the masterpiece nor the failure that some have suggested, it is too loose, too long (as was *Do the Right Thing*), but still has enough verve to hold the whole thing together. Denzel Washington, whom Lee correctly identifies as having 'matinée idol' potential, plays Bleek Gilliam, a young jazz trumpeter dedicated to his craft. Indeed, his dedication overrides everything, even his relationships with women and with the members of his band. Nothing or no one will come between him and his horn.

Lee artfully sets up several jazz myths only to have them

destroyed by the end of the movie. Bleek's self-absorption is, after all, part of the whole macho musician trip that routinely excuses selfishness as genius. Both the women in Bleek's life — Indigo, a sensible teacher (Joie Lee), and Clarke (Cynda Williams), an aspiring singer — put up with this for a while. They know about each other but, on confronting Bleek, he can only come up with the smugly pathetic reason, 'It's a dick thing.' He is in the enviable position of having his cake and eating it.

It's the same with the other members of the band whom he refuses to listen to. While the other musicians are getting pissed off with playing to packed houses while making little money, Bleek ignores them. The only person he seems to have any time for is his childhood friend Giant, played by Lee himself, who is steadily gambling himself into real trouble.

The film has a timeless feel, a mix of bebop fashion and VDUs, pork-pie hats and portable phones. Its lush score underlines the lifestyle of the musicians, which appears to be far from struggling. They live in enormously stylish apartments and dress to kill. But Giant's gambling leads to Bleek's downfall. At the same time, Indigo and Clarke decide they have had enough and leave him. And Bleek is left alone to realise the error of his ways. After the purposeful ambiguity of *Do the Right Thing, Mo' Better Blues* is an enormously moral and romantic film as Bleek learns painfully that love conquers all, its final scenes telescoping love, marriage and childbirth as the answer to Bleek's problems.

Along the way though, there are the now familiar Lee trademarks and themes: an episodic structure, wonderful improvised sequences with magnetic performances, interspersed with less successful scenes which drag on way too long; a brilliant score composed by Bill Lee, Spike's jazz-composer father, and Branford Marsalis. Bubbling just below the surface are the usual racial conflicts — one of the musicians has a white, rich-bitch girlfriend whom the other members of the band laugh at. And Bleek himself has to choose between the dark-skinned Indigo and the light-skinned Clarke.

But it is the portrayal of the two Jewish clubowners — the Flatbush brothers — who own the club in which Bleek's band plays that has caused so much offence. Undoutedly caricatures of money-grabbing Jews, the other characters in the film are treated with far more respect. 'What they say, the way they speak, their body gestures, the *gelt* in their eyes, make for quintessentially crude anti-Semitism. It's the kind you see on the walls of toilets,' writes Nat Hentoff. Certainly there are no other Jewish characters to offset them.

Lee denies he is an anti-Semite, but points out that many black musicians were ripped off by white businessmen over the years. What Lee has tried to do is to make a black jazz film, to reclaim jazz as a specific part of black heritage. This is important. After all, the last big jazz film, *Bird*, was made by a very white, white man, Clint Eastwood. Eastwood, whatever his liberal intentions at the time, gave many interviews in which he talked about jazz being one of the few authentic *American* (rather than black) cultural forms.

Lee's love of jazz is certainly up there on the screen and hard to resist. But whether that compensates for his use of stereotypes and the ending of the film, which is as glowing an endorsement of family values as you will see this year on screen, is quite another thing. So is it the wrong thing? I don't think Lee has it in him to make a movie that is not complex, thought-provoking and irritating all at the same time. Films that demand to be struggled with sound pretty much like the right thing to me.

Great expectations

Black Audio Collective's first feature, *Testament*, is a difficult film. It's not easy to watch or write about. Admittedly, the prize-winning *Handsworth Songs* is a hard act to follow. Taken together with the cluster of independent black films, such as Sankofa's *Passion of Remembrance*, it has signalled a resurgence in black film-making that Paul Willemen described as 'the most intellectually and cinematically innovative edge of British cultural politics'. But this kind of praise can become another kind of pressure. Apart from the 'burden of representation', whereby one low-budget black film has to speak for all black experience, it has also got to be better than everything else.

It is one thing to have great expectations, but political sympathy alone cannot carry a film — and, in the end, it is judged by the muddle of supposedly objective and daftly subjective prejudices that make up much film cricitism in this country. And, of course, by audiences.

When confronted with a film like *Testament*, which blurs the categories that we usually lump films into, the criteria that we use to discuss cinematic value look increasingly redundant. *Testament* has been approached as though it were simply a black British film, an African film, a historical documentary, an avant-garde travelogue, when it is in fact much more. Its low-production values are chastised in the *Independent*, which seems particularly unfair when one compares its budget with that of the average Hollywood film. And the peculiarly flat performance of Tania Rodgers, as the central character Abena, has been seen as simply bad acting or as some typically pleasureless avant-garde device rather than, more realistically, to do with the lack of experience most workshop productions have in actually directing actors.

Testament shares with *Handsworth Songs* a complex documentary structure though this time the central story is fictional. Abena, a television presenter, left Ghana after the coup in 1966 when Nkrumah was overthrown. The end of Nkrumah's nine-year rule of Africa's first independent black state, tears Abena — then a student at the Ideological Institute — apart. After believing in Nkrumah's espousal of pan-Africanism and socialism, she feels politically adrift as she returns much later on to a film a documentary about Werner Herzog's *Cobra Verde*. As she wanders through the empty landscapes and stilted conversations with old friends, she meditates on what has happened, on her guilt at leaving, her disillusionment, her despair, her anger and her over-whelming sense of exile. She belongs nowhere and yet even the past is no longer a comfortable place to be.

The difficulty of representing the experience of exile is overcome by another kind of splitting, and *Testament* contrasts Abena's intimate memories with a larger sense of time full of river goddesses and ancient mythology. It is almost as if this cyclical psychic time, a mystical and feminine space, is her refuge after the loss of the father — her real father died at the time when her political idealism was stripped away from her. But, between personal memory and collective myth, are the inter-subjective, everyday relations between people — something *Testament* seems unable to deal with.

Mixing archive footage with dramatic sequences and oddly disturbing images that suggest half-forgotten dreams, the film is slow and, at times, hard to follow. While *Handsworth Songs* demonstrated a wonderful precision of imagery, *Testament* suffers from images which are so loaded with universal meaning they eventually become meaningless. The separation of two siamese twins, for instance, may stand for all separation or separation of the most final kind, but it runs against *Testament*'s attempt to give a diasporic experience a specific historical context.

Maybe this is an impossible task. John Akomfrah's script is

a poem to doubt, uncertainty, dispossession and loss. At times wilfully obscure, at others as painful as only the sharpness of memory can be. Yet the script lacks a certain pace or lightness of touch and threatens to drag the film down to a tedious formalist experiment. If this is the price of trying to work through a new aesthetic that is neither identifiably 'black' or 'European avant-garde' or 'third world', here *Testament* makes demands not just on critics, but on its audiences. As Judith Williamson rightly remarked: 'Audiences do matter. I don't see how you can talk about oppositional or political film without talking about audience.' Yet, as this new wave of black film illustrates, just as there is no single black identity, there is no single audience. The polarity that is often hinted at between a white progressive art-house audience which understands this sort of thing, and some mythical inherently reactionary black community which doesn't is, to say the least, misguided.

Director Akomfrah talks more sensibly of making 'a series of alliances' between different kinds of audiences. This is not to say that there won't always be people who find any kind of anti-realist film too arty-farty and boring.

What is exciting about *Testament*, though, is that the struggle — and it feels like a struggle — to find new forms does not come out of a purist desire to follow the European avant-garde into its own blind alley, but that the old language for exploring these issues sounds like a worn-down record with the needle stuck in a groove. We don't describe much black music, with its postmodern eclecticism scratching together old and new forms, its sampling of all kinds of identities, as avant-garde, but as *popular*. This kind of breaking up low and high, marginal and centralised culture calls into question the resonance of a term like avant-garde.

It just so happens that the material that many black film-makers are working with — the construction of ethnicity, the relation of a colonial past to a post-colonial present, the experience of racism in all its subtle forms, the impossibility of national identity, of Britishness, is never a clear linear narrative that leads from the past to the present. Instead it is a cluttered journey filtered through memory, myth and many other texts. As Stuart Hall has pointed out, the return of 'roots', both politically, emotionally and aesthetically, is a profoundly intertextual one that is always mediated through the forms of the present. This is the stuff of which post-modern dreams are made and it pushes ethnicity to the centre of these debates, right into the eye of the storm. In another context Toni Morrison questions the historical specificity of postmodernism when she talks of the condition of slavery as *the* postmodern experience.

So, if *Testament* suffers from the same cultural dislocation it attempts to chart, it isn't really surprising. 'The end of innocence', or the end of the 'essential black subject', as Hall describes, plunges us all into 'a critical politics, a politics of criticism'.

Flawed as it is, *Testament* is part of that transition, a brave film that stimulates as many questions as answers. For that reason alone it is worth seeing.

POPULISM

Postmodern paralysis

This week *Smash Hits* included a pull-out poster of Jason Donovan. They also ran a feature 'Is Jason Donovan a dunderhead?'. They asked the hapless but ever-happy Jason to do a general knowledge test. He scored a rather miserable four out of ten. No comment was made. There was no need.

By contrast the *Guardian* ran a lengthy profile on him in the space normally reserved for political figures. In the rather bemused way that papers like the *Guardian* approach popular culture, they tried to analyse the secret of his success. It was, they concluded, his incredible blandness. You don't say?

Yet Jason *is* very ordinary. Somehow his fame has to be accounted for. Shouldn't we be glad that all those progressive ideas about people's everyday culture being valuable and relevant and worthy of serious discussion have, by the end of the decade, permeated the mainstream? Shouldn't we rejoice that you can't move for arts programmes and colour supplements that deconstruct every cultural product from Kylie to Koons, from Perrier to Potter?

If it was all done with the panache of *Smash Hits* things might be OK. But it's not. *Smash Hits* engages with its readers from *within* pop culture and in this way can provide a kind of auto-critique, a running critical commentary without being patronising or pretentious. Isn't this what it really means to take popular culture seriously?

Throughout the 80s we have moved to culture in a big way. Meaghan Morris wrote: 'In 1975 everything was, oppressively, Political. By 1985 everything has become, obscurely, Cultural.' On television a whole run of arts and culture programmes were introduced. Some good, some bad. But we're talking quantity not quality here. Now we could talk culture non-stop, Alice Walker and Andy Warhol in the same breath. Wow.

Then, just as we'd managed to separate culture from politics completely — something that the right knew never to bother to try — someone burned a book, and culture got banged up against not just politics, but religion, race, the whole damn kaboodle. A generation of intellectuals and academics creaked into action. Magazines like this one could even relive their youth. OK so I know about fundamentalism and there is nothing more fundamental than freedom of speech, but I can't help wondering what would have happened if Barbara Cartland had written *The Satanic Verses*.

Instead it was Salman Rushdie. A literary man with impeccable class credentials, a proper author. Would the same eloquent and moving defence have been proffered if the offending writer was the author of trashy novels? If she wore leopard print shoulder pads and stilettos? When the shit hits the fan you're better off being a fan of high culture, of Art with a capital A.

This might seem surprising because we do endlessly read about the P-word (postmodernism) and how there is no longer any distinction between high and low culture. Theoretically, at least, postmodernism seems to contain the seeds of a cultural democratisation. We all have access to this incredible jumble of ideas and styles that is the twentieth century. In theory we can all read these multiple texts, play with our identities and have mystical experiences in shopping malls.

Problems with straightforward sexism in the latest block-buster? Hey, try these amazing 3-D postmodern spectacles and you'll see things differently. What you thought was sexism was actually an incredibly ironic and nuanced inter-textual reference to a film which was itself a pastiche on commodity fetishism. Confused? Fine, that after all *is* the postmodern condition.

Whatever its uses — and I think these ideas are at times extremely valuable — the one thing that postmodernism is unable to deal with is relationships between people. It's very good at talking about the complexities of subjectivity, but hopeless at talking about intersubjectivity — the actual relations between people. It is as if we are at the point where we can only relate to a screen: a television, a computer, an image and never ever to each other.

Instead, as we go into the nineties a reverse, or at least slowing down, of some of these trends seem to be happening. After the days when you could win a chunk of the Berlin Wall in a competition in the *Sun* (what could be more cultural politics than that?), there will have to be a reassessment of what has passed for left cultural politics. After the free-for-all idea that it was somehow intrinsically radical to discuss popular culture, old questions are again being asked. Questions about cultural value, about the quality of the culture that we make and take. Just because we understand the appeal of James Bond, does that mean we have to embrace it?

Ann Barr Snitow said that in matters of popular culture, you are not what you eat and it's true. But that doesn't mean you don't get sick of it. Even *The Face*, the root of all evil or an inconsequential style magazine depending on how you see it, has ended the decade asking us to send faxes to China. Issues like China, eastern Europe, the green movement, another famine, are so obviously about more than style, more than superficiality, more than images, that everyone now has to 'get real'.

Part of that reality will, I hope, involve a cultural politics which is what it says it is — a politics of, from and within culture. The eighties have been a celebration of popular culture through tracing the spurious and fleeting strands of resistance that can be found. The result, though dressed up in all kinds of ways, has been a degree of acceptance that culture as we know it is unchanging, so that we might as well get used to it, warts and all.

But, in the 90s, I don't want my culture warts and all. And I certainly don't want Jason Donovan. Is that really too much to ask for?

___

Britain's macho man

It's not really surprising, when you think about it, that James Bond movies are a key text in the study of popular culture. With the aid of Open University notes on Ian Fleming's fabulous creation, most of us could trot off some sort of essay about how the character, James Bond, reflects certain attitudes about class, gender and nationality. It's almost as if Bond was written for the purpose of being read for his ideological incorrectness by angsty academics who felt decidedly uncomfortable that they actually enjoyed these unsound films.

Where could you find a better example of xenophobic, chauvinistic behaviour? Whether as a fantasy of post-colonial or masculine power, James Bond films are rampantly reactionary. So how do you explain their popularity? Of course you can't without recourse to words like 'pleasure' and 'fantasy', words which these days can at least be spoken out loud rather than slipped in as a footnote in the analysis of culture.

This overall lightening up, this acceptance of old-fashioned virtues like entertainment and escapism means that James Bond fans can sleep sound in the knowledge that they no longer have to feel embarrassed about getting off on the cunning stunts of this most British of macho men. After all having a rape fantasy doesn't actually mean that you want to be raped and watching a Bond movie doesn't necessarily mean that you want to be James Bond. Or does it?

It takes a dour feminist indeed — a part I certainly don't relish — to insist that the fantasies that films like this engender are unacceptable. Yet reaction to the Bond movie *Licence to Kill* is interesting in that it points to a kind of *critical paralysis* (what Meaghan Morris has described as banality) in left cultural analysis. It's a sign of the times that Sally Hibbin, writing about the film in *Marxism Today*, is ultimately less censorious about the film than many articles that have appeared in the press and in commercial women's magazines such as *Elle*.

While I wholeheartedly embrace the move towards accepting the complex and fascinating thrills and spills of pop culture, it's not enough to say of a Bond movie it's a 'fantasy world' and leave it at that. Without some idea of how these fantasies intersect with the 'real' world, we might as well pack our bags and go home.

But then if the postmodern condition means the negation of critical distance, why bother in the first place? There will always be more of where that came from which we, in our incredibly smug postmodern way, can remain knowingly immersed in. It doesn't matter whether you switch on or off, it doesn't matter whether you like it or not, and it doesn't really matter if *Licence to Kill* bored the arse off me. Because, as they say, it's just a 'fantasy world'. I guess it's just not mine.

What is really curious though, is that while we have downed our critical tools, exploring rather than castigating popular pleasures, those pleasures have themselves changed. Even fantasies like James Bond have to reflect changes in the 'real' world. Several components of the Bond formula have been revamped in the new movie. (*Licence to Kill* was initially called 'Licence Revoked', a title considered too difficult for the American market.)

Glasnost has meant that it's no longer plausible to have Bond battling against an evil empire of nasty Russians. Instead, a new stereotype has to be found. This time it's slimy South American drug barons and, as in so many recent action movies, drug dealing has become the crime *par excellence*, that is quite literally, the root of all evil.

Organised crime mirrors organised capital — its multi-national, global nature requires villains who can transcend national boundaries, both in terms of plot and audience. It also has that tinge of morality and shifts Bond's character out of the world of espionage and into the realms of the more traditional hero. In the film, dollar bills are forever being strewn around and yet Bond wants none of it, presumably his mind being on higher things.

Bond himself — the second outing for Timothy Dalton — is more realistic, more human (he bleeds), more caring (he nearly cries), less of a bastard than he used to be and consequently less charming. Yet the move towards realism pulls against the essential fantasy of the film. Those Bond hallmarks such as the stunts and the gadgets also seem less amazing and the stuff of any one of a thousand cop films. There is the obligatory mid-air stunt, the underwater fight and the car chase where Bond hangs on to various moving vehicles and then kicks out the driver. The gadgets, a hangover from the 60s obsession with technology, are even more disappointing. In days when eleven-year-olds are already expert hackers, exploding toothpaste just won't do.

But the biggest, and most publicised change is in the treatment of women. *The Living Daylights*, the last Bond movie, was described as a safe sex film which seemed to mean that it had no sex in it. *Licence to Kill* follows on from this, with a 'liberated' heroine and remarkably few sex scenes.

Carey Lowell plays Pam Bouvier as a tough modern, but modelly, woman. She gets to make a couple of secretary jokes and wants to be called Ms, which seems to generate laughter in itself. As a token feminist she is, I suppose, better than nothing, though naturally she succumbs to Bond's charms in the end.

As the fantasy has altered to accommodate reality, the fantasy has becomes less *fantastic*. Heralded by many critics as a return to the original essence of the Fleming novels, the new James Bond seems to be a combination of what Raymond Williams called the residual and emergent aspects of cultural life. To ignore the distasteful elements in our rush to celebrate its popularity, its power as fantasy, is as bad as the older, left position of dismissing much popular culture on the grounds that it was popular. Just as this film rethinks its old formulas, substituting realism for wishful thinking, we must rethink ours.

On the side of the man in the street

Question: When is a documentary not a documentary? Answer: When people enjoy it. Or so it would seem in the strange case of *Roger and Me*. Michael Moore's film has been a hit with the American public, raking in over six million dollars, and scotching the myth that documentaries automatically mean box-office death. It has secured a distribution deal with Warner Bros, which no one thought would take on this kind of film, and has appeared on scores of critics' top ten movies of 1990.

The Roger of the film's title is Roger Smith, chairman of General Motors. The 'Me' is Moore himself who, for three years, pursues Roger Smith in order to ask him why he is closing down car plants in Moore's home town of Flint, Michigan. He wants him to visit Flint to see firsthand the consequences of mass redundancies — poverty, evictions, rising crime and general desperation that have hit the town.

Moore never gets that interview but instead uses this device to weave together a series of quirky, acute and funny observations about what happens when the American Dream 'goes down the toilet'.

But the tide of acclaim for the film turned when Harlan Jacobson, then editor of *Film Comment*, claimed that Moore had juggled with the truth — that the film was not chronologically accurate. Since then the debate has raged not only over the validity of Moore's film but implicitly over the role of documentary itself.

Moore uses archive material full of images of a happy and prosperous working class, interviews with local residents, and offers his own, idiosyncratic version of events. Though he presents himself as a bumbling but good-hearted smalltown boy in a baseball cap who only wants to bring Roger Smith to justice, Moore was in fact a political journalist for over ten years — you can't help feeling he could have got the interview if he had really wanted it. When asked for accreditation he proffers his Chuck E Cheese fastfood discount card. This is exactly the kind of thing that has offended some critics because Moore is playing to the audience when documentaries are supposed to record events rather than manipulate them for easy laughs.

Yet this ploy of the little man up against corporate America does work because however self-indulgent Moore can be accused of being, he is so obviously on the side of the little man. And he unearths a series of bizarre interviews with local people such as the Bunny Lady — a woman who breeds rabbits for 'pets or meat' and skins them with amazing dexterity in front of the camera. He charts the decline of the town through its desperate measures to set itself up as a tourist attraction by building an indoor theme park, Auto-World, just as it is closing down its real car factories.

The local sheriff's brutal pragmatism as he evicts mothers and children is as hard-hitting as the interviews with the well-to-do, who hire local people to be 'human statues' at their Great Gatsby party. As houses are boarded up a new jail is built. Celebrities such as Pat Boone and the terrifying Anita Bryant are brought in to mouth inanities about 'attitude' in a town that has just been named in *Money* magazine as the worst place to live in America.

That all these things happened is not in dispute but the charges that have been levelled against Moore is that they did not happen in the time-span or order he presents them in this film. Events which took place over a ten-year period have been telescoped into three-years. Reagan visited Flint before the plant closures, not after them. The ridiculous drive to promote Flint as a tourist centre also took place before the major-lay-offs.

This tampering with chronology in the name of entertainment, combined with the influential Pauline Kael's proclamation that *Roger and Me* was nothing more than 'a piece of gonzo demagoguery', have put Moore on the defensive. He claims that his intention was to make 'a movie' not a documentary, something that would be seen in shopping malls as well as art houses. Even more controversially he has argued that all journalism re-arranges sequences of events for its own ends.

The popularity of the film compared with the prissiness of the critics again puts Moore on the side of the 'man in the street'. Yet however naive Moore may appear in his film, *Roger and Me* is ultimately a very sharp piece of film-making. His manipulation of events manages to make some very heartfelt and sophisticated points about the workings of contemporary capitalism. You may be able to name another film that encompasses the end of the manufacturing base, the rise of service industries, the relocation of corporate capital in less developed countries, the creation of themed environments that shut out the poor. But I doubt if you can honestly say it makes you laugh too.

What Moore achieves is an essential truth, a reality that is recognisable however this film is viewed. What he has done is simply to reverse the processes of modern capitalism for his own ends. Giant industries personalise their products through personal endorsements, so Moore goes after Roger Smith as personally responsible for the devastation of Flint. He puts a face on to this huge unwieldy process. He may simplify it but he makes us care — he makes himself an innocent in order to show who is guilty. In making Roger Smith a villain, he inevitably makes himself a hero. This is a fundamentally populist strategy but one that I think he gets away with.

Indeed, the most interesting of recent documentaries such as Errol Morris's *A Thin Blue Line* are bending the rules of documentary making. They deny that there is an incorruptible version of truth out there that merely has to be recorded. Instead they make their own truth in the telling, no longer separating the medium from the message. If Moore is to be held accountable for this then to whom? To other journalists, to the people of Flint, or to General Motors? Are some truths so great that they can afford to dispense with smaller ones? If fact is stranger than fiction, Moore's only crime is that he has made it even stranger. He has described his film as 'docucomedy' but there is already a word for it: info-tainment — the dramatising of real-life events by some American news networks. It has been regarded universally as a 'bad thing'. Go and see *Roger and Me* and think again.

Against the sober grain

Pedro Almodóvar, Spanish director of the much acclaimed *Women on the Verge of a Nervous Breakdown*, seems to be all things to all men. The National Film Theatre describes him as 'a wonder kid'. Alexander Walker dubs him an 'Iberian buffoon' in the *Evening Standard*, which is a sure sign that Almodóvar is doing something right. Anyway, how can you resist a man who once made a film with the poetic title of *Fuck, Fuck, Fuck Me, Tim*? He has been touted variously as the new John Waters, a successor to Buñuel and 'a woman's director'. Negotiations are under way for *Women on the Verge* to be remade as a star vehicle for the newly divorced and de-ribbed Jane Fonda.

What Hollywood will do with him is anyone's guess. For a start, one of the best things about his films is that they go completely against the current clean and sober craze that permeates every other American movie. His characters have all kinds of sex and take all kinds of drugs as a matter of routine rather than regret. And his film *Tie Me Up, Tie Me Down* has been given an x certificate in the States, a category usually reserved for pornography, though it is still managing to do good business.

Tie Me Up, Tie Me Down is simply dripping with controversy. The press have talked of 'German feminists'

267

storming out of the film at the Berlin Film Festival, conjuring up the usual image of dour dungareed types, while Almodóvar has played the part of the misunderstood film director with great charm. It is the basic storyline of the film which has given so much offence. Ricki (Antonio Banderas) is a twenty-three-year-old who has spent most of his life in institutions. When released from a psychiatric hospital, he goes straight to a filmset in order to woo Marina (Victoria Abril), the woman of his dreams. She is a B-movie star, an ex-porn actress and ex-junkie, who has already spent a night with Ricki though she can't remember it. He breaks into her apartment, hits her and ties her to the bed, waiting for her to reciprocate his love.

And she does, even at one point asking to be tied up. Is this a savage dissection of marriage or a paean to female masochism indicated by the Sacred Heart pictures in the title sequence? And, more importantly, can Almodóvar, previously acclaimed for his empathy with women, get away with it?

Well, you want him to, not only because no one else is making films about things like this, but also because no one else is making films that look like this. Amodóvar finds colours and faces that you never usually see on the screen: all those wonderful blues and oranges, all those beautifully ugly faces you could look at for ever. His films hover somewhere between reality, fantasy and wish fulfilment. So as Ricki tracks down Marina, who is already being pursued by the wheelchair-bound director of her film, you want it all to work out. He ties her up so tenderly, buying special tape to gag her with. He goes out to buy her drugs to take the edge off the pain of her toothache. He busies himself with small domestic tasks — a new washer for the tap — as he tells us he just wants to marry her and have babies. And when he comes home after being beaten up himself, in a fine parody of every wounded man sequence from the Bible to the classic western, they make bruised love until Marina realises that this is the man for her.

It helps no doubt, that the man who has kidnapped her is a good-looking hunk. It also probably helps that Marina appears to have no life of her own. Yet it is her pragmatic acceptance of the situation that rings true only at the level of pure fantasy. Though Almodóvar doesn't flinch in showing us the violence, I flinched when I saw it. As Ricki pushes her through the door he hits her hard enough to break a tooth. While Almodóvar plays with his cinematic references, including *Dressed to Kill*, Marina is not just playing at being a woman in peril. She *is* a woman in peril.

This is something that Almodóvar's camp sensibility cannot recognise. Despite the presence of the feisty Lola, Marina's sister, and an upbeat ending, *Tie Me Up, Tie Me Down* is an uneasy film, almost aware of its own limitations. Almodóvar has dismissed criticisms of the film as 'crude and primitive' and yet his defence has been equally naive. The ropes that Ricki ties Marina up with, he has insisted, are a simple metaphor for the ties that bind any two people together. All relationships involve mutual constraints.

While it may be the case that feminists have shied away from dealing with the murky area of female masochism, this graphic representation of it in the name of a love story, cannot help but jar. This may be why Almodóvar has been accused of staging a homosexual fantasy using a heterosexual couple.

Mabye it's a heterosexual fantasy that power relations magically vanish between people of the same sex, but such an imbalance of power would not be so politically or physically loaded. After all, Ricki is a big man and Marina a small woman. But Almodóvar wants to discuss passion not politics. Passion is his god. Passion is seemingly oblivious to the machinations of gender — it obliterates such details in its irrational quest. His company is called, appropriately enough, El Deseo.

A few years ago, even in his bleak land, desire became an intellectual buzz word. You couldn't move for books or talks with the word 'desire' in the title. Rooms full of people would nod seriously as some French philosopher would spout on about the impossibility of desire, as though being told that you would never have what you wanted was the most enjoyable thing in the world. Eventually however, it became clear that even such an unbounded psychoanalytic concept had its boundaries. That there were other things to consider. Like who gets to express their desire and how.

In other words, desire or passion may feel transgressive, able to cut through social systems, but they are still as much a part of that system as anything else. What Almodóvar sacrifices on the altar of passionate camp is the question of power. But, as Sontag wrote in her seminal *Notes on Camp*, camp incarnates a victory of aesthetics over morality. And: 'It goes without saying that the camp sensibility is disengaged, depoliticised — or at least apolitical.'

Nowadays camp is moving fast into the mainstream. Everyone knows what it is. Yet, at the same time, it is still held up to be subversive — it relies on artifice; postmodern long before the word was invented. But as we all become more fluent in the language of camp (Almodóvar's and John Waters's success, among others, bear witness to this), it's worth asking just how disruptive this 'sensibility' is. While the radical edge of camp allows us to change the world, if only superficially, *Tie Me Up, Tie Me Down* asks us only to accept it.

POSTMODERNISM

Politics Of Seduction

Your latest book is on America and you have commented that: 'All of the themes explored in my previous books suddenly appeared stretching before me in concrete form.' Questions about the loss of reality, the primacy of the image and the passivity of 'the masses' all recur and you say that there is no hope in American society. But what gives you hope?

I've said in the past that hope is a rather unimportant value. We are in a period when hope is not a very lucid idea. I realise that utopias are very active in the US — the green movement, the feminist movement and so on. These are the so-called hope-bringing movements that aspire to be revolutionary but in actual fact in the American hyperreality they are part of the same publicity game. They may not be part of the official power but nevertheless they play a role in the mega-publicity operation that is America.

They are not innocent of this or uncontaminated by it and in this way they have an enormous superficiality about them. They keep changing. Movements disappear or emerge not because the ideas are good or bad but simply as a sign of vitality — the physical vitality of American reality which is in constant flux. I can't see that this sort of thing can really be described in terms of politics.

I don't believe in the ecological movement but I *do* it. One doesn't have to believe in it to do it and I would like to say that I do it! In America it's the doing that is important and it doesn't matter whether the ideas are good or bad. As an example of energy, transformation and transmutation America is still extremely alive. Much more than Europe.

In America *you describe American culture as 'vulgar but easy', as a culture which its own intellectuals are unable to analyse. Doesn't this imply a nostalgia for European culture, particularly academic culture?*

Yes. The European position is very ambiguous. The European model sees American culture as a superficiality and it analyses it in a superficial way. But American culture or rather non-culture is in itself completely original. It's not just a lack of culture and doesn't need to be interpreted negatively. The word superficial should really be in inverted commas because I've taken the banal, the normal way of looking at America and turned it around. This non-culture is in itself positive and shouldn't be viewed through the eyes of European nostalgia.

If American intellectuals can't understand their own culture do you agree with Umberto Eco who says that American professors should be pensioned off? Is it possible that high school kids have an intuitive understanding of their own society that the intellectual can never have?

Yes. There is a possibility of understanding by intuition. But the American intellectual cannot understand his own culture because he is locked into an intellectual ghetto, his defensive style is to mimic European culture which is why there is such a great divide between the American intellectual and American culture. Of course young people have a much livelier intuition and are not put in this false position.

When I wanted to investigate American hyperreality for myself, my colleagues refused to participate so I wouldn't say along with Eco that they should be pensioned off. I would actually send them into the desert.

Ah yes, the desert! You say that: 'Deserts are sublime forms distanced from all society, all sentimentality, all sexuality.' And you also suggest: 'One should always bring something to sacrifice in the desert and offer it as a victim. A woman. If something has to disappear there, something equal in beauty to the desert, why not a woman?' What is the point of such a gratuitously provocative statement? Is the corollary to sacrifice a postmodern philosopher in the centre of the city?

It would be a very good idea to publicly sacrifice a postmodern philosopher.

Naturally there is a certain amount of provocation in the image of sacrificing a woman, but I don't necessarily regard the term sacrifice negatively. I see it as a positive thing. There is a certain amount of reciprocal sacrifice in seduction for instance. Something has to die but I don't see it as having to remove someone — perhaps desire or love must die. Sacrificing a woman in the desert is a logical operation because in the desert one loses one's identity. It's a sublime act and part of the drama of the desert. Making a woman the object of the sacrifice is perhaps the greatest compliment I could pay her.

In New York recently there was a show called Resistance *(Anti-Baudrillard) to which a number of prominent artists contributed. How did you feel being confronted with your own work as something to be struggled against, as something to be contested as melancholic, full of inertia, as offering no way forward?*

As I said before, there is always an element of provocation in what I write. It is a sort of challenge to the intellectual and the reader that starts a kind of game. Naturally if you provoke then you must expect some counter-provocation and some negative reaction. The fact that it is so virulent is really quite interesting. It shows that in a way my negativity has passed on to them, subliminally perhaps, which is what I expected. I would say that there has been a *hyper-reaction* to my work and from that point of view I have succeeded.

So what about the position of women in your work. Are they experts in seduction?

I am not in agreement with hardline feminist ideology which says that woman as seducer is a degrading role. In my view the strategy of seduction is a happy, liberating power for women. It feeds into the simulation. Unfortunately in feminism everything that happens to be female is defended — *l'écriture feminine*, poetry, any kind of artistic creation and this makes it a kind of mirror of masculine simulation. This is a negative simulation, an unfortunate simulation. It seems to me that the feminine strategy of seduction is not an alienation of woman as the feminists believe. One must rise above the battle of the sexes and get away from sexist alienation. Men and women shouldn't oppose each other. I believe one can regain feminine seductiveness as a positive virtue and that this is one way to rise above it. But of course I risk being misunderstood.

Isn't that just a romantic view of woman as transcendent? A lot of feminists have already critcised the essentialism that you criticise.

It's important to make a critique of woman as woman. Seduction is not just a sexual strategy and it's not one-sided. More a complicity. There are rules to the game. It's a very physical game and one of equality. Both sides are deeply involved and the stakes are high. It's almost an ideology played out to the detriment of democracy. Right now men are striving themselves to find an ideology which defines them and I think that femininity should go beyond its narrow confines, beyond the way that it sees itself at the moment.

Is there such a thing, then, as love?

There is an acting-out, but I don't really know. I don't have a great deal to say about love.

Do you have children? Do they make you feel optimistic?

I had two. Today they are grown-up. Perhaps I was a bad father because I didn't project my own personal hopes on to them so they were carried along by their own impetus. They do their own thing.

Do you gamble?

Yes I do in Las Vegas. Sometimes I am not a gambler.

Is your work a gamble? If so what are the stakes?

I don't know whether you could call them cultural stakes. You must not confuse the stakes with the results. The problem is to not destroy the work — perhaps the work doesn't have a stake — it spins around itself until it's exhausted. The stake I think would be its potential for energy. It's almost like a game of poker. The stake is, in a way, a game beyond the bidding in order to see other people's hands. And the stake is for other people to show their hand.

In The Ecstasy of Socialism *you denounce 'the unbelievable naivety of . . . socialist thinking'. Does this position simply reflect a total disenchantment with post-'68 politics? Haven't you just exchanged any engagement with the political for a fascination with the mindlessness of consumer culture?*

There is a certain problem because the generation of '68 brought everything into play. There was a spectacular negation of culture, a sacrifice of political values. Of course after a sacrifice there is always a vacuum, a cultural vacuum. In America this vacuum has been replaced not by a culture but by *events* which have a reciprocity with the '68 political scene — a cultural fireworks.

The radicalism of '68 has passed into major events like the stock exchange crash, the advent of AIDS — that is American radicalism. That is a radicalism in which the intellectual has no place, the intellectual in the traditional sense. Intellectual radicalism has passed into events so the intellectual has been neutralised.

The intellectual has no future.

Getting a bit of the other – the pimps of postmodernism

If I Was Your Girlfriend Would You Remember 2 Tell Me All
The Things U Forgot When I Was Your Man
If I Was Your Best Friend Would U Let Me Take Care Of U
And
Do All The Things That Only A Best Friend Can
If I Was Your Girlfriend Would U Let Me Dress U
I Mean, Help U Pick Out Your Clothes Before We Go Out
Not That You're Helpless, But Sometimes Those Are The
Things
That Bein' In Love's About
If I Was Your One And Only Friend Would U Run 2 Me If
Somebody Hurt U, Even If That Somebody Was Me
Sometimes I Trip On How Happy We Could Be
If I Was Your Girlfriend Would U Let Me Wash Your Hair
Could I Make U Breakfast Sometime Or Could We Just
Hang
Out Go To The Movies And Cry Together
2 Me Baby That Would Be So Fine
Sugar Do You Know What I'm Saying 2 U This Evening?
Maybe U Think That I'm Being A Little Self-Centred
But I Want 2 Be All Of The Things U Are 2 Me
Surely U Can See

Prince, If I Was Your Girlfriend

If I was your girlfriend . . . so sings Prince on the hit single taken from his *Sign of the Times* LP. Prince, precocious and perverse — the perfect Postmodern Man. Slithering between hetero and homosexuality, blackness and whiteness, masculinity and femininity. Simultaneously embodying a desire that in its urgency becomes disembodied, this song gives voice to an overwhelming want that pays no heed to sexual difference. Until he reaches the place where man and women can really be best friends and more . . .

To hell with New Man, here's a True Man — one that can be all things to all women. And just as I'm packing my bags and getting ready to leave for the Promised Land, to this other world, the song ends. And it is only a song and Prince is only a pop star. And anyway he isn't my girlfriend. He isn't actually anyone's girlfriend.

A sign of the times indeed. This strange love song is about a yearning far deeper than simply wanting another person. Like all the best love songs it is about loss, about the self-defeating nature of desire. He wants to assert himself, his desire, his identity at the same time as dissolving away the masculine identity that constricts him. To travel to another place, another country, another identity; to fuse with it, be it and take it over — that seems to be his goal. Far from being the centre of the world, masculinity appears to be just a place on the map.

The dark continent that he wants to visit is naturally the world of the feminine. There lies the key to the perfect union — with himself, with another. But in sensing the possibilities of this kind of gender travel Prince both recognises the limitations of masculinity whilst clinging to them.

These days of course it's much easier for all of us to travel — through strange places and other cultures. We try to be polite to the 'natives' and then return with anecdotes about how well we got on with the people. No, we weren't like those other tourists, we really got the feel of the place. We buy a piece of 'otherness' and bring it home to put on the mantelpiece. We didn't steal it, we bargained for it in the market place . . . in their language. We were kind and cautious. Colonisation is a cruel word for such harmless holidays.

Yet the whole point about going on holiday is that you know you are coming back. You may *be* another person while you are away. You may feel different but that is because your identity is firmly established elsewhere.

What I want to look at here is the new kind of gender tourism, whereby male theorists are able to take package trips into the world of femininity. The glossy tourist brochures of contemporary theory offer cut price entry into these exotic places. The land of milk and honey is waiting for you. The price is right. Come on down!

> '*Myth and Utopia: the origins have belonged, the future will belong to the subject in whom there is something feminine.*'
> Roland Barthes, *A Lovers Discourse*

> '*Being an incomplete female, the male spends his life attempting to complete himself, become female*'.
> Valerie Solanas, *The SCUM Manifesto*

Barthes, like Prince, certainly knows how to whisper sweet nothings in many a feminist ear. At times his work offers us a utopian vision of a world where sexual difference as we know it has disappeared. Bodies simply glide in and out of varying subject positions — sometimes male, sometimes female, sometimes neuter. No more fighting, no more politics, only the body and its pleasures. What a wonderful world it will be . . .

Barthes' position is by no means unique. Freedom from the 'binary prison' is what many of us interested in sexual politics have been fighting for. A whole feminist culture has been built upon exploring ways of escaping the rigidity of masculinity and femininity. Through novels, plays, films, paintings, this imaginary world of no-man's land has been conjured up. And central themes have been myth and utopia.

Myth and utopia, the past and the future. These are the times when things have been or will be different. What Nietzsche called 'A new way of thinking, a new way of feeling' is envisioned in Barthes' work through the metaphor of femininity. Yet this projection of the past into the future neatly sidesteps the present where there exist actual subjects in whom there is *already* 'something feminine' — women.

What makes Barthes' work so seductive is that he always stresses plurality, multiplicity, fluidity, above the values of linearity and hierarchy. These are the qualities traditionally defined as female. The pleasures he describes in his erotics of reading and writing are those of 'writing the body' — the physicality of human communication. The 'grain of the voice', the 'rustle of language'. His celebration of *jouissance* (bliss, coming), a pleasure so intense that it disrupts cultural identity, where the subject literally loses itself, has come to be seen as a celebration of the ultimate female pleasure. For Barthes writing itself is an essentially Oedipal activity — making love to one's mother tongue. Instead of a phallic morality based on binary opposition, Barthes invokes a sexual pluralism. This emphasis on the pleasure of the body, the link between the mother's body and the mother tongue all resurface in the work of Irigaray and Cixous who, unlike Barthes, are concerned with the specific relationship of women to culture.

One consequence of Barthes' rejection of phallocentrism is an essentialising of all that is 'feminine'. As many critics have pointed out the whole problem with essentialism (biology as the source of behaviour, anatomy as destiny) is that it cannot recognise specificity. All women become subsumed into the category of Woman which then comes to stand for a mythical and other worldly space. Barthes seems to think that to enter this world is transgressive in itself but he does not do so unselfconsciously. 'Who knows if this insistence on the plural is not a way of denying sexual duality?' he asks.

But what is at stake here is not his denial of sexual duality *per se* but the denial of women. For if we all share the goal of escaping from this binary prison then part of that escape must involve the acknowledgement of women and their desires. We need neither an idealisation or impersonation of them. The valorisation of feminine pleasure in Barthes' work which is common also to Kristeva's, Irigaray's and Cixous' writing fails to recognise that female sexuality is experienced differently, at different times, in different cultures.

As Ann Rosalind Jones writes in her essay 'Writing the Body': 'I wonder again whether one libidinal voice, however nonphallocentrically defined, can speak to the economic and cultural problems of all women'.

This recognition of difference, not just of sexual difference but of all the other kinds of difference, has been a continual problem for feminism. Women first realising just how different their lives were from men's experience, were claiming a separateness, demanding a voice, insisting on their own identity. This led to a politics based on identity, on the feeling of authenticity, of at last having found oneself and then of having found others the same as you. Then a new layer of difference disrupted any cosy feminist or gay identity — differences of race, class, age and experience. So difference becomes painful, difficult and unsurprisingly we want to do away with all of it. We dream instead of indifference. We fantasise or theorise a world like that of Barthes — where oppositions no longer exist, where every small difference is simply the starting point for our desire. Stephen Heath describes it thus in *Men in Feminism*:

> Difference as desire: no difference, only differences, no
> one and other, no his-her, man-woman, nor hetero-homo

(another difference definition drawn up from the man-woman norm), a new sociality, deferring places, in that sense a utopia.

But whose desire?

For whether it's Barthes writing about desire or Prince singing about it, the desire in question is, in all its confusion, still *his* desire *their* desire, *male* desire. So what I want to know is this — if Prince wants to be his girlfriend's girlfriend, what does *she* want to be?

The work on subjectivity to which Barthes has contributed, has become of increasing importance to sexual politics. It is no longer so easy to talk of the individual or the self as an autonomous and coherent unity but instead we have come to understand that we are made up from, and live our lives as, a mass of contradictory fragments. It is paradoxical that a politics premised on identity, on self-assertion, should produce and appropriate theories that undermine the very notion of a secure identity. Yet this is a contradiction that is valuable in many ways as it stops politics becoming the 'other' of theory and vice versa. Feminists began to try to unravel the construction of gendered subjectivity — how we acquire the social characteristics associated with masculinity and femininity — not out of a desire to read lots of complicated books on psychoanalysis, but so that we might find out how we could construct ourselves differently. In other words, to unmake the processes which we feel are oppressive we first have to understand how they work and why they feel so powerful.

This kind of thinking is a direct challenge to the various ideologies which say that men and women are naturally different, that they are born with innate male and female qualities (men as aggressors, women as carers, etc). Instead it questions many fundamental assumptions about what is often regarded as natural or 'just the way things are', and puts social and cultural conditions above considerations of biology.

Some feminists, though, cling to what they see as distinctly female traits, and claim for them both mythical and mystical properties. Women are supposed to be more peace loving and closer to nature. One particularly nauseating example of this is Susan Griffin's book on *Women and Nature* in which she claims that women are akin to cows, goats and even shellfish! Mary Daly, another high priestess of radical feminism, makes similar arguments: every wrongdoing is a symbol of patriarchal power which is monolithic and ahistorical, so that footbinding in China becomes the same as a hysterectomy in Los Angeles which becomes the same as witch burning in the seventeenth century etc, etc. An analysis based on such a scenario has difficulty in dealing with how we might live with men on a daily basis or indeed how anything might actually change. We are offered once more wonderfully utopian visions of a matriarchal future; but by collapsing all women, regardless of race or class, into the category of Woman, we find ourselves faced yet again with an essentialist and essentially patronising view of women.

Rather we need to understand how particular subjectivities are lived at particular times. The recognition that femininity is an ideological construction does not make it possible to simply cast it off as a worn out piece of clothing. It informs every aspect of our lives, our dreams and our fantasies in a way that runs much deeper. Sensing this has led to many theoretical excursions into psychoanalysis in order to provide us with a theory about the unconscious. If we talk about femininity as an ideology then we also have to explain how it actually gets into our heads (and hearts) so that we often seem to be colluding in our own subordination.

Talking about the unconscious has proved as difficult and unsettling as it has productive. Juliet Mitchell's resuscitation of Freud (see: *Psychoanalysis and Feminism*) and the influential work of Lacan has problematised not just the question of gender but the whole nature of identity itself. Crucial to these theories is language, language as absolutely central in the formation of gender, as the way that we not only represent ourselves to each other, but as the only way we have of representing our selves in the first place. These discussions about language are more complex than some of the debates about the sexist nature of words themselves, and the power of naming (eg think of the different connotations of master/mistress, or bachelor/spinster), for they question the actual structure — the form of language not just the content.

In Lacanian theory the baby's self creation as a human being involves the perceptions it makes about its body, which are primarily sexual. The baby experiences itself as a mass of drives unaware of the boundaries of its own body. It has to learn to differentiate between inside and outside and so, as Mitchell describes, it is around the openings or gaps in the body (mouth, anus, etc) that meanings cluster, and these become charged with erotic significance. The first difference the baby learns is the absence or presence of satisfaction (of the breast then later the mother) and this difference is the primary difference that is later recreated in language. When the child enters the symbolic realm through the Oedipus complex, it is into a world already structured through language. Language operates as a system of differences, but the chief signifier of difference in our culture, according to Lacan, is the phallus, and therefore the child has to position itself in relation to this. Absence/presence of the phallus/breast thus becomes transformed into feminine/masculine. The baby assumes a gender position, for the only way we can make sense in language is to adopt a subject position by learning to say 'I' — pulling all the fragments together under one name. Yet this nominal identity is always a misrecognition of ourselves as unified, coherent subjects — as the origin of meaning, the speaker of the sentence. Contained within such a misrecognition though is always the reminder of the original loss that caused us to enter the signifying chain (language) in the first place — the first splitting from the mother. It is through language then that the unconscious comes into being and it is in the gap between language and the unconscious (the unconscious comes about because of the repression of desire) that desire exists. In Lacanian theory then desire can never be satisfied as it always carries within its expression traces of the original loss.

From this brief outline I want to emphasise three points. The first is this notion of the decentred subject, the subject-in-process, the subject as a site of contradictions — the 'I' of a dream can be someone else. Unlike the driving ego of some American interpretations of Freud, the ego is 'necessarily not coherent'.

The second is that *if* the phallus is the key signifier of difference, and that's a big if — many feminists have argued cogently against this — then masculinity becomes set up as the norm and femininity can only exist as absence, as what masculinity is not. Of course no one actually possesses the phallus but men are able to make identifications with this symbol in a way that women are not. Femininity thus becomes, as Kristeva argues, that which cannot be represented, that which always remains unsaid — how else can you represent pure absence? And so women become objectified in every sense of the word in order to shore up men's subject position.

Thirdly is this still nagging question of desire. Desire is always desire for the other, the unobtainable — surely not always reducible to desire for the mother? Desire as a concept then is genderless, asexual, neither one thing nor the other. Its expression and object, though, must be, for we have all been through the Oedipus complex and have all learnt the grammar of gender.

Yet obviously men and women enter the symbolic world of

language from different positions and always somewhat precariously. To assume a masculine subject position, alongside the phallus as guarantor of authority — as integrated into the symbolic realm — or to take a feminine position, as that which is outside or marginal to it, is not simply a question of biology. For both Lacan and Kristeva show that this feminine terrain of lack, of marginality, is open to men as well as women. It is this mobility of subject positioning that allows access to *jouissance* that is beyond the phallus, beyond man, and that can therefore undermine and disrupt all representation. Feminine *jouissance* then is where the phallus is revealed as the completely arbitrary rather than transcendental signifier of difference — there exists no difference, only differences. But is the unconscious, from which *jouissance* comes, itself gendered? For Lacan the answer is yes. The unconscious is the space of the other, it is woman. In the words of Alice Jardine: 'Feminine *jouissance* is therefore posited by Lacan as an ultimate limit to any discourse articulated by Man.'

Psychoanalysis was itself founded by Freud who listened to the voices of hysterics. Heath describes hysteria as the oscillation between female bodies and male subjects — women trying to find some way of speaking their desire. But Lacan, who Gallop calls, appropriately enough, the Ladies Man, declares himself to be 'a perfect hysteric'. He can speak from the place of a woman though he actually enjoys the power of a man. Like so many of these new hysterics he can claim a feminine subjectivity; so if it's no longer necessary to be a woman to speak as a woman, how do you speak as a feminist? Alice Jardine tackles such questions in her brilliant book *Gynesis*. By Gynesis she means the putting into discourse of 'woman' or 'the feminine' as a metaphor for all that Western thinking has not been able to represent.

'In France, such thinking has involved, above all, a reincorporation and reconceptualisation of that which has been the master narrative's own non-knowledge, what has eluded them, what has engulfed them. This other-than-themselves is always a space of some kind (over which the narrative has lost control) and this space has been coded as feminine, as woman.'

Significantly for us however it is this new rhetorical space of woman that is 'inseparable from the most radical moments of most contemporary disciplines', that is perceived as politically revolutionary in its ability to disrupt the very foundations of our existing order. But what has this conception of woman got to do with actual women? And how might it affect our ideas about sexual politics?

For although such radical claims have been made at various times by feminists of all persuasions, many of the so called thinkers of postmodernism remain unaware or truly indifferent to the voices of real women. Indeed why should they when they have neatly managed to step into the space of the 'other' without ever having to talk to a single woman? Why should they be interested in a sexual politics based on the frightfully old-fashioned ideas of truth, identity and history?

For if psychoanalysis has problematised identify from the inside out, then theories of postmodernism have problematised it from the outside in, until it no longer makes any sense to talk of inside/outside or the subject in society. If marxism gave us the alienated subject and psychoanalysis gave us the decentred subject, postmodernism proclaims the death of the subject — though it seems to have been on its last legs for a very long time now.

'*You make me feel . . . mighty real*' Sylvester

It is both impossible and in a sense improper to try to pin down the term postmodernism to a single meaning or definition, but if anything it can be characterised by a sense of 'profound binary crisis'. Every opposition that is central to Western thought has been blown apart — essence/appearance, truth/ideology, time/space, signifer/signified, etc. Fredric Jameson describes this as the rejection of all depth models, a sense of the end of everything, while Baudrillard talks of the 'death of meaning' and the 'loss of the real'.

The term postmodernism originates in connection with new styles in art and architecture where the purity of modernism has given way to a plethora of quoted styles and historical fragments that are brought together into a facade that revels precisely in its artificiality. Yet the critic Fredric Jameson sees it as more than a style and refers to it as the cultural dominant of late capitalism. He links it explicitly with multinational capitalism. He describes the feeling of living in a post-industrial society in terms of schizophrenia, dislocation and depthlessness. This schizophrenic 'structure of feeling' is one in which what was once separated into distinct categories becomes blurred. The old boundaries between art and mass culture, reality and spectacle, self and other, have broken down until everything takes on an almost hallucinogenic quality. Our culture, he argues, has become the culture of the image. As the mass media and information technology have come to dominate our lives, image has replaced reality. Our experiences are always mediated by and through images. For instance, the news is now news of soap opera stars, an actor is now president of the United States and we all have the feeling at some time or another of playing a part in a movie scripted by someone else.

Another characteristic of the postmodern experience is the transformation of time into a 'series of perpetual presents'. History, which requires a sense of continuity, has instead fragmented into a vast repertoire of images of the past that can be cut and pasted at will. The tampering with, not of the distant past but of recent history, and the sudden creation of old 'traditions' is something that those of us in Thatcherite

Britain or Reaganite America know only too well. The media, whose function it is to turn everything into appearance, is instrumental in this process.

If political rhetoric is now formed from a cut-up, a collage of bits of the past, this is only possible because what Lyotard calls the 'Grand Narratives' of our culture have broken down. By this he means that the big stories we told ourselves (or were told to us) about progress, science, truth, socialism, no longer seem plausible any more. The idea that things would progress in a predictable and linear fashion has been shattered and been replaced instead by lots of smaller, more localised narratives. In other words these big stories have been revealed *as* stories rather than absolute truths and have become somehow meaningless or irrelevant. In the process through which their narrativity becomes visible they lose their power of legitimation.

Lyotard links this both to a general crisis in representation and to a crisis within scientific thought. He argues that through the commodification of knowledge via information technology, knowledge and power have become two sides of the same coin. Instead of science being self legitimating it has had to face up to the question, 'Who decides the conditions of truth?'. The notion of objective truth is no longer viable —the observer always changes the outcome of the experiment. The 'value' of knowledge is thus always relative. Instead the exchange value of knowledge/information has taken over from its use value and it becomes the new commodity form. An obvious example is trading on the stock exchange, where actual goods are never exchanged but merely information about them.

This questioning of the status of knowledge and of the dissemination and legitimation of certain knowledges above others, are implicitly feminist concerns. For if it is true that the Grand Narratives are breaking down, the question we have to ask this time is not whose desire, but whose grand narratives? And what will replace them?

Grand narratives, narratives of mystery, master narratives (you take your pick according to both translation and position): Jardine reads Lyotard's crisis of legitimation as implicitly gendered, as 'the loss of the paternal fiction'. For Baudrillard this crisis is not just the explosion of the master narratives into smaller particles, but the folding in of all meaning on itself. The sign system itself is in crisis. The fundamental distinction between the map (representation) and the territory (reality), between signs and what they refer to in the real world, has broken down. He cites four successive phases of the image:

> It is the reflection of a basic reality
> It masks and perverts a basic reality
> It marks the *absence* of a basic reality
> It bears no relation to any reality whatever:
> it is its own pure simulacrum.

So signs are no longer tied to one-to-one relationships with their referents, but have become adulterous, producing illegitimate offspring wherever they go — pure simulacrum. Meaning is carried weightlessly around this circuit which is no longer involved in exchange with the real, instead, in this 'liquification of all referentials', signs refer only to each other and reality becomes redundant. The threat of illegitimacy has undermined the paternal fiction — for these bastard signs reproduce amongst themselves, not knowing or even caring who their father was. In a system that is based on exchange, as is our system of representation, a system which rests on the Law of the Father, two things undermine it more than any other — illegitimacy and incest. So if the postmodern condition is for Lyotard linked with a crisis in the authority of the father, it is also for Baudrillard about the loss of the transcendental signifier (the phallus, God, Man) as guarantor of meaning.

But does this withering away of the phallus and its power have different implications for men and for women? For if as Lacan argues women enter the signifying chain in a position of lack (of the phallus), then what can it mean to be told that this negative relation is in fact the condition of humanity? Does it mean that desire unrestrained by a binary morality (having or not having) can be released? And is this untrammelled flow actually liberating? For whom? Men, women or both? It seems to me then, that we have to stop talking as though this crisis was somehow universal and neutral, and ground it more firmly in the terrain of sexual politics; otherwise it does what so much philosophy does and simply ignores or subsumes both questions of sexual difference and political practice.

Here, though, I want to say a couple of things about this whole concept of 'crisis' itself. Firstly, whether there *is* actually a crisis of/in representation is still debatable. What is certain however is that there is much representation of the crisis (including this essay!) In fact so much contemporary theoretical work takes for granted this notion of crisis, that it has become almost the new transcendental signifier. Maybe this is because, as Umberto Eco says in his essay 'On the Crisis of the Crisis of Reason', 'Crisis sells well'. He goes on to say:

> But even admitting the considerable age of the crisis, I still don't understand what the hell it means. I cross the street on a red light, the cop blows his whistle and fines *me* (not someone else). How can this happen if the idea of the subject is in a state of crisis, along with the sign and reciprocal?

Secondly, if there is a crisis, is it symptomatic of the breakdown of everything as we know it — including capitalism and 'patriarchy'? Or is it in fact simply a by-product of capitalism readjusting itself? This question is important if we want to pursue any political possibilities — for, in much of the so-called postmodern work, going with the flow, so to speak, is seen as a more positive strategy than trying to stop it.

For example, the letting loose of the primary impulses of desire, the 'Becoming — woman' that Deleuze and Guattari describe in their 'On the Line', may not necessarily be detrimental to capitalism. This metaphor of becoming woman — the necessity of entering a feminine subjectivity in order to have access to the *jouissance* of the maternal body — is a way of 'being' sexuality that escapes sexual difference (that does not pass through the Oedipus complex). So even women have to 'become woman' in order to express desire that is free of the constraints of gender. The becoming-woman of the male subject is an osmosis into the space of the minority of the other. Woman acts as the place and the boundary of this otherness, but in this process she will lose her identity as the boundary is permeated. As her terrain is taken over, all boundaries dissolve and so in turn she is able to 'reterritorialise' what was once 'Man'.

Yet it may be argued that this dissolution of all boundaries produces a kind of psychosis that is absolutely necessary for capitalism to reform itself. As Dick Hebdige comments, the ideal consumer is now the 'psychotic consumer' — completely decentred, unanchored and irresponsible. The model of consumption that had at its core the sexually repressed worker has given way to a new consuming subject. Stuart Hall describes this historical process that started to take place after the Second World War as the 'libidinisation of consumption'.

Hebdige writes: 'The Ideal Consumer as extrapolated from a barrage of contradictory interpellations from advertising billboards to magazine spreads to TV commercials is a bundle of conflicting drives, desires, fantasies, appetites'.

In real terms we can see that consumption is being

redefined as an activity that is suitable for men — rather than simply a passive and feminised activity — so that new markets can be penetrated. More products are being aimed at young men and shopping is no longer a means to an end but has acquired a meaning in itself.

So far then I have suggested that much postmodern theory seems to be about a shifting in the position of masculinity, an uncertainty about manhood, a loss of faith in patriarchal authority. It comes then as no surprise that the strategies for living in this brave new world are 'feminine' ones. Baudrillard's work is particularly interesting in this respect, so let's look at it more closely.

'I consider woman the absence of desire. It is of little import whether or not that corresponds to real women. It is my conception of femininity.'

Jean Baudrillard

In Baudrillard's world, reality is mediated by the image, it has become replaced by a system of simulacra. At times this simulation of reality appears more real than real — hyper real. In this strange place truth melts into falsehood and the imaginary into the real until no one can tell the difference any more. In a parallel move to Lyotard, who discusses the commodification of information. Baudrillard describes the ultimate commodity fetishism of the image. The exchange value of signs, freed forever from fixed meanings, from their use-value, is what enables simulation. So for Baudrillard meaning is no longer produced or consumed but *simulated*. As Meaghan Morris points out, the work-ethic and the theory of value enshrined in the marxist concept of production gives way in Baudrillard's work to this model of simulation.

The word simulation comes from Plato and refers not to a replica of something that actually exists but to an identical copy for which there has never been an original. According to Baudrillard, for instance, Disneyland is a simulation, but its function in proclaiming its status as unreality is precisely to make the rest of America look real. So if everything has become for Baudrillard a 'precession of simulacra', simulation becomes a technique for getting by. No longer should we oppose this by looking for some underlying reality or fighting for truth — instead we should actively participate in the simulation — take it to the limits, as it were. We should push everything as far as it will go, into excess, into 'hyperlogic'. As in much of his work, the concept of reversibility comes to replace that of opposition.

Well, of course, simulation as a technique for living or even understanding is incredibly problematic in many ways, but I want to again discuss this question of sexual difference. For who are already experts in simulation if not women? Femininity itself has come to be understood as existing only in and through representation, as constructed discursively rather than as being a reflection of some inner state of being. Femininity is the perfect simulacrum — the exact copy of something that never really existed in the first place. There are strong correspondences here with the psychoanalytic concept of femininity as masquerade. There is a decidedly postmodern feel in the blurring of essence and appearance, in Joan Riviere's essay 'Womanliness as a Masquerade', written in 1929, in which she describes womanliness as a mask. Stephen Heath comments:

> In the masquerade the woman mimics an authentic — genuine — womanliness but the authentic womanliness is such a mimicry, *is* the masquerade ('they are the same thing'): to be a woman is to dissimulate a fundamental masculinity, femininity is that dissimulation. The masquerade shows what she does not have — a penis — by showing the adornment, the putting on of something else.

This showing of what she does not have is what, for Irigaray, makes the masquerade a way of women participating in male desire at the expense of their own. For the question remains in these dizzying spirals of inauthenticity, where is female identity? Where is female desire? If femininity is the perfect simulacrum, what happens if women refuse to play this game? Heath describes the failed masquerade as in fact hysteria — the hysteric 'misses her identity as a woman'. Simulation (what Morris fittingly calls 'the ecstasy of making things worse') as a techinque, then, has very different consequences for men and women. In a sense it is what women have always been doing, still do. Their refusal to play this game (or their decision to play it according to their own set of rules) has come about through the political impetus of feminism and has often led to them being denounced as hysterical.

But for Baudrillard the feminine is only ever lack, only ever appearance. That is the only truth. Feminism, which in many ways refutes this, which says women have identities, women have desires, is for Baudrillard fighting a losing battle, for the power of the feminine lies in this superficiality rather than in chasing after the falsehood of depth. Or to put it another way the postmodern condition has always been women's condition. Yet because he has no coherent theory of power relations, Baudrillard cannot conceive that this is far from the ideal position.

His hostility to feminism is made even more explicit in his theory of seduction. Seduction is always in reality an oscillation between activity and passivity — you let yourself be seduced, you actively play the passive role. For Baudrillard seduction is not just a leading away from truth, an adulteration of production, it is the only truth. This is of course contradictory, for if the value of seduction is that with its artifice and superficiality it always undermines truth — then how can it be the truth? In an essay called 'French Theory and the Seduction of Feminism' Jane Gallop dissects Baudrillard's position with a scalpel sharpened by feminist frustration. If seduction is a threat to the masculine world, which he defines as against appearance, then how come he is in a position to tell women the whole truth about it? As usual he places himself above sexual difference and from this lofty position advises women how best to combat masculine power:

> Now, woman is only appearance. And it's the feminine as appearance that defeats the profundity of the masculine. Women instead of rising up against this 'insulting' formula would do well to let themselves be seduced by this truth, because here is the secret of their power which they are in the process of losing by setting the profundity of the feminine up against that of the masculine.

So women instead should listen to what he says, be seduced by him! As Gallop wryly comments, 'A line if ever I heard one'.

The whole principle of seduction is that of reversability — the ability to swing one way or the other. So the best way to be seduced is also to seduce. Reversibility again replaces the concept of opposition, but Baudrillard, though he wants to seduce feminism, will not let himself be seduced by it, so he ends up making the kind of irreversible and absolute statement that he wishes to undermine. When it comes right down to it, for all his talk, he doesn't want to go both ways.

In another piece he writes:

> Imagine a woman who faints: nothing is more beautiful, since it is always at one and the same time to be overwhelmed by pleasure and to escape pleasure, to seduce and to escape seduction.
>   Please follow me.

No thank you. This ridiculously Victorian idea of a woman

who swoons with pleasure, who is corpse-like and beautiful, betrays Baudrillard's reputation as a thoroughly modern man. I have never met a woman who fainted with pleasure — these days if people pass out it's usually because they feel sick!

This conception of femininity as passivity occurs also in his book *In The Shadow of the Silent Majorities or the End of the Social*. The title itself is interesting, for although he describes the masses as the silent majority, historically there are in fact lots of different silent or silenced majorities/minorities. So while the 'end of the social' may be good news for him, what about all those fighting precisely to be accepted within it?

The masses, which he nonetheless refers to as an undifferentiated body, are, he says, no longer interested in socialism or liberation but know somehow instinctively that 'a system is abolished only by pushing it into hyperlogic . . . You want us to consume — OK let's consume always more and anything whatsoever: for any useless and abysmal purpose.'

Hyperconformity is for him 'an impenetrable simulacrum of passivity and obedience, and which annuls in return the law governing them'. This silent mutiny of the masses is a 'fantastic irony' which he says is 'akin to the eternal irony of femininity'.

So again Baudrillard follows the path of least resistance and his ecstasy in this is obscene — obscene is another of his buzz words referring not to the obscenity of that which is not usually seen but instead to the 'obscenity of the visible, of the all-too-visible'. It seems as if in his role of the disappearing theorist sitting and watching the demise of Western civilisation, he somehow believes himself to be outside the processes he describes. Otherwise how can he tell us about them or why would he want to? If the 'masses' are so wonderfully annulling that which governs them, why do they need a Baudrillard to chronicle their strategies or give away their secrets? Surely that old-fashioned and deeply romantic separation of the critic and society, the outsider and his/her culture, is one that he cannot sustain. This separation has been attacked from many directions — marxism, feminism, structuralism, post-structuralism, psychoanalysis, and within the physical sciences as well. Indeed opposition to such a notion is central to anything that we might call postmodern thought.

Still, I suspect that Baudrillard for all his talk, in his heart of hearts does not really want to disappear, though he subscribes to the art of the disappearing theorist. One can view his work as an example of what he is describing — it is a simulation of theory, that always self-implodes, that is always seductive. It is an elaborate game and he says he likes gambling. Gambling is a favoured metaphor because, he says, there is always a sense of forgetting oneself involved. In gambling, he says, money becomes detached from social reality — one becomes seduced into a game of pure appearance in which a sort of metamorphosis occurs. The transmutation that occurs is the goal of his methods of seduction and simulation — a coming through to the other side: 'Becoming-animal, becoming — woman. What Giles Deleuze says about it seemed to me to fit perfectly.' Gambling, a perfectly masculine metaphor, always presumes that you have something to gamble with. Money as social reality, rather than appearance, a sense of worth, of value, these are luxuries for some people. You can only play Baudrillard's game if you have something to play with. Baudrillard prefers to sit, paralysed, hypnotised, but amazingly not struck dumb, by the spinning of the roulette wheel.

'What are you going to do now that you know how the other half lives? I mean the other half of you?'

Lulu, *Something Wild*

So far I have been trying to describe how the theoreticians of the postmodern subject seem also to be describing their own crises about heterosexual masculinity. Rosa Braidotti asks the crucial question about this:

'I wonder what it is that makes them want to embark on this sudden programme of de-phallicisation? What is being exorcised by male thinkers in the act of their becoming 'feminised?'

To this I would answer that what is left out, what is not spoken about, is the uncomfortably prickly notion of power. Male power. In deciphering the language of the 'other' and then claiming it for themselves, these theoretical drag queens don the trappings of femininity for a night on the town without so much as a glance back at the poor woman whose clothes they have stolen.

In these theories psychic space becomes the primary site of inquiry until it almost subsumes any social context. This is the true 'end of the social'. It then becomes almost impossible to talk about social relations (and of course politics) except in a kind of totally abstract but crude way. Power is always the power of the mother, the phallus, the signifier, the simulacrum and so on. And yet Foucault, who describes power in a far more complex way — as a fine network of relations rather than as a possession — is useful here, for he also insists on the materiality of discourse. In other words, ideas are always embodied in the particular discourses and institutions which produce them, in all our ways of writing and speaking. That these theories repress the actuality that men are in a position of power over women means that this power can go unchallenged and resurface elsewhere. The silence about such matters is deafening. This is not to say that feminists or the left should ignore such theories and hope they go away. On the contrary I think it is crucial that we engage with them, use them, exploit them completely for our own ends . . .

One of the ways we can do this is to look at how the

mechanisms that I have described operating at a theoretical level can also be seen within popular culture.

Much of our enjoyment of music and films often seems to be bound up with experiencing something other to our daily lives. This 'getting a bit of the other' seems also to depend on women as the gateway to the other world, but increasingly black people and black culture is used to signify something radically different. Some kinds of 'otherness' remain just too threatening to be colonised in this manner — homosexuality for example seems to be seen as far too disturbing and difficult to offer this kind of escapism.

Escaping from, or at least exploring the constraints of, masculinity is a common theme of what the press has dubbed the 'Yuppy Nightmare Movie'. This whole sub-genre of films offers men at least the kind of nomadic subjectivity that allows a masculine identity to be dissolved only so that it may be resumed and reassured by the end of the film. *After Hours, Blind Date, Blue Velvet* and *Something Wild* are all examples of this. Judith Williamson's excellent review of *Something Wild* in the *New Statesmen* made explicit what such a film might tell us about the male psyche.

The plot of *Something Wild* starts with the kidnapping of a nice middle executive (Charlie) by a 'wild' woman (Lulu) for an afternoon of exotic sex. So begins Charlie's voyage into a whole other world and the souring of a classic male fantasy. Throughout his voyage this other world is signalled largely through blackness — black cultures and black music. At various points in the film we see rappers, ghetto-blasters and gospel singing. But although Lulu has facilitated Charlie's entry into this world, by the middle of the film she has become a pawn between two men — Charlie and her psychopathic ex-husband Ray. In fact the central relationship of the film is really between Charlie and Ray or perhaps at a symbolic level between Charlie and the repressed aspects of himself. Though forced into a passive role by the outrageous

Lulu (not simply sexually — he also finds himself caught up in her lies to her mother), as soon as another man appears on the scene Charlie has to prove once more that he is in control, that he is man enough to fight and more importantly to win. One of the twists of the film is that Lulu's appearance is only a masquerade. She reveals herself later as Audrey — a much more 'ordinary' woman.

This theme, that of masculinity having to face up to its darker side is one that is shared with *Blue Velvet*. Here too a similar plot structure is used — two men are brought together through their relationship with a woman. In both *Something Wild* and *Blue Velvet* this is made visually explicit in shots where the good man and the evil man are literally mirroring each other. As Charlie knifes Ray, they stand for seconds facing each other. Their similarities rather than their differences are apparent. There is a comparable shot in *Blue Velvet* where naive college student Jeff comes face to face with the terrifying Frank. This caricaturing of innocence and evil, which occurs in both films, is carried all the way through *Blue Velvet* which operates with a series of simplistic oppositions — pretty-pretty suburbia versus inner-city decay, night versus day, virginal romance versus sadistic sex, purity and horror, and so on. As Jeff makes his Oedipal journey into the underworld, in this cartoon psychoanalytic drama, it soon becomes clear that these two versions of masculinity, the dark and the light, are really two sides of the same coin.

The catalyst that brings these two halves together (Charlie with Ray, Jeff with Frank) is the female character. But both Lulu in *Something Wild* and Dorothy in *Blue Velvet* end up as pawns in the struggle between the two men. As Judith Williamson writes: 'the gateway to the other world/underworld/innerworld is women or more explicitly sex with women'.

As with the theories that I have been discussing, the world of the feminine becomes a way of men exploring, rejecting or reconstructing their masculinity, of 'getting a bit of the other' at the expense of women. At one point in *Something Wild*, Charlie has to buy new clothes in a gas station. He ends up literally dressed as a tourist in shorts, cap and a T-shirt which says 'Virginia is for Lovers'. As with the gender tourists of post-structuralism and postmodernism, he returns back home to a familiar environment and his own clothes, respectable once more. Wild woman Lulu has also now been turned into prim Audrey — who now knows her place and in a reversal of the beginning of the film hands him the keys to her car, lets him drive and sits demurely in the passenger seat.

Although the insecurity of identity that these films offer is pleasurable, it can also be unsettling if security is not restored by the end of the film. It is thus inevitable that these wild women either have to be revealed as basically nice girls or punished in some way or another — look at what happened to Simone, the black prostitute in *Mona Lisa*. Lulu can be something wild but ultimately not so wild as to actually threaten the underlying order of things. Something really wild is the Glenn Close character in *Fatal Attraction*, in which the whole horror of the feminine is unleashed in the form of this monstrous witch woman who challenges and destroys all that is secure.

I wanna be black I wanna be a panther
Have a girlfriend named Samantha
Have a stable full of foxy little whores
I don't want to be a fucked up middle class college student
anymore
I just wanna be black
Wanna be like Martin Luther King
Get myself shot in Spring
And lead a generation too
I wanna be black
I wanna be black like Malcolm X

And cast a hex
Over John Kennedy's grave
And have a big prick too
I just wanna be black

Lou Reed

Lou Reed's song, a parody not of blackness but of white people's perception of it, is apt when we come to looking at another way of getting a bit of the other. For if women's function then is to represent those parts of themselves that men cannot speak about, blackness also increasingly becomes a signifier of authenticity, of naturalness, for white men no longer so sure of their own identities. Black music is often seen simultaneously as both authentic and rebellious. Soul music, especially if it is at least twenty years old, has now been reinstated as some kind of truth in a world full of artificiality. Its sound is organic rather than machine made. The fatal irony is, though, that this expression of self-assertion, of pride, was a form of resistance against oppression; although these songs were part of an historical struggle to claim an identity, they are now being used as the soundtrack for an identity based on consumption of everything from jeans to lager. Removed from their historical context, their 'otherness' becomes more marketable.

Obviously black music is not a unified entity but is full of different musics, and at the other end of the spectrum from soul is hip hop — the music of the 80s. Unlike soul, hip hop can be read as being about the fragmentation of any identiy whatsover. Simon Reynolds, in his music criticism, maps postmodern theory onto popular music with interesting results. He argues that if soul is about the Grand Narratives of truth, progress and morality, hip hop and house have abandoned their narrative structure for a different beat that dispenses with storyline altogether. Time is chopped up into Jameson's 'a series of perpetual presents' rather than bound by linear narrative structures. Much of this music is literally machine made and does not have a wholesome, warm or reassuring sound to it. Instead it is made of shattered fragments and contradictory voices. On top of all this is often blatant, almost paranoid, aggression — the rappers message 'I can do everything better than you.' Frequently criticised for its glowering sexist lyrics, this music may tell us a lot about masculinity. If things seem to be breaking down, or feel insecure, it is the male ego that will fight its way to the forefront with its mean self-assertion at the expense of everyone else.

This is a music born originally of poverty, of desperation, so maybe it's wrong to read it in terms of the individual psyche, but what does it mean to the white youth who dance to it every weekend? How does a different social context alter its meaning?

Reynolds, who prefers hip hop to soul, writes:

> To the oppressed, the cry 'I am somebody', the struggle
> to become the subject of your own life, has resonance. As
> someone who's been brought up to be aspiring,
> motivated and in command of myself, I'm fascinated by
> failure; I get my fix from cultural representations of self-
> squandering, drift and dispersal. Strong voices don't
> reach me, broken voices do.

Postmodernly ironic (which means never having to say you're sorry), Reynolds tells us here that his pleasure is in this 'otherness' which for him is somehow the Real Thing. Whether blackness, like femininity, represents authenticity or disintegration is not the question. It is the way that they are always defined in other people's terms that makes them an object rather than a subject.

Williamson asks at the end of her review of *Something Wild*; 'If sexy women and laid back blacks can be made to stand for repressed facets of the middle-class psyche — what of their own social reality?'

Exactly. Irigaray asked a similarly 'scandalous' question of Lacan — yes, but is woman the unconscious or does she have one? When confronted with postmodern theory we still have to keep asking these questions for the coming together of what Gallop calls 'theory and flesh' will only be possible when female desire is recognised. If the whole question of power cannot be tackled, it is because these new hysterics with their male bodies and optional feminine subjectivities cannot speak of a desiring subject who is actually a flesh and blood woman.

Flesh, blood, power — these have become the really dirty words. Mention them to your postmodern man and he will try to change the subject. But the subject never can be changed until these issues are addressed. It's not enough to lay back and think of Baudrillard and fake a good time — instead ask yourself, Who's fooling Who?

Bibliography

Gilbert Adair   *Hollywood's Vietnam: From the Green Berets to Full Metal Jacket*   William Heinemann 1989

Helen Baeher and Gillian Dyer   (eds) *Boxed In: Women and Television*   Pandora 1987

Roland Barthes   *A Lover's Discourse*   Jonathan Cape 1979

Roland Barthes   *The Pleasure of the Text*   Hill and Wang 1975

Roland Barthes   *Roland Barthes*   trans. Richard Howard Hill and Wang 1977

Jean Baudrillard   *Forget Foucault*   Semiotexte 1987

Jean Baudrillard   *In the Shadow of the Silent Majorities*   Semiotexte 1983

Jean Baudrillard   'Please Follow Me' in *Art & Text*   March–May 1987

Jean Baudrillard   *Selected Writings*   (ed) Mark Poster Stanford University Press 1988

Philip Brophy   'Horrality — The Textuality of Contemporary Horror Films' in *Screen*   vol. 27/no. 1 Jan-Feb 1986

Patricia Campbell   *Hearst, Patty Hearst—Her Own Story* Corgi 1988

Erica Carter and Simon Watney   (eds), *Taking Liberties, AIDS and Cultural Politics*   Serpent's Tail 1989

Rosalind Coward   *Female Desire: Women's Sexuality Today*   Paladin 1984

Elizabeth Cowie   'Fantasia' in *m/f* no. 9 1984

Guy Debord   *Society of the Spectacle*   Rebel Press 1987

Deleuze and Guattari   *On the Line*, Semiotexte 1983

Mary Ann Doane   'Film and the Masquerade: Theorising the Female Spectator' in *Screen*   vol.23 no.3/4, Sept-Oct 1982

Andrea Dworkin   *Pornography: Men Possessing Women* Women's Press 1984

Richard Dyer   'Don't Look Now' in *Screen*   vol. 23 nos.3/4 Sept-Oct 1982

Richard Dyer   *Stars*   BFI 1982

Anthony Easthope   *What a Man's Gotta Do: The Masculine Myth in Popular Culture*   Paladin 1986

Umberto Eco   *Travels In Hyper-reality*   Picador 1986

Mark Ellis   *Visible Fictions*   Routledge and Kegan Paul 1982

Mark Finch   'Sex and Address in *Dynasty*' *Screen* vol.27 no.6. Nov–Dec 1986

Michel Foucault, 'Afterword: The Subject and Power' in H.L. Dryfus and Rabinow (eds) *Michel Foucault: Beyond Structuralism and Hermeneutics*, Harvester 1982

Michel Foucault *The History of Sexuality: An Introduction* Penguin 1984

Sigmund Freud *On Sexuality, Three Essays on the Theory of Sexuality* Penguin 1977

Carl Gardner and Julie Sheppard *Consuming Passions: The Rise and Fall of the Retail Culture* Unwin Hyman 1989

Christine Gledhill (ed) *Home Is Where the Heart Is* BFI 1987

Albert Goldman *John Lennon* Bantam Press 1988

Susan Griffin *Woman and Nature: The Roaring Inside Her* Women's Press 1984

Alice Jardine *Gynesis: Configurations of Woman and Modernity* Cornell University Press 1985

Stephen Heath 'Joan Riviere and the Masquerade' in *Formations of Fantasy* Methuen 1986

Stephen Heath *The Sexual Fix* Macmillan 1982

Dick Hebdige *Hiding in the Light: On Images and Things* Comedia 1988

Barney Hoskyns *Prince – Imp of the Perverse* Virgin Books 1988

ICA Documents 6 *Identity: The Real Me*

ICA Documents 7 *Black Film, British Cinema*

Fredric Jameson *Postmodernism or the Cultural Logic of Late Capitalism* Verso 1991

Alice Jardine and Paul Smith (eds) *Men in Feminism* Methuen 1987

Ann Rosalind Jones 'Writing the Body: Toward an Understanding of L'écriture Feminine' in *The New Feminist Criticism* Elaine Showalter (ed) Virago 1986

Mark Le Fanu *The Cinema of Andrei Tarkovsky* BFI 1987

Jean Liedloff *The Continuum Concept* Arkana 1989

Jean François Lyotard *The Post Modern Condition: A Report on Knowledge*, Trans G. Bennington and B. Massumi Manchester University Press 1986

Angela McRobbie and Mica Nava (eds) *Gender and Generation* Macmillan 1984

Marks and Courtivron (eds) *New French Feminisms* Harvester 1980

Juliet Mitchell *Feminism and Psychoanalysis: The Daughter's Seduction* Macmillan 1982

Tania Modleski   *Loving with a Vengeance: Mass Produced Fantasies for Women*   Methuen 1982
Toril Moi   *Sexual/Textual Politics*   Methuen 1985
Dave Morley   *Family Television: Cultural Power and Domestic Leisure*   Comedia 1986
Meaghan Morris   *The Pirate's Fiancée: Feminism, Reading Post Modernism*   Verso 1988
Frank Mort   'Boy's Own?: Masculinity, Style and Popular Culture' in *Male Order, Unwrapping Masculinity*   Lawrence and Wishart 1988
Laura Mulvey   'Visual Pleasure and Narrative Cinema' in *Screen*   vol. 16, no. 3 autumn 1975
Stephen Neale   'Masculinity as Spectacle: Reflections on Men and Mainstream Cinema' in *Screen*   vol. 24 no. 6, Nov–Dec 1983
Simon Reynolds   *Blissed Out: The Raptures of Rock*   Serpent's Tail 1990
D.N. Rodowick   'The Difficulty of Difference in Wide Angle' in *Screen*   vol. 5 no. 1, 1982
Jaqueline Rose   *Sexuality in the Field of Vision*   Verso 1986
Ann Barr Snitow   'Mass Market Romance: Pornography for Women is Different' in Ann Snitow Christine Stansell and Sharon Thompson (eds), *Desire: The Politics of Sexuality*   Virago 1984
Valerie Solanas   *SCUM Manifesto*,   Black Widow
Susan Sontag   *Against Interpretation*   Andre Deutsch Ltd 1987
John Stoltenberg   *Refusing to Be a Man*   Fontana 1989
Andrei Tarkovsky   *Sculpting in Time*   The Bodley Head 1986
Fred and Judy Vermorel   *Starlust*   W.H. Allen 1985
Margaret Walters   *The Male Nude: A New Perspective* Penguin 1979
Judith Williamson   *Consuming Passions: The Dynamics of Popular Culture*   Marion Boyars 1988
Peter York   *Modern Times*   Futura 1984

The articles in *Looking for Trouble* were originally published as follows:

Marxism Today
Politics of seduction   January 1989
Prince   August 1989
Men against men again   October 1990
And now the news   December 1990
Political poison   January 1991
Deviant laws   February 1991
Birth and death   March 1991
Killjoy culture   May 1991
Material girl   June 1991

New Socialist
Target man   January 1987

Women's Review
Hi, I'm Anneka – fly me   no 19. May 1987
Reach for the stars   no 21. July 1987

I to I
Modern romance   February 1990

National Student Magazine
Good vibrations   Summer 1987

The Observer
The odds of getting even   3 June 1990
Close-up as the cookie crumbles   9 June 1991

The Guardian
Green light spells danger   3 May 1990
A call to underarms   31 May 1990
Something to stay home about   5 July 1990
The merry life of Windsor   20 September 1990
Soft soap   December 1990

New Statesman and Society
Mini-politics: saying no in public   1 January 1988
Politics of choice   2 September 1988
Filming by numbers   9 September 1988
Hiding in the wardrobe   23 September 1988

Unhappy families   7 October 1988
The money game   25 November 1988
Jazz junkie   2 December 1988
To hell and back   16 December 1988

A problem of identities   13 January 1989
The great awakening   24 February 1989
A screw of convenience?   3 March 1989
The death of intimacy   10 March 1989
Nothing but the truth   24 March 1989
Film slobs   31 March 1989
Kidnapped by the counter-culture   14 April 1989
Never really at home   28 April 1989
Junk culture   12 May 1989
Torch Song tightrope   26 May 1989
Fatal fantasies   9 June 1989
Everyday eroticism   16 June 1989
All night long   7 July 1989
Toy soldiers or wicked willies   14 July 1989
Sculpting in time   21 July 1989
The metal age   18 August 1989
Great expectations   8 September 1989
Belushi's last high   13 October 1989
Starship stories   27 October 1989
Postmodern paralysis   22 December 1989

Playing Jesus by night   26 January 1990
Sun rises in the east   2 February 1990
Fag ends   16 March 1990
Eternal childhood   23 March 1990
On the side of the man in the street   27 April 1990
The brothers grim   4 May 1990
Against the sober grain   13 July 1990
One big act   27 July 1990
Brand loyalty   3 August 1990
The struggle for safe endings   7 September 1990
Maternal melodramas   14 September 1990
You can't do the right thing all the time   21 September 1990
Electric shocks   28 September 1990
Understimulation   12 October 1990
Happiness is a warm gun   16 November 1990
Heroes in a half-shell   30 November 1990

Beating Times   12 April 1991

Getting a Bit of the Other:The Pimps of Postmodernism first
appeared in *Male Order: Unwrapping Masculinity* edited by Rowena
Chapman and Jonathan Rutherford. Lawrence and Wishart 1988

Here's Looking at you, Kid first appeared in *The Female Gaze:
Women as Viewers of Popular Culture* edited by Lorraine Gamman
and Margaret Marshment. The Women's Press 1988.